FOOTPRINTS OF COURAGE

Our Family's Struggle for Justice

Jan Jenkins

ISBN: 978-0-615-29722-4

Heaven's Ink, Incorporated
PO Box 294
Savage, MN 55378

Photo credits
Page 27, Photo courtesy of Jonah Nielsen for the *Minnesota Daily*
Page 35, Photo courtesy of Martin Ludden for the *Racine Journal Times*
Page 59, Photo courtesy of Andrew Thomas for the *Minnesota Daily*
Page 62, Photo courtesy of Trish Brunner, master photographer, Legacy Studio, Sheboygan, Wisconsin
Page 209, Photo courtesy of KSTP Channel 5 News, St. Paul, Minnesota
Page 256, Photo courtesy of Todd Moen for the *Carver County News*
Page 291, Author photo, courtesy of Cayman Imaging: www.caymanimaging.com
All other photos from the author's collection.

To order additional copies of this book
U.S. destinations: www.FootprintsOfCourage.com
Canadian and other international destinations: www.itascabooks.com
Bookstores and other resellers: www.itascabooks.com

Contents

Part III. Seeking Justice

Part IV. Living with Hope

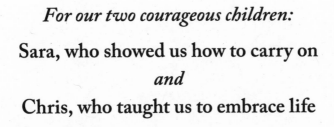

For our two courageous children:

Sara, who showed us how to carry on
and
Chris, who taught us to embrace life

We will be together again someday.

Chris Larson

When I was a coach, discussions with my teams had a number of common themes. Primary among them were teamwork and family.

Teamwork is a cooperative or coordinated effort on the part of a group of persons *acting together or in the interests of a common cause.* The power of the team is so great, and it is so readily identified, that the language of sports has permeated business, educational, and other environments. *Family* is traditionally defined as parents and their children, but a family can also be a group of people who are not related by blood but who share common attitudes, interests, or goals. However narrowly or broadly we define it, the family is the base unit of our society; it is an idea with which almost everyone identifies.

It's important to get players to buy into these concepts if you want to succeed. All the goals you set are based on the development of a sense of teamwork and belonging to a family: sharing responsibility for completing the tasks that will lead to the common goal, accepting additional responsibility without complaint when someone else cannot meet theirs, lessening the pain of failure, embracing the joy of victory.

Famous athletes almost always extol the virtue of the "team," and they always miss the "fellas" after they retire. What is it about teamwork and family that make success that much sweeter? I think it's that the experience is shared among people who have dedicated themselves through sacrifice and determination to that common goal. It can be challenging to relate to people who have not set out on this most difficult path.

A vital component of both those concepts is leadership. Without leaders there's no one to set goals and steer the family or the team toward its goals. Our society is rich with leaders—political, industrial, religious, and athletic. How does someone get to a position of leadership? Often it's through a desire to affect positive change, sometimes it's inherent in a personality, and some leaders ascend based on their performance under pressure. You will notice in this book that Chris Jenkins is described again and again as a leader—of his lacrosse team, in social settings, and in the classroom. What knowing Chris taught me is that some leaders rise to their position as a result of the environment. Knowing Chris's parents, it's easy to see that his family and their example shaped Chris as a leader.

Leadership isn't always easy, and perseverance through difficult times is a measure of greatness in a leader. Leaders are the ones who need to make tough decisions and take the blame for failure. As you read this book, I want you to think about how leadership, as well as teamwork and family, shapes the events Jan Jenkins describes. The results of effective leadership are usually positive, but at other times, a lack of solid leadership results in failure and frustration.

Steve and Jan have carried on through and against unbelievable obstacles and odds. They are inspirational leaders who keep us going even when it seems like there's nowhere else to go. Their leadership, along with all the people involved in seeking justice for Chris (who have become a new family), has resulted in amazing things. We've worked together as a team, to the best of our collective ability, to find the truth. To celebrate, we get together to run a race, share memories, maybe even toast a friend. I'm sure Chris couldn't be prouder of his family and the team that came together on his behalf.

Chris shares a moment with his parents before the Madison lacrosse tournament.

Coach Larson and son Casey contemplate Chris's game strategy.

Straight from a Mother's Heart

Be not afraid.
JOSHUA 1:9

My husband, Steve, and I taught our children, Sara and Chris, to believe in themselves, act with courage, and tell the truth. As parents, our commitment to those values would be severely tested when we learned on November 1, 2002, that our twenty-one-year-old son was missing. Chris was on top of his game as a senior honor student in the Carlson School of Management at the University of Minnesota, as well as goalie and co-captain of the University's lacrosse team. We knew our son well: he would *not choose* to disappear. Our family nurtured a close relationship: Steve and Chris spoke virtually every day. The Minneapolis police told us they would not initiate an investigation for seventy-two hours because Chris was older than eighteen. We trusted our instincts and began our own investigation immediately.

Missing? It didn't compute. The dynamic leader his friends counted on, respected, and loved, Chris offered compassion and support at any time day or night. Dozens of people told us Chris loved life more than anyone they had ever met. He lived fully, savoring even routine experiences and making everything an adventure. Searching for a lost dog might look like a treasure hunt; walking paths at the zoo transformed into an intriguing safari; peering into the pond for frogs could become a fishing expedition; running a drill in lacrosse practice often resembled a game of tag. Chris's positive energy and infectious smile lifted those who came in contact with him. His silly antics easily captivated an audience, while his genuine goodness kept people by his side. Chris's kindergarten teacher told us Chris was often the first to run to her desk, asking to help his wheelchair-bound classmate Jimmy. Though Jimmy

"I'm the only one who ever caught a fish in my cousins' pond."

had difficulty talking, he and Chris understood each other effortlessly. At a young age, Chris had already mastered the art of making people feel good about who they are.

Chris adored children and delighted in making Halloween—his favorite holiday—a memorable event for everyone. As a child, he loved dressing in a costume and ac-

Christie loves piggyback rides from cousin Chris.

companying his dad every year to the local Sam's Club to buy oversized candy bars and footlong licorice ropes for trick-or-treaters. With great enthusiasm, Chris attended what would turn out to be his last class at the University of Minnesota dressed in costume on October 31, 2002. He celebrated the evening by spending time with friends at the Lone Tree Bar in downtown Minneapolis. Tragically, a series of heartless and preventable events occurred in the bar, forcing Chris outside on a bitterly cold night and leaving him utterly alone. Once on the street, without his cell phone, wallet, or house keys, Chris fell prey to evil lurking in the darkness.

Sara, only twenty-four, bravely faced the harsh reality that her beloved brother, personal comedian, and best friend might never come home. Her resulting strength and focused energy became testaments to how much she adored her brother. Steve, Sara, and I formed a tireless trio with a rock-solid purpose: find Chris. We led hundreds of brave volunteers in repeated organized searches. These amazing people supported us through endless media appearances, frantic days, and sleepless nights. We remain eternally grateful to every one of these generous individuals, including thousands of people around the world who prayed for Chris's safety and for our strength to persevere.

Steve and I grew acutely aware of the endless courage and resilience demanded of parents who must bear the horror and raw anguish of not knowing the whereabouts or status of their child. Due to a decided lack of effort and shameless resistance from local law enforcement personnel, we felt catapulted into the agonizing role of lead investigators in our son's disappearance. On February 27, 2003, after four long and tortuous months, Chris's body was found in the Mississippi River, less than a mile from the Lone Tree Bar.

Our persistence in seeking the truth over the next several years prevailed in the face of overwhelming adversity. To some degree, we unraveled the mystery of Chris's murder and paved the way for federal involvement in the possible serial homicides of more than seventy victims in eleven states over the preceding twelve years. In the process, we demonstrated thousands of times—to ourselves and to others—that a parent's love is a force to be reckoned with.

Parents, we implore you to know your children and advocate for them when circumstances arise that demand your involvement. Act courageously when nothing less will evoke the truth. No stranger can be an expert on or for your child.

We passionately hope Chris's legacy and our struggle for justice will inspire others to believe in themselves and to trust their instincts. Empowering ourselves gives us the courage to stand up for the truth. Our tragic story can serve as a wake-up call to parents, students, law enforcement, water rescue and recovery personnel, medical examiners and coroners, bar owners and employees, and the community at large. The loss of one life affects thousands of people. Murder is the ultimate crime where so many lose.

In a press conference on November 20, 2006, Chief Tim Dolan of the Minneapolis Police Department apologized to our family and announced that Chris's death was indeed a homicide. As of this writing, no one has been formally charged, and little progress has been made in bringing a killer or killers to justice.

When the light of Chris Jenkins's life was extinguished at the hands of sick and twisted murderers, our lives changed forever. Steve and I lost one of our two greatest miracles. Sara lost her beloved brother and only sibling. Steve, Sara, and I will be Chris's voice until the day we join him in heaven.

Part I

Believing in Chris

When we honestly ask ourselves which person in our lives means the most to us, we often find that it is those who, instead of giving much advice, solutions, or cures, have chosen rather to share our pain and touch our wounds with a gentle and tender hand. The friend who can be silent with us in a moment of despair or confusion, who can stay with us in an hour of grief and bereavement, who can tolerate not knowing, not curing, not healing and face with us the reality of our powerlessness, that is a friend who cares.

HENRI NOUWEN, *OUT OF SOLITUDE* (1974)

CHAPTER I

Missing

November 1–2, 2002

You gain strength, courage, and confidence by every
experience in which you really stop to look fear in the face . . .
you must do the thing you think you cannot do.

ELEANOR ROOSEVELT

November 1, 2002, started as one of those fabulous Fridays. Energized by an exciting project with a new client, I looked forward to spending the evening with my husband, Steve, in front of a crackling fire at our home in Burlington, Wisconsin. We eagerly anticipated the weekend visit of our daughter, Sara, arriving the following morning from Cincinnati. The three of us planned to relax and simply enjoy being together. While sectioning fruit for a shrimp and cheese platter, I called in to the family room: "Steve, have you talked to Chris yet about his car insurance?"

"No."

"Why don't you give him a call and before you hang up, let me talk to him, OK?"

The television droned in the family room, so I heard little of the conversation. For some reason I heard the word *missing*. I froze. I literally stopped breathing. Instinctively, I started taking deep breaths to calm myself. Missing? Hey, Chris probably lost his car keys or his wallet. I forced myself to walk to the family room and ask, "What's going on?"

As I stared at Steve's blank face, he answered slowly, "Chris is missing." Time stopped.

Steve spoke with Chris's roommate Ben Kroon, who said they were just about to call us. Several of Chris's friends were trying to locate him, but no one knew where he might be. Ben also said Chris's Halloween costume wasn't in his room, so Chris had not made it home from the Halloween party at the Lone Tree Bar in downtown Minneapolis the

3

night before. I stared at Steve: "What's the plan?" Steve said Ben would call back in an hour. Every cell in my body registered red alert as I grabbed the phone and called Ben. "Ben, what do you *mean* Chris is missing?"

Over the next couple of hours we phoned several of Chris's friends, seeking in vain to understand the situation. One person I spoke with was Ashley Rice, Chris's date who accompanied him to the Lone Tree Bar along with three other friends. Ashley told me she did not leave the bar with Chris. After several vague responses from her, I could hardly control my anxiety. I finally blurted out, "What kind of friends leave their friend at a bar?" She hung up. Steve and I had just met her the previous weekend following a business trip to Minneapolis. We shared time with Chris and Ashley at a great restaurant, and I presented her with a gift from our recent vacation. I ached for honesty, not an abrupt disconnection.

My body already knew what my mind wanted to deny: Chris was in serious trouble. After three attempts, I finally reached Sara. I quickly shared the few facts we had learned while resisting the panic pulsing through my body. Sara immediately wanted the names of everyone with Chris on Halloween night, as well as the phone numbers of his closest friends. She told me to chill out as she assured me she would get to the bottom of things. Sara hung up and then, surprising herself, began throwing things at her mirror, screaming, "You can't take him from me now!" Clearly, she experienced the same initial numbing dread I felt, but her sense of the harm that had befallen Chris raged even stronger than mine. Sara was so freaked out by her atypical reaction, she didn't tell me about it for several months.

Meanwhile, cell phones continued to buzz as several friends gathered at Chris's residence near the University of Minnesota campus in Minneapolis to call everyone they could think of who might know his whereabouts. They also phoned local hospitals, taxi services, even detox centers, in hopes of finding him. Christian Bailey arrived at Chris's house about 5:30 p.m. to help. Christian, Ben Simms, and our son served as co-captains on the UMN Men's Lacrosse team. Christian remembers Ashley Rice walking in with two of her roommates shortly after he arrived. She had worked her shift at the Lone Tree Bar earlier that day. Christian told us he thought it was strange that instead of helping locate Chris, Ashley sat on the sofa chatting with her room-mates, acting indifferently toward Chris's disappearance. Shortly there-after, Christian recalls Ashley heading up the stairs to Chris's room with her roommates. He asked, "Hey, Ashley, where are you going?" She replied, "Oh, I'm going up to Chris's room. I need to get a few things." Her response seemed a bit odd to him, but he didn't question her further.

At about 10:00 p.m., Steve telephoned the Minneapolis Police Department to request help in locating a missing person. After hear-ing several times, "Your son will probably show up," my husband was finally told about filing a report. Informed that he had to complete the report in person, Steve repeatedly explained that we lived six hours from Minneapolis. I suggested we ask the local sheriff to come to our home to identify us to the MPD. Deputy Matt Prochaska arrived within fifteen minutes. He spoke with the MPD, verifying our names and address. Deputy Prochaska treated us with kindness and compas-sion. He gave us a ray of hope in a very dark night, his only regret being he did not know what else he could do to help us. After receiving the missing person report, we completed it and faxed it back to the MPD, with the understanding that the report would be sent to law enforce-ment agencies throughout the state of Minnesota at midnight.

We phoned the MPD to be sure they received the fax. They had. When we inquired about next steps, time stopped again. Shock and despair swept over us when we learned that since Chris was over eigh-teen years old, the MPD would not start an investigation until he had been missing for seventy-two hours. By now, Steve and I felt numb. This can't be happening. Chris has been missing almost twenty-four hours and we live 350 miles away; why isn't law enforcement forming a posse to hit the streets? Parents have a sixth sense about their chil-dren. We knew beyond the shadow of a doubt that this was an all-out emergency. What parents ever think that one day their child will be missing, much less that the disappearance would not be taken seri-ously by law enforcement just because that child is over eighteen years old? To make matters worse, we had to complete the missing person report two additional times before it was sent throughout the state. We learned from a source inside the MPD that the report sat on a desk. Chris disappeared on October 31 and it was not until November 5 that the report was finally distributed. A dedicated UMN student athlete, an incredible young man, did not return home. Yet it took five days for a statewide alert to activate! Why was there no sense of urgency from law enforcement?

Shortly before midnight, on November 1, we spoke with Sara for the third time, and she relayed the data she had gathered. We decided we must go to Minneapolis immediately, taking with us contact lists with the names and phone numbers of everyone we knew. Sara would leave Cincinnati on the first flight to Milwaukee the following morning; we'd pick her up at the airport and proceed to Minneapolis.

Sara did not tell me for at least one year what happened at her house that night. As she continued phoning key people in an attempt to find Chris, her anxiety increased dramatically. So Sara decided to call her friend Tara for moral support. Realizing Sara's tension, Tara drove immediately to Sara's house, taking her two little dogs with her. From the moment the dogs entered Sara's house they started racing around, literally slamming themselves against the walls. Their frantic behavior continued the entire evening. Tara assured Sara that her dogs had never done anything even remotely like that. Sara felt the dogs sensed Chris's spirit in the room, fueling her fears that her brother was already dead.

The lively fire that had been lit in joyful anticipation a few hours earlier was now reduced to glowing embers. The clock showed almost 1:00 a.m. I noticed Steve staring at the untouched food, wringing his hands. It was time to turn to God. I took our picture of Jesus off the dining room wall, brought it into the family room, and placed it in front of the fireplace. We sat side by side on the sofa, gazing into the eyes of Jesus as we held out our arms with palms up, praying desperately for our son's safety. We begged for wisdom, grace, and strength. By this time both of us were shaking; tears flowed down our cheeks. As I put the picture back and climbed the stairs to throw a few clothes into a suitcase, I began bargaining silently with God: *Dear God, Chris is in serious trouble, I know it. Please God, let me be wrong.* The knot in my stomach warned me otherwise. Finally my mind had to acknowledge what my body already knew: I might never see my precious son again. Steve and I held each other tight through a sleepless night.

Day Two without Chris: Saturday, November 2

After collecting Sara at the Milwaukee airport, we sped to Minneapolis. At one point Sara and I tried to lighten things up a bit, saying we were like three Yosemite Sams on a mission, the difference being that we had blazing cell phones instead of blazing guns. During the drive we made more than three hundred calls.

One of the first calls Steve made was to Rick Stein, my brother-in-law. Steve asked him to rent several rooms at the Holiday Inn Metrodome in Minneapolis. Once Rick understood the situation, he told Steve, "Let me take it from here." Then Rick proceeded to establish search headquarters. He set the tone with a refreshing can-do attitude and behavior that typified the next two weeks as one individual after another bravely faced the disturbing facts.

Whether we spoke to people or left messages, we told everyone the same thing: "Chris is missing and we're on our way to Minneapolis. If you are available, be at the Holiday Inn Metrodome in Minneapolis by 2:00 p.m. Rick Stein, Jan's brother-in-law, is setting up search head-quarters there. Bring everyone you know. We only have a couple of hours before it gets dark, so we must start searching immediately."

In Minneapolis, temperatures were now falling into the twenties at night, and the wind chill could fall well below zero. If Chris lay somewhere injured and unable to move, every minute counted. Since the MPD had already told us they would not consider starting an investigation for seventy-two hours, we knew we were on our own until Monday morning, November 4.

Early in the drive, Sara, Steve, and I agreed on the two most important actions: hire a private investigator and engage the media. Steve thought immediately of contacting his lifelong friend, Officer Mike Blood, for a recommendation regarding a private investigator.

One year earlier, Mike had been shot in a bank robbery in Edina, a suburb of Minneapolis. Chris called his dad immediately when he heard about the tragedy from the evening news. Bullets had hit every major organ in Mike's body except his heart, yet not one major organ was destroyed. Hanging on to life, he received 124 units of blood (approximately fifteen gallons) in the first forty-eight hours alone. Mike spent ten months at Hennepin County Medical Center in Minneapolis,

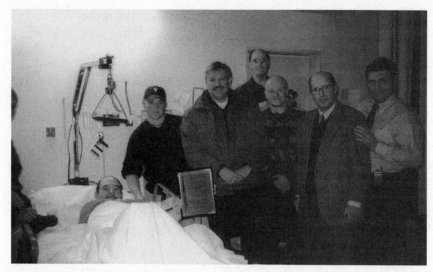

Chris presents the Lifetime MVP Award to Officer Mike Blood from turkey bowl gang.

undergoing dozens of surgeries. Chris joined the team of men who took turns spending the night with him to help Mike through unrelenting pain and terrifying drug-induced hallucinations. Through this experience, Chris told us he had gained even more respect for police officers.

Mike Blood recommended we contact Detective Eric Kleinberg of the Edina Police Department. In a conversation with Steve, Detective Kleinberg named Chuck Loesch as his number one recommendation. He said Loesch had worked as a successful PI since 1978, earning a reputation for integrity and fairness. During my brief conversation with Chuck, he answered questions in a factual and direct manner. I hired him on the spot. He agreed to meet us at search headquarters as soon as we arrived in Minneapolis.

Loesch's results demonstrated his strong work ethic and passion for truth. What he accomplished in the first two weeks alone established a baseline that would eventually crack the case wide open. He worked far beyond the call of duty and probably charged five cents on the dollar, considering the effort he poured into Chris's case.

Anxiety ripped through me during the five-and-a-half-hour drive. My hands shook as I tried to hit the numbers on my cell phone, and the knot in my stomach seemed to grow. Once again, I began silently bargaining with God. During a call with my older sister Deborah I stated in a flat, quiet voice, "I may never see my son again." That statement jarred both of us. Logic pushed me to keep asking myself, *What are the facts? Jan, get a grip. By tonight this will be over, you will be hugging Chris, and making him promise to never let this happen again.* I tried to push away the fear that we were already too late to help our son.

Saturday Afternoon: Building a Solid Team

As we pulled up in front of the Holiday Inn Metrodome in Minneapolis, now search headquarters, Steve saw a dark blue Ford Crown Victoria at the far side of the hotel parking lot. As we drew near, we noticed the antennas on the rear trunk deck of the car and decided this was the unmarked vehicle of a private investigator. Sure enough, it was Chuck Loesch with another man he introduced to us as Don Enger, a retired, thirty-seven-year law enforcement veteran. Loesch explained that Enger often worked with him as a consultant and, at least initially, they would work as a team. We quickly exchanged a few key facts. While Steve and I parked the car, Sara hopped into the back of Loesch's car to share everything she had learned from the phone calls initiated the night before.

We checked into the hotel, went up to the third floor where Rick had reserved several rooms, and saw dozens of people waiting to help. Rick said at least one hundred people had arrived, and search teams were already out canvassing the area between the bar and Chris's house for clues. We felt overwhelmed and blessed by this positive response. The questioning, coupled with the confused looks on so many of our friends' faces, only served to affirm our own fears. The most difficult pairs of eyes to look into were those of my mom and dad, known to everyone as Grandma Rose and Grandpa Gene. Chris was their first grandson; they knew him well and loved him dearly. The three of us didn't say much. Our anxious eyes and tight hugs revealed words we were not yet willing to speak. My five sisters and members of their families arrived one by one over the next several days, three sisters coming from across the country. The first moment I saw each one of my sisters, we ran toward each other, embraced, and sobbed the un-spoken horror.

Chris's uncle Rick took charge. He seemed to work miracles by making things happen fast. Like so many of the volunteers, he hardly slept. Rick said he did what he thought we would have done if his son Eric were missing. Though he didn't tell us at the time, Rick phoned the MPD many times over the next several hours begging an officer to at least speak with parents who were growing increasingly frantic while attempting to locate their son. He was told no. At one point, Inspector Robert Allen of the First Precinct in Minneapolis said to him, "Back off, Rick. Go back to the suburbs where you belong."

That first weekend, leaders emerged as key roles evolved from on-the-fly strategy sessions conducted by Rick, Chris Larson (Chris's lacrosse coach), and Steve. Coach Larson (known to all as Coach Lars) took charge of the actual searches. He pieced together maps that outlined the likeliest paths between the bar and Chris's residence. He then divided the path into smaller, numbered areas, each one overlapping the surrounding areas. We had strength in numbers with our volunteers, so over the next several days, each area was combed at least twice by different teams, guaranteeing new perspectives from fresh sets of eyes. Both sides of the Mississippi River and Nicollet Island between the bar and Chris's house were searched extensively for any possible clues.

John Wood, an executive at Mortenson Construction, knew Chris's character through his son Matt, a close friend of Chris's. Hence, John understood the need for speed and came immediately to search head-quarters. He listened carefully and determined what was needed most in the first few critical days. He helped strategize a search plan, raise money, seek assistance from a media coordinator, and identify the locations of security cameras in the area. John made himself available for anything we needed. His invaluable intelligence, compassion, and calm demeanor balanced constructive action with our mounting tension. One critical task John accomplished was speaking with personnel at the Federal Reserve Bank of Minneapolis, which sits next to the Mississippi near the Hennepin Avenue Bridge. That building has two powerful surveillance cameras that capture the entrance to the bridge from Minneapolis toward the University campus—a logical route if Chris had elected to walk home from the Lone Tree Bar. At night, the bridge is illuminated almost as bright as day, allowing the sweep of the cameras to catch pedestrians and vehicles on the bridge. Keith Lange, a supervisor at the Federal Reserve Bank, told John that the tapes from 11:00 p.m. on October 31 to 4:00 a.m. on November 1, 2002, had been examined. Chris was not seen on that bridge.

John Wood also knew Chris's work ethic. He had recommended Chris for summer construction work at Mortenson, a rare commendation for a college student. Chris was proud to be part of the team that completed the Excel Energy Center in St. Paul, Minnesota, in the summer of 2002. He told family and friends that on his last day on the job, the day before the grand opening of the center, he left his work gloves up on one of the catwalks. Those gloves are likely still there. Chris wanted to leave his mark. Over the ensuing years that mark, Chris's remarkable legacy, has been shared with us by hundreds of people in their stories of the indelible footprints Chris left on their hearts.

That very Saturday afternoon, Steve, Sara, and I began speaking to the public, seeking information regarding Chris. We knew the importance of making the media our new best friend. We created flyers and oversized posters with Chris's picture, contact information, and a reward up to $50,000. We didn't have a clue how to raise $50,000; we would figure that out later. In the next twenty-four hours, our son's picture papered downtown Minneapolis. The first flyer I saw taped outside on the window of a public building was gut-wrenching. I looked at Chris's picture, and, as I struggled to deal with the harsh reality, I felt a crushing weight on my chest. *Dear God, please guide us to Chris.* My mom, Grandma Rose, kept her rosary in her pocket. I knew she prayed continuously. We thought if we could just hold on until Monday morning, the end of the seventy-two-hour wait, the police would arrive with direction and expertise to launch a full-scale investigation. Our hope was that we would be hugging Chris long before that point.

Hundreds of amazing people came to help: family, friends, colleagues, coaches, Chris's professors, and other University staff, even total strangers. Busloads of lacrosse players came from Duluth, Minnesota, and Stevens Point, Wisconsin. Those young men knew Chris and his contributions to the game of lacrosse in the Upper Midwest. As did other young people, they demonstrated their unwavering belief in Chris and eagerness to help locate him. Their energy, confidence, and persistence inspired and uplifted us. Over the next several days, countless people commented on how these incredible young adults "restored their faith in American youth." We heard those exact words several times. Every single person served as a lifeline for us, each one contributing in his or her own special way. The love, commitment, and selflessness of others gave us strength and courage to bear the unbearable.

Many psychics and intuitives phoned search headquarters. Though the psychics had good intentions, their grisly stories of what they thought had happened to Chris tore our hearts. In the early days, a few told us Chris was still alive, but unconscious, or lying in pain close to death. Someone on our team would have to listen to each atrocious story, then recount it to us. We'd head out to yet another location only to come away with nothing but numbing despair. After a few weeks, we came up with a plan. We told every psychic who called that since they knew Chris's whereabouts, they could go to that location and call us. We'd come to pick up Chris, and they'd receive the $50,000 reward. No one ever took us up on it. Again, they seemed like compassionate people trying to help and not one of them asked for money. But no results ever came from dozens of hours of unnecessary trauma.

We lost precious time and focus following such distractions. Yet we did not have hours to analyze every move we made. We did our best at a time when law enforcement had not engaged *and* we were living every parent's worst nightmare: a missing child. Let's get real. If we were staring at a pile of manure and someone told us the answer to Chris's whereabouts was beneath the manure, we'd have eaten it if we had to. Nothing on earth mattered more to us than finding our son, and we were prepared to do almost anything.

Late Saturday night, one of the psychics led us to Hudson, Wisconsin, where we searched along the St. Croix River with at least a dozen determined volunteers. We walked up and down riverbanks, peered into deserted buildings, walked along railroad tracks, and poked through log piles. The psychic strongly felt Chris's presence. I wanted so badly to believe; I even brought a blanket to wrap him in when I found him. I shouted his name until my voice left me: "Chris, this is Mom. I love you. We're all here. Please let us know where you are." It wasn't long before I was sobbing as I struggled through the words. Everyone called for Chris and offered each other encouragement. Periodically some of us went back to one of the cars to warm up. Everyone felt uncomfortable in the bitter cold, even with coats, hats, and gloves.

We continued the search until roughly 2:30 a.m., when a police officer drove up and asked us what we were doing. Though we explained the situation, he was curt and told us to leave. In desperation, we asked him if he would just drive to the end of the parking lot and shine the lights from his squad car so we could see if we missed anything in the area. Even though Steve and I, the parents of the missing child, were speaking with the Hudson police officer, he refused and was clearly annoyed with us. On public ground looking for our missing son, we kept trying to control our anger, thinking it would only exacerbate the situation. What a mistake! Over the past several years life has taught us that cooperation is not a behavior exhibited by many in law enforcement. We got results when we pushed back and refused to be intimidated.

CHAPTER 2

What Happened Halloween Night?

November 3, 2002

Hell is empty. The devils are all here.

WILLIAM SHAKESPEARE

Chris, where are you? Such questions became our desperate plea over the many sleepless nights. At different times during the night, Steve or I stood in front of the windows of our room at the Holiday Inn, peering through teary, swollen eyes at the lights of Minneapolis. *Chris, where are you? We know you're out there. Please guide us to you. Chris, we love you more than life itself.* The wrenching sobs came from a place so deep inside, we didn't recognize our own voices. Ours were the anguished cries of parents at the bottom of hell.

Day Three without Chris: Sunday, November 3

Sara's incredible strength and insight inspired all of us. By Sunday morning, the third day of our agony, the three of us had hardly slept since awakening Friday morning. Yet I watched a determined Sara sitting on the floor leafing through the Yellow Pages, desperate to locate a bloodhound. She secured vans from her employer, Ford Motor Company, for the searches. She combed Chris's room with Amanda Steppe looking for clues.

Just one month earlier, Amanda and her husband, Pete, had asked Chris to be the godfather of their new baby boy, Grantly, who was born premature and required almost constant care. To give Amanda a chance to rest, Chris frequently took care of Grantly during his lunch hour from his 2002 summer job at WSI Sports Inc. Amanda shared with us that she sometimes found Chris rocking Grantly, telling him stories about the awesome game of lacrosse. She watched Chris give

Godfather Chris celebrating Grantly Steppe's baptism.

Grantly a big kiss, promising to help him become a superstar lacrosse player.

Amanda gave Chris a journal about six months before he disappeared—a *Chicken Soup for the Soul* journal, personalized with many phrases written with bright colored markers. Several of us knew Chris wrote regularly in his journal because he talked and laughed about it. He told me he was turning into a "writing nerd." Chris's roommates told Sara Chris left his journal next to his bed. Sara and Amanda became even more concerned when they couldn't find the journal or Chris's PDA. Sara promptly packed up his DVDs so they would not disappear as well. None of this made sense because Chris's roommates were great, trustworthy guys we knew well. In addition to Ashley Rice and her roommates, who else might have been in Chris's room? Who would take a personal journal and a PDA, both potentially containing data that might help us locate Chris?

Early Sunday afternoon, our private investigators, Chuck Loesch and Don Enger, came to search headquarters to share what they learned the night before when they interviewed Lone Tree Bar employees who had worked Halloween night. To elicit as much truth as possible, they questioned employees who actually saw Chris that night, starting with those in entry-level positions. Loesch and Enger disclosed the following documented statements and details to Steve, Sara, and me.

Thorman's Account

As they approached the Lone Tree Bar, Loesch and Enger saw a large male wearing a black winter jacket and dark stocking cap standing on the sidewalk in front of the entrance/exit door (closest to Hennepin Avenue) on Sixth Street and Hennepin. They introduced themselves to the man, and he identified himself as Ryan Thorman. Thorman stated he had worked as a bouncer on the sidewalk in front of this exact door on Halloween night, and he did see Chris in costume standing on the sidewalk at this same door, sometime after midnight on Halloween. Thorman confirmed he had received and followed instructions by radio communication from Tony Norris, a security supervisor on duty that night, not to let the person dressed in the Indian costume back into the bar. Enger and Loesch then requested names of other Lone Tree personnel who had worked on October 31, 2002.

Krause's and Hollister's Accounts

Thorman referred them to a manager, Jill Krause, whom they met inside the bar. Krause stated that she had seen Chris in costume, adding that he may have been escorted out by a security person named Tony Norris, through the same door described by Thorman. She agreed to get a list of personnel who had worked at the bar on October 31, 2002, as well as the names of Minneapolis police officers present that night. Then Krause pointed to and identified a young woman named "Natalie Hollister," a bar server, who worked Halloween night. Hollister gave a clear description of Chris in his costume and stated she had seen a bouncer/security person escort Chris out of the bar through the door Thorman had worked. Hollister expressed confidence in her responses because on Halloween night, she was stationed next to that door, standing on an elevated platform behind a tub of beer.

Enger and Loesch learned that Hollister substituted for Rice at the Lone Tree Bar on Halloween night. She had recounted the same story about Chris being escorted out of the bar to Rice, who then communicated the information to a trusted adult volunteer at search headquarters. More than one person said they thought Chris was unable to reenter the bar because he had no identification.

Krause returned with the names of bar personnel and of two MPD officers—Mike Casey and Grant Johnson. Confirming that the bar had held a staff meeting Halloween night from 1:30 to 1:40 a.m., which Rice did attend, Krause added that she believed Officer Mike Casey gave Rice a ride home after the meeting.

Stohlberg's and Roth's Accounts

Loesch and Enger then questioned security guard Chris Stohlberg, who described Chris's costume, including the headband with a single feather in the back. Stohlberg said he worked the door on Sixth and Hennepin on Halloween night and saw a security supervisor escort Chris out that same door. As Stohlberg continued to speak, a large man walked up and identified himself as Ryan Roth, the head of security who had acted as roaming security in the bar on Halloween night. When Roth said he was 99 percent certain Chris was *not* escorted out, Stohlberg shot Roth a puzzled look as if to say, "What are you talking about?"

Norris's Account

Tony Norris then approached Enger and Loesch. Loesch closely observed Stohlberg's and Roth's facial expressions when Enger asked Norris whether Chris was escorted or thrown out of the bar. As Roth stared at Norris, Loesch felt he was signaling Norris not to say anything. Initially, Norris told Enger he did not think Chris was asked to leave or removed from the bar. Loesch asked Norris if he had instructed any other security person not to let the person dressed as an Indian back in the bar. Only after Roth left the area and Enger continued to speak with Norris, did Norris say that perhaps he did tell some other bouncer or security manager not to let the person dressed as an Indian back in the bar.

Four employees working Halloween night stated that they had seen Chris in costume being escorted out of the Lone Tree Bar by a security person through the entrance/exit door; three of them worked at that same door (two inside the bar—one elevated on a platform next to the door—and the third outside on the sidewalk in front of the door). Though rumors that Chris was not removed from the bar have circulated, we have never heard or seen a statement from anyone who actually saw Chris walk out on his own. Nor have we heard a single account of Chris's causing trouble, behaving badly, or in any way bothering or hurting another person that night. Chris's friends have told us he would never leave a date stranded. Furthermore, if Chris had decided to walk home, he would not have left his house keys, wallet, and cell phone behind.

While all the statements collected by Loesch and Enger, two seasoned professionals, certainly raise serious questions, the story they told us they heard from Krause is even more disconcerting. First, Krause explained that if anyone is escorted out of the Lone Tree Bar, the entrance/exit door (closest to Hennepin) on Sixth and Hennepin, or a rear door would be used. She described Chris as being calm and explained that if patrons are removed for unruly behavior, they are escorted out the rear door, where Minneapolis police officers are usually stationed. Krause observed Chris having a brief conversation with MPD Officer Mike Casey around 12:30 a.m. After Chris walked away from Officer Casey, Krause observed Officer Casey speaking with Norris, who subsequently escorted Chris out of the bar. Krause repeated her account of what happened to Chris from the time he was singled out by Officer Mike Casey until he found himself on the sidewalk in front of the Lone Tree two or three additional times.

Gag Order

Loesch and Enger fully intended to continue interviews in the bar that Sunday evening, but discovered that the bar was closed on Sundays and Mondays. By the time they could get back into the bar, the window of opportunity for questioning key people had slammed shut. The owner, Rob Rankin, had already required bar employees to agree to a story saying that Chris left the bar on his own and that they would not speak without an attorney present who represented the bar. If any employee did not agree to this stipulation, he or she would be fired. Several employees verified the existence of the gag order and its terms. Ashley told Sara that she had spoken with one of the bouncers from the Lone Tree, and he stated that he had definitely seen Chris being escorted out of the bar and had received radio communication from a bar employee not to let Chris back in the bar. He also allegedly said the owner and/or a manager of the bar had instructed bouncers to cover the truth.

Trying to confirm the facts, Loesch phoned Krause requesting an interview. Krause returned Loesch's call and reported that she had contacted Lone Tree Bar owner Rob Rankin, who instructed her not to speak with anyone involved in this investigation. He said all requests must go directly through him, and then possibly through his attorney.

Ashley and one of her roommates who also worked at the Lone Tree Bar approached Sara for advice. They told Sara they had been asked to sign the gag order and didn't know what to do. Sara told them not to sign it.

Officer Casey and Ashley Rice

On October 31, 2002, MPD Officers Casey and Johnson worked off-duty security jobs at the Hennepin Center for the Arts, adjacent to the Lone Tree Bar. Each one of their written statements, part of the official MPD report, says that Ashley introduced Chris to them as her boyfriend shortly after her group of five arrived at the bar around 11:00 p.m. Both officers' accounts contain numerous comments regarding Chris's behavior, people with him, and even where Chris stood in the bar that evening. Why did they observe Chris so often, especially when Officers Casey and Grant were being paid to work in the adjoining building? Though not included in either of the officers' written statements, Ashley revealed in her first interview with Loesch and Enger on November 2, 2002, that she wore Officer Casey's official MPD shirt, complete with badge and patch, as part of her Halloween costume. Her costume, described in detail, is also mentioned in interviews in the MPD report. In fact, before her mother whisked it away, several of us at search headquarters saw a photo of Ashley wearing the police shirt and hat on Halloween night.

More than a dozen people who had been at the Lone Tree Bar on Halloween night told Loesch and Enger, as well as several others, that they had seen Ashley and Officer Casey flirting openly throughout the evening. Ashley admitted this in separate interviews with Loesch and Enger. The bar manager, Jill Krause, stated that an after-hours employee meeting at the Lone Tree Bar was held in the early morning on November 1, 2002, to address the fact that employees had been intoxicated while working. She verified that although Ashley did not work that night, she attended the meeting with three of her roommates who did work Halloween night. Officer Casey's report states that he drove Ashley home in his personal car because she did not have a ride home and she was a friend. No ride home? She had just attended an after-hours meeting with three of her roommates. Even Sergeant Jackson, who was assigned to Chris's case on November 9, admitted to Grandma Rose that he knew this was not the first time Officer Casey had taken Ashley home.

Steve and I have asked the MPD on numerous occasions why Officer Casey has never been questioned. We continue to receive the same disingenuous response: "He's a married man with children. We don't want to break up a family." If you were Chris's parents or his sister, how might you feel? Officer Casey was one of the last people to speak with Chris alive. If Chris had been allowed to go home with his friends, he would be alive today. Who is being protected? Who is being served?

Officer Hokanson

Finally, late Sunday afternoon on November 3, Officer John Hokanson came to search headquarters to speak with Steve and me. He sauntered into the main room asking, "Where's the mother?" Grandma Rose did not ignore his patronizing tone or cavalier attitude. With an edge in her voice, she walked up to him and asked, "Are you looking for my daughter Jan, Christopher's mother?" Officer Hokanson basically slid by her and proceeded to tell us, "He's off on a road trip, he'll be back." A few moments later he turned to Steve and said, "Come on, Steve, he's sowing his oats." I don't think Hokanson intended for me to hear his comment, but I did. With angry tears falling, I turned, looked up at Hokanson, and asked, "Are you willing to listen for five minutes to understand Chris's character?"

Spotting Ashley Rice across the room, Hokanson virtually ignored my question. He went over to Rice, put his arm around her, and said, "Hey, I know you." The two of them went into an adjoining room and did not return during the twenty minutes we stayed in the main room. Several people witnessed this bizarre scene unfold. Some of those people were Chris's friends, who later told us they were so disgusted by the entire episode, they left search headquarters for the day.

By Sunday evening we held on to the shred of hope that Chris would be found in a hospital, unconscious, listed as a John Doe. Though not a pleasant or likely possibility, at least we'd know he was alive.

Monday morning, November 4, marked the end of the seventy-two-hour waiting period. We convinced ourselves that with their expertise and experience, surely law enforcement would make rapid progress with the facts we gave them. To make certain we did everything possible for a successful start the following day, Steve spoke with the inspector of the Second Precinct, Rich Stanek, at about 10:00 p.m. Sunday. I sat in the room with Steve when he made the call. An angry Stanek immediately challenged Steve because members of our team were contacting politicians, including U.S. Congressman Jim Ramstad, State Senator Roy Terwilliger, and others, requesting assistance. Steve explained that he could not possibly be aware of all the activity our team had generated. The bottom line was that hundreds of people were determined to find Chris, already missing more than forty-eight hours, with no help of any kind from the MPD.

I watched Steve pace back and forth as he spoke, sleep deprived and frantic over our son's disappearance. He was trying valiantly to understand what we needed to do the next morning to jump-start an official investigation. Stanek kept insisting that Steve address him using his proper title of Inspector. Steve kept messing up by saying "Investigator." After being corrected three times, Steve finally blurted out, "Hey, I'm not in your industry. I'm just a guy who sells plastic. Cut me some slack here." Tensions escalated when Stanek retorted in a condescending voice, "I'm not used to speaking with people like you at this time of night." Steve shot back with, "Well, I'm not used to losing my son in your city."

CHAPTER 3

Loaded in Trunk

November 4–6, 2002

*A friend is someone who knows the song in your heart and can
sing it back to you when you have forgotten the words.*

AUTHOR UNKNOWN

"Well, I love you, Mom!" Those were the last words I heard from Chris
when I spoke with him on October 30, 2002. That phone call was the
last earthly connection I would have with the remarkable son we had
raised and loved for almost twenty-two years. How we all prayed for
good news. It was not meant to be; Chris would not come home ever
again.

Day Four without Chris: Monday, November 4

The seventy-two-hour wait ended. Since we had not heard a word
from the Minneapolis Police Department, Steve phoned them at about
ten o'clock Monday morning. He was told that Sergeant Denno would
be the investigator on Chris's case. However, he was told further, Denno
was working on another case and would not contact us until he started
Chris's. When Steve hung up, he looked as if he had been kicked in the
stomach by a horse. The commitment by the MPD to begin a proper
investigation seventy-two hours after Chris disappeared was not being
honored. We had no idea when Chris's case would be opened. No one
had seen or heard from him since Thursday night and still there had
been no action, no concern, and certainly no sense of urgency from the
Minneapolis police.

Understandably, our shock at this lack of support from the officials
we had trusted devastated us. Trying to determine next steps, our despair gave way to utter disbelief and anger. Once again Steve phoned

the MPD and eventually spoke with Denno, who told Steve he saw no reason to meet with us—Chris would probably show up.

Since the MPD did not take Chris's disappearance seriously, they would not release their official search dogs. Sara pushed forward in her quest. She met with success after following a suggestion to contact the Ramsey County Sheriff's Office. The RCSO offered six cadaver dogs, the caveat being that the Minneapolis officer assigned to the case must approve Sara's request. The request, however, was denied. Sara's stormy eyes showed her outrage that one of the most obvious methods for locating her missing brother—using search dogs—was initially dismissed, and now denied, by the very people she and Chris were taught to respect—the police.

Amidst tears of frustration and fear, she plopped back down on the floor with the Yellow Pages. Her efforts produced results. Sara found a bloodhound handler, Annie Sharma, who agreed to help. Sharma told Sara that her dog, Scrumpy, was young and consequently did not have a lot of experience. Sara assured her that we had no other options and we desperately needed to start working with a search dog. They agreed to meet later in the week.

Grandma Rose contacted Father Tim Power, our priest for eighteen years at Pax Christi Church in Eden Prairie, a large suburban community southwest of Minneapolis. Father Tim had already seen the news coverage and agreed to come to search headquarters that very afternoon. Fourteen years earlier, Chris had received his First Communion from this compassionate priest. Now, Father Tim sat with us, leading a prayer for Chris. His presence created whatever calm was possible in an increasingly anxious environment. In one of those quiet moments, I looked over at a huge poster of Chris leaning against the wall. I allowed myself to gaze into my son's eyes, imploring him silently for answers. His eyes, so full of life, love, and happiness a few days before, what would they reveal now? I sensed him telling me he was OK. Yet that answer could be interpreted in more than one way. How desperately I wanted it to mean he was coming back, healthy and unharmed. My intuition knew otherwise. I could not disconnect from his eyes, nor could I stem the flow of tears.

We welcomed the genuine support of Dr. Robert Seybold, from the University of Minnesota Counseling and Consulting Services, who

"Father Tim, I'm so excited to have my picture taken with you."

arrived at search headquarters with a colleague. For two days they made themselves available in one of the rooms for anyone who needed a listening ear, an encouraging word, or an idea about how best to cope.

Our team continued searches along the Mississippi River between the downtown area and the University campus, checking every dumpster, garbage can, shed, and log pile. Imagine the courage it took for friends and family members to open a dumpster, knowing Chris might be in it. Steve recalls lifting the lid of a huge garbage can and being startled by what he thought was a squirrel. When it jumped, so did Steve. Repulsed, he realized it was a large rat.

My heart ached for the amazing young adults who bravely faced new challenges each day with renewed hope. By Monday afternoon, their shoulders and heads drooped with the burden of not realizing their collective goal: finding Chris. Each night everyone returned to the main room at search headquarters so that our family could share updates on the day's events, answer questions, encourage comments and suggestions, thank the volunteers, and remind them not to skip class, miss work, or shirk other responsibilities. At the end of those gatherings, Grandma Rose and Grandpa Gene led us in prayer. The volunteers may have suspected we were rallying the team at the end of the day to help them hold it together. In actuality, being with everyone held *us* together because it compelled us to stay strong for them—and for Chris. We needed each other. Through this surreal tragedy, I appreciate the bonds that connect human beings in pain. I am convinced our deepest connections to others are forged in the worst of situations when we stand strong together.

Shaking Off Fear

Levity became a way to shake off the fear, to stay grounded enough to keep moving forward. We used it whenever we could. I grew up with five sisters, all born within ten years. My sisters were truly impressed with the character and spirit of Chris's friends at search headquarters. So, of course, I told them to eat their hearts out because these cool guys had hung out at our house for years. It eased the tension a bit to hear my sisters argue over who got to ride in the Ford vans "with all the cute guys." The forced banter kept us functioning so that we could focus on our mission. The alternative would have been to float aimlessly in a cloud of denial and almost certainly accomplish nothing. Never once did Sara, Steve, or I question whether we should act. We knew our why, our mission stayed crystal clear. The only question was, what do we do next? We remained confident that the "how" would take care of itself.

Who would have guessed that underwear would become a humorous issue? Steve, Sara, and I packed for only a couple of days, as did other family members. It was probably our way of pretending everything would be OK. Clean underwear quickly became a distant memory. Ingenuity came to the rescue: it occurred to us to "just flip it," and so we did. Nothing mattered more than finding Chris. The underwear issue became even quirkier when my sister Linda McCoy arrived from San Francisco at the end of the week. Mom had waited to call her until Linda finished running a scheduled marathon. Linda had just purchased underwear and in her haste to pack, she threw the whole bag of it in her suitcase before rushing to the airport. That bag of underwear was stashed in a drawer in her room at search headquarters and then it simply disappeared. Hmm, an underwear thief in our midst. (It showed up in housekeeping many days later.) No one really cared. This episode engendered brief laughter, a therapeutic gift in the midst of horror.

Humor also found its way to our radar screen in the form of a spy. My friend Diane, who is also the mother of one of Chris's closest friends, came to search headquarters to help. Due to a health condition, she rests every day for an extended spell. She fell asleep on one of the sofas and a few people suspected she was a spy (likely misinterpreting a comment passed from one person to the next) who was only pretending to sleep. I went to check out the spy theory and discovered my dear friend Diane fast asleep. Her son Jonathan, the only person who did not find the situation amusing, grumbled, "Yeah, right: my mom the spy. If she heard something, she wouldn't remember it anyway!"

"Loaded in Trunk . . ."

On Monday afternoon, four days after Chris disappeared, Brenda Olsen found statements written on one of his flyers taped up just two blocks from the Lone Tree Bar. Brenda, a key volunteer, was also one of the five members on the board of trustees who managed the newly created Chris Jenkins Search Fund. Some of the handwriting on the flyer read, "Loaded in Trunk . . . Paid for by dollars green." Brenda carefully removed it with the tape, hoping fingerprints could still be found. She brought it to search headquarters and immediately phoned the MPD to suggest they check nearby security cameras in hopes of catching the author. They told her the writing had no value whatsoever, that it was simply gang talk. The police refusal to check security cameras in the area where the flyer was discovered stunned and angered many of us. Sara, Grandma Rose, and I had a gut feeling the writing on that flyer provided clues to what had happened. The hateful message intensified our worst fear: Was Chris kidnapped? Then what? Why? Those cruel statements still haunt us and the flyer remains in our possession. What does it take to get help from law enforcement when a young male adult is missing?

Armed only with hidden microphones, my brothers-in-law and other adult male friends walked the streets at night, canvassing the areas in Minneapolis where homeless people gathered. They questioned those who lived in the area, believing these were the likeliest people to have seen or heard something. Some of the activities we engaged in were dangerous. But the alternatives—to wait for Chris to show up, or to presume law enforcement would suddenly move aggressively forward—seemed too ridiculous to voice. Chris was an integral member of our family; we would not leave one of us behind, ever.

Sara and Jan— profound grief.

A Late-Night Visitor

One of the late-night hunts surfaced an individual who said he had information. Shortly thereafter, he arrived at the Holiday Inn, our search headquarters, and was promptly interviewed in the lobby by Rick Stein. Another brother-in-law, Bob McCoy, hung out in the lobby to cover Rick's back, just in case things went south. At one point, the informant whispered to Rick, asking him if he knew someone was watching them, adding it was probably the FBI. The informant was referring to Bob, now affectionately known in our family as "FBI Bob." The name fit him well. His ability to observe, strategize, and interview proved invaluable during the critical first two weeks our family faced the harsh reality of our missing child. Moreover, his compassion touched us deeply. Ultimately, the information provided that night did not net results. We just kept moving forward, making the best decisions we could.

Meanwhile Chuck Loesch and Don Enger continued their investigative work. They learned that someone had been brutally beaten by several gang members on Halloween night in front of Times Square Pizza, across the street and down about half a block from the Lone Tree Bar. It made us crazy to think people hurt Chris that fateful night, yet we tried to piece together the most probable scenarios from the facts gathered. Sara asked a few friends what happened to someone when they were severely beaten. She heard that at some point, a person doesn't experience pain. *We* felt that pain, and we still do. We've had to face hundreds of ways Chris may have died, and it is as gut wrenching today as hearing it for the first time.

By late Monday night, both Enger and Loesch decided the entire situation had escalated so much that homicide at the MPD needed to take control of the situation. They believed the following glaring facts, among others, demanded a serious homicide investigation: Chris Jenkins, a responsible twenty-one-year-old student athlete, had not returned home; several witnesses had seen Chris being escorted out of the bar by a security supervisor; the Lone Tree Bar owner had issued a gag order on employees; a person was severely beaten around the corner from the Lone Tree Bar on Halloween night; one of Chris's flyers had a tormenting message; and key volunteers were continuing to search in unsafe areas. At about 10:00 p.m. Enger went straight to MPD homicide to share all the information and strongly advised them to take over the investigation.

Still looking for support, we secured a meeting with Minneapolis Mayor R. T. Rybak the following morning. Rick Stein and John Wood (John is the father of Chris's close friend Matt) accompanied us to that meeting. Mayor Rybak listened and extended his sympathy. Yet in terms of specific support (viewing of surveillance videos, release of search dogs, putting search boats on the Mississippi River, contacting the National Guard to search steep areas along the riverbanks, putting pressure on the MPD to investigate), he made no concrete commitments. Consequently, none of us felt confident that meaningful action would ensue. Just before we left his office, exiting through the back, he gave us his cell phone number and told us to use it. Over the next several days, we did just that. We never received a response, however, so it was as if that meeting never occurred. The mayor of Minneapolis left it to us to figure out how to motivate the police.

My parents, Grandma Rose and Grandpa Gene, would have climbed a mountain if the answer to their grandson Chris's disappearance were located at the top. They had not received a kind word from anyone in law enforcement, even though they had faithfully contributed to society their entire lives, including raising six responsible children, volunteering with numerous organizations, paying taxes, and leading lives of integrity. In their time of need, they received next to nothing from Minnesota law enforcement. They had to watch their family struggle without the support that should have been there from the first day of this ordeal.

Out of sheer desperation, Grandma Rose contacted the Jacob Wetterling Foundation for assistance. Known as the Jacob Wetterling Resource Center (JWRC) since 2008, the center is a national non-profit organization that was founded in 1989 by Patty and Jerry Wetterling after their son was abducted at gunpoint near St. Joseph, Minnesota. In 2002, JWF was part of a coalition to launch the AMBER Alert program in Minnesota. (See Notes)

On Tuesday afternoon, Patty Wetterling came to search headquarters with her sister Peg Overturf (interestingly enough, Peg taught Sara in sixth grade at Eden Prairie Middle School shortly after Jacob disappeared), and the executive director of the Jacob Wetterling Foundation,

Nancy Sabin. They provided a lifeline for us, giving us what we needed most—compassion, encouragement, and hugs, after little sleep and nearly unbearable anxiety for several days. They also came armed with suggestions: stay visible in the media (every station, every day), and build a bridge with law enforcement. From the very beginning we labored to build that bridge with the MPD, but we achieved little success. We kept trying, hoping a leader would emerge, or at least someone with an open mind. Our efforts eventually spanned three chiefs of police.

Shortly after Patty, Peg, and Nancy left search headquarters, my mom showed me a book those wonderful women had left for us. The book contained numerous steps to follow when searching for a missing person. As I leafed through its pages, I recognized the value of that pertinent resource. Yet I simply could not read it. My anxiety level had hit overload and I could hardly function. The disappearance of a child creates a chasm of profound loss and horror from which there seems no escape. Sleep eluded me. I had already stopped driving a car because exhaustion left me unable to find my way in a city I had known for thirty years.

Speaking for Chris—Begging for Information

We spoke to the media several times a day, almost every day, during those first two weeks. Each station wanted a private interview, and we tried to accommodate that request as often as possible. On Wednesday afternoon, I remember freaking out just as we started the third consecutive interview. Begging for Chris to come home, for someone to let him go, for someone to come forward was bad enough. But by now, we started admitting that the likelihood of ever seeing Chris again dwindled with each passing day. Stating that continuously to the public felt like the words created a grievous outcome. I remember screaming to no one in particular, "I just can't do this anymore!" I left the room and went racing down the hall. I ducked into an area near several vending machines. Hiding was my only thought—escaping the images my spoken words created. Without thinking, I squeezed behind a vending machine.

Moments later I heard my longtime friend Jackie Woll calling my name. I finally answered her in a weak voice. She told me I had to come out, but I refused, asking why. She had already arranged our interview via satellite from the FOX affiliate station in Minneapolis with Greta Van Susteren of FOXNews New York for that evening. Jackie reminded me we had to go shopping for clothes because all I had was the grubby jeans and muddy shoes I had been wearing when climbing the riverbanks. I still resisted and said I didn't care. In exasperation, Jackie said I had to come out and when I asked why again, she answered in a determined, direct voice, "Jan, let me put it to you this way: if Connie Chung calls back, we have to tell her you are already booked tonight." The truth of her statement jarred my senses. Covered with dust and cobwebs, I slowly inched my way out from behind the vending machine. Oh dear, I'm a public speaker, and I'm hiding behind a vending machine because I no longer want to face the media. Time for some serious self-talk: *Jan, pull it together, for Chris.*

After brief interviews with local media, we returned to search areas along the St. Croix River in Wisconsin. Based on leads that had come in, we decided to work that area one more time. I vividly remember walking in the shallow water along the shoreline when I heard Sara from the top of the steep embankment: "Hey, Mom, get out of the water." I yelled back, "OK, in a minute," and kept right on going. Suddenly I realized I couldn't feel my legs from the knees down in the bitterly cold water. Something inside told me Chris was in the water somewhere; frozen legs were irrelevant. About ten minutes later, Sara admonished in a more determined voice: "Mom, get out of the water. I really mean it this time." I tried to get away with saying "OK," but she wouldn't budge until I climbed up and stood next to her. There she stood with her hands on her hips, giving me a scolding look. The role reversal amused both of us.

Along with several of Chris's friends, we searched until dark when fatigue, cold, and hunger dampened our spirits. Steve and I took everyone to dinner; it was the least we could do to thank these incredible young adults for their continued efforts. We walked to each of the tables during dinner, checking in with every individual. We projected a positive attitude in an attempt to reassure them that we intended to do whatever was necessary to bring Chris home. Likewise, they voiced their determination to stay by our side. We held on to hope and each other.

We left the restaurant looking for a store to purchase clean clothes and shoes. T.J. Maxx was still open, so we stopped. As Sara and I walked down the aisles, we looked at the trail of mud we were leaving behind us. I lamented to Sara, "Oh no, look at the mess we're making." She gave a classic Sara reply: "Mom, you worry about the dumbest things! Besides, we'll be spending money here. We better move it, we've got ten minutes." Her comments brought a smile to my face as I realized the wisdom of her words. I had momentarily lapsed into "normal" behavior. Right then, mud didn't matter.

We returned to search headquarters and quickly changed. FBI Bob waited for us in a van in front of the hotel. I arrived first and jumped into the backseat. As we waited for Sara and Steve, I glanced out the window. I was staring at the back of one of Chris's flyers taped on the van window. Chris's picture drew me in as I sensed his presence. His words surrounded me: "Mom, I'm so sorry." As with the first time I had sensed him speaking to me, this message could have many interpretations. I felt his sorrow for all the agony his disappearance caused, yet he seemed to communicate even more. Feeling his message enveloped in sadness, my leaden heart knew he wasn't coming back. I tried to tell FBI Bob what had just happened, but I choked on the words and never finished.

Sara and Steve hopped into the van and we headed out for our first studio appearance on national television: live with Greta Van Susteren. We were on our way to tell the world our beloved Chris had been missing for almost a week. We wanted to express gratitude to all the volunteers and beg for someone to come forward. A few days earlier, in a brainstorming session with Steve, several of Chris's friends had come up with the tagline "Someone Knows Something."

Law Enforcement Finally Interviews Us

Almost a week after Chris's disappearance, Steve, Sara, and I were interviewed by the authorities. Each one of us was questioned at the same time in separate rooms. MPD Sergeant Denno interviewed Steve, MPD Liaison Officer Lisa Davis questioned Sara, and FBI Special Agent Dan Otterson spoke with me. Anger flashed through Sara's huge blue eyes when she exited her interview and strode toward Steve and me. She told us that she was asked several times, "What did the police find when they searched your brother's apartment?" She kept responding that no one from the MPD had searched Chris's house. Sara told Lisa

Davis: "My brother doesn't even live in an apartment. He rents a house with his friends." When Davis asked the same question a third time, Sara's frustration burst forth: "Which part of 'no one from law enforcement ever went to my brother's house' isn't clear?"

Steve's recounting of his interview with Denno riled Sara and me. We did not think he used good judgment in telling Denno that Chris had talked with a psychologist a few times after a breakup with his first love almost two years earlier. Chris and Crystal had dated for three years, and she was like a member of the family. Sara supported Chris through the inevitable heartache of losing someone he loved, and she suggested he seek professional help. Chris trusted her judgment and did just that. He didn't miss a beat that spring semester. He still maintained a high GPA and earned the trust of his teammates as a co-captain and starting goalie on the University Men's Lacrosse team.

When Sara and I learned that Denno had really pounded Steve with questions after he mentioned Chris's tough breakup, we knew our fears were realized—it sure seemed as if the suicide theory was born that day and grew legs. Steve told us that he became annoyed with the continued questioning about Chris's mental stability and that he had intended to present an example of Chris's resilience. Now, however, Denno saw Chris as a depressed individual. Steve sensed no concern or caring from Denno; consequently, he did not believe much of an investigation would ensue.

My interview with Otterson went well, yet nothing surfaced to give us direction. FBI agent Don Thompson had appealed to the FBI office in Minneapolis, asking for a professional courtesy since the MPD had not yet engaged and Chris was his nephew. Otterson appeared sympathetic, yet the FBI did not have jurisdiction in the case. Hence, I understood that their ability to act was extremely limited. We still felt alone in our desperate search for Chris.

A Prayer Vigil for Everyone's Child

Chris had become everyone's child. The public craved details, as evidenced by more than 100,000 hits on Chris's Web site the first three days it was up. Many left messages of hope for his safe return. Perfect strangers captivated by Chris's story (particularly those living in the downtown areas of Minneapolis and St. Paul, both papered with flyers) shared insightful and supportive messages. One poignant example:

> Just a stranger: I don't know Chris but his absence is noted in my everyday life: Every trip downtown I'm surrounded by his face. It follows me on my way home, at least an hour from the Cities, where I see the poster on car windows during the commute and then in the parking lot of where I work. Going to a concert on Nov. 2nd, I kept looking at the faces I would see in the crowd, the blondes with the short haircuts, I imagine to be his face in the corner of my eye . . . We're all watching, looking, and praying.

Prayer from all over the world sustained us. Human beings are simply not equipped to handle relentless terror without drawing on a power much greater than them. The Jacob Wetterling Foundation helped organize a prayer vigil for Thursday evening, November 6, at Northrop Mall on the University's Minneapolis campus. Approximately four hundred people came with flashlights, sorrow, and prayerful hearts. We brought candles for anyone who wanted one.

The flame from one of those candles will shine forever in the heart of Christy, a dear friend of Chris's. She clung tightly to her candle at the prayer vigil as she clung to hope for the safe return of Chris. Christy suffered from seizures, so she wore a helmet to protect her head. Four years earlier at Eden Prairie High School, where both were students, Chris had heard a boy teasing Christy because of her helmet. Chris couldn't stand to see people being ridiculed or taken advantage of, especially when they weren't able to defend themselves. Seeing the hurt in Christy's eyes, Chris confronted the boy, telling him in no uncertain terms that Christy wasn't any different from anyone else and that if the boy ever teased Christy again, he'd have to deal with Chris. A freshman challenged by a solid senior makes an impression. Deeply touched by that gesture, Christy began referring to Chris as "The Bodyguard." On the side of her candle, she wrote, "Bodyguard."

Where is Chris the Bodyguard? Is anyone helping him now? Did anyone help him Halloween night or was he simply handed over to cold-blooded killers?

Several of us struggled through our brief speeches at the prayer vigil. We spoke of our belief in Chris, his love for life, our desperate plea for his safe return, and our gratitude to all the volunteers who had put their lives on hold for us. We begged for someone to come forth with any information, no matter how trivial they thought it might be. As we shivered in the cold, the wind strengthened, dimming or extinguishing flames in dozens of candles. Those fading flames felt like a mirror to our souls where hope began to falter; a happy ending would be nothing less than a miracle.

Sara's prayer: "God, please bring Chris home."

CHAPTER 4

The Decision

November 7–November 16, 2002

Strength does not come from physical capacity.
It comes from an indomitable will.

MOHANDAS GANDHI

Sara, Steve, and I fled Minneapolis at midnight after the prayer vigil. Though we had little fear of our surroundings, my parents' troubled eyes expressed a different story. Other family members also became concerned for our safety; they heard grumbling in the streets as they walked. We received a few threatening calls at search headquarters. Apparently some folks didn't appreciate our presence in their world. We soon realized our naïveté regarding this world of gangs, turf, and drugs, all right in the middle of the entertainment district in downtown Minneapolis. Thousands of people now recognized our faces after almost a week of begging for information regarding Chris several times a day in the media and in the streets. For everyone's peace of mind and safety, the three of us tossed our belongings into suitcases, loaded them onto a luggage rack, and vacated search headquarters through a back entrance.

We headed toward Eden Prairie, the location the four of us called home for eighteen years. Although Sara and Chris had grown up in Eden Prairie, now Steve, Sara, and I instinctively knew the concept of home would never be the same again. One of our family members, 25 percent of our family, was missing. Without much thought, we pulled into the Courtyard by Marriott in Eden Prairie. Luckily, a room was available.

Ensconced in our undisclosed location, Sara flopped on one of the double beds in the room and unleashed. "So, a few short days ago, I'm on my way to Wisconsin to visit my parents, and just chill. But, oh no, my dumb brother has to go missing! So instead, I'm searching

for him in hospitals, dumpsters, abandoned buildings, and along riverbanks in Minneapolis. Why me? Oh, that would be because the cops
in Minneapolis aren't even looking for Chris. They told us he's on a
road trip or shacking up with a new 'chick.' They don't even know him!
I haven't slept or been able to eat for days. Chris, where are you? I love
you so much. I want you back." With her face buried in a pillow, Sara's
anger turned to despair and she sobbed uncontrollably. When she lifted
her head and stared at me, confusion and torment inundated her red,
puffy eyes. "Mom, what's going to happen to us? I can't live without
him, Mom, I can't."

Swirling emotions calmed inside me as they seemed to form the
trunk of a mighty oak. I gathered Steve and Sara around me as we
stood and formed a football huddle. As if to infuse my thoughts into
their hearts, minds, and souls, I leaned forward and they did likewise
until our heads touched. I heard myself affirm slowly and confidently,
"We are making a decision, right here, right now, to support each
other, no matter what. We will build each other up, not tear each other
apart." As we stood with arms grasping each other's shoulders, and
heads bowed forward, we felt our bond strengthen into an inseparable
covenant. We became a gift to each other, a gift wrapped and tied with
a bow by the hands of God. This decision propelled us forward; we
didn't look back or second-guess each other. Luckily, we had no idea
of the nonsense we would need to challenge, or the insults and broken
promises we would endure. Blatant resistance to our efforts compelled
us to blaze a trail, an uncharted path through the thick woods of evil,
deceit, and political fools. Along this treacherous, unpredictable path,
we often felt utterly alone.

Living this nightmare 24/7 threatened our bodies and minds with
an unrelenting panic we named red alert. Each night loomed as fore-
boding as all the others, with sleep coming only in short bursts followed by instant panic upon awakening. Sara, Steve, and I experienced
the same terrifying state: the moment our conscious minds ascended
from sleep, we immediately trembled with the realization that our beloved Chris had vanished. In fact, the dream world of restless sleep
seemed like real life. Waking up and going through the motions of the
day felt like the dream. To the very core of our bones, we knew life had
taken a vicious, untimely turn.

Sara spoke of her desperate, albeit irrational, attempt, to connect with her brother. She said food tasted like poison, and if Chris couldn't eat, she wouldn't either. Her mind reasoned that by starving, she would know when Chris's body started to shut down because hers would too.

Sara and Chris's cousin Jeffry Twidwell brought us a small statue of the large hand of Christ cradling a young boy. Jeffry's class at Benilde-St. Margaret's wanted us to have it. I pressed that statue into the palm of my hand, holding it tightly every night. To stay sane, I had to believe God held Chris in the palm of His hand. Yet periodically, I harbored anger toward a God who allowed this to happen. At times, I even felt God had abandoned us, dumped us on our heads, and left us alone to figure things out. Once in a while during the night I dropped the figurine. Upon any slight awakening, I'd curl my fingers tightly around this symbol of the only peaceful image of Chris I envisioned. If I couldn't feel the statue, panic overwhelmed me. My hands would grope for the light. I'd crawl on my hands and knees trying to find the physical image of Chris cradled in God's hand. Usually, I'd locate it under the blanket where I slept. I had already lost so much; this was my desperate attempt to hang on to something, anything, that offered a shred of comfort. Profound loss and the subsequent helplessness threatened the very fabric of life itself.

Day Seven without Chris

The Break-in

Early the following morning, November 7, Sara phoned Annie Sharma, the bloodhound handler she had contacted a few days earlier, confirming their 9:00 a.m. meeting to begin the bloodhound search. Shortly after we arrived at search headquarters, Sara went to her Ford Expedition parked behind the Holiday Inn Metrodome, only to discover a busted front window on the driver's side. Someone had broken in and stolen Chris's cell phone. Late the previous night, in her haste to vacate search headquarters with Steve and me, Sara had left the phone on the front passenger seat. She also left in the vehicle Chris's athletic bag filled with his sweaty, smelly lacrosse clothes and pads, ready for use as scent items in the bloodhound search. The bag lay opened. Someone had rummaged through it, but it did not appear anything was missing. Vandals had broken into other vehicles parked behind the hotel that same night, including the tour bus of a rap musician. A targeted theft of Chris's cell phone, or a crime of opportunity? Chuck Loesch reported the incident to the MPD and the FBI.

Scrumpy

Annie Sharma arrived at search headquarters with her bloodhound, Scrumpy, and an associate. They met Sara and Chuck, briefly discussed a strategy, and then everyone drove to the last place Chris was seen (also known as the place last seen, or PLS), the Lone Tree Bar. They scented Scrumpy in front of the bar with some of Chris's lacrosse gear. One block away, the hound picked up Chris's scent in front of Times Square Pizza. Following the scent, Scrumpy entered the indoor parking facility just north of that establishment. The dog circled the small main floor, and then continued down a ramp into the lower level. Scrumpy went immediately around the corner to the right, heading to an area behind the wall separating two parking sections in the lower level. He proceeded to stall eighty-nine, where he reared up on his hind legs, producing what Annie interpreted as a solid hit. A hit, or alert, is a generic term used by many dog handlers across the United States. The term refers to a canine indication or response to the scent of the person/object being tracked. The group exited the parking structure and scented the hound again. Scrumpy circled a bit, then continued in a straight line, moving rapidly; he stopped in front of the Lone Tree Bar.

After a short time out, the team restarted the process. Scrumpy took the same route into the parking facility, proceeding to stall eighty-nine, where he produced another solid hit. Next the team headed in the direction of the Hennepin Avenue Bridge over the Mississippi River. Scrumpy exhibited no interest whatsoever in the area between the Lone Tree Bar and the bridge. Yet about halfway across the bridge, Scrumpy stopped and sharply turned his head. Annie thought this alert might indicate a scent picked up in the air—coming from the bridge, or possibly from the river. Since Scrumpy was a young, inexperienced hound, Annie interpreted his alerts with caution. After crossing the bridge, Scrumpy went to and into the river directly below the north end of the bridge. Annie felt that alert was significant since the hound didn't even like water, and worked it with great effort. She believed the dog was picking up Chris's scent from the flowing water, indicating Chris or his body may have been in the vicinity, or upriver. The entire search is detailed and documented in Loesch's case notes.

A Red Feather

Loesch notified Sergeant Denno of Scrumpy's work. Denno and other agents then went to the parking facility, where they spent a couple of hours and found a portion of a red feather. A few days earlier, Loesch had spoken with the parking attendant who was on duty October 31. The attendant recalled sweeping up a red feather, which he described as similar to the one in Chris's headband, part of his Halloween costume.

Starting Over

Sometime that Friday, Chris's case was reassigned to Sergeant Jackson, MPD homicide. After meeting Jackson, we felt renewed confidence that progress could be made at last. He told us he basically had to start from the beginning. We shared all the information we had gathered, including twenty-six pages of notes documenting activities and interviews conducted by Chuck Loesch and Don Enger.

We left search headquarters late in the afternoon on Friday because Steve had received permission to announce Chris's disappearance and request information at the Eden Prairie High School football game that evening. It felt good to drive west and leave Minneapolis behind. Though hundreds of wonderful people had come to help, we had also experienced deceit, mockery, and indifference from a city we thought we knew so well. Chris had fed the homeless with his Grandma Rose and Grandpa Gene in this city where he was thrown out on the street, straight into the hands of cold-blooded killers.

Football: A Strong Father-Son Bond

Football represented a tight bond between Chris and Steve, one that had strengthened throughout Chris's life. Steve had coached every football team from the time Chris was five until he played in high school. Chris

"Hey, Dad, let's throw the pigskin."

played on three state championship football teams at Eden Prairie High School during his sophomore, junior, and senior years. Grandma Rose and I even painted our faces and fingernails red and black (Eden Prairie's colors) during the state championship games in 1999 at the Metrodome in Minneapolis.

The Eden Prairie football team, Class 5A, is legendary. Chris's coach, Mike Grant, is the son of Bud Grant, the respected eighteen-year head coach of the Minnesota Vikings from 1967 to 1983, with a final stint

Carrying Dobbins—our left OT. "Dude, are you losin' weight?"

in 1985. Over the years, Coach Grant established a solid football program in Eden Prairie, enabling him to suit up more than 120 players for high school games. At five feet eight inches and 195 pounds, Chris played offensive right tackle on the first string his senior year. Playing with passion and great enthusiasm, he held back guys a hundred pounds heavier and much taller than him. His success in that position was rare indeed for someone his size. Chris told us he felt honored to be chosen by his teammates as one of the senior co-captains. He loved football and we never missed a game. Grandma Rose and Grandpa Gene didn't either; a loud clanging cowbell always announced their arrival. For Steve, football symbolized a powerful and wonderful connection to our son. In fact, outside work, Chris's sports largely defined Steve's life. Chris and Steve were pals, quite a fun-loving pair!

At the last minute, I decided to let Sara and Steve brave the Eden Prairie football game. A massive migraine had settled in, leaving me extremely weak. It felt like a tight band compressing my head so hard, my eyes even watered. I thought if I took a shower and rested, maybe I'd recover a bit. I knew Steve and Sara would return crushed by the weight of yet another inconceivably difficult experience. Steve's face showed steely resolve as he prepared his brief speech. We both knew he would have crumbled without psychologically bracing himself for the inevitably painful and surreal experience he must now endure.

A Painful Plea

Before the players came onto the field to start the game, Steve spoke from the press box with Sara at his side. Sara told me it ranked as one of the most difficult traumas of the first two weeks without Chris. She described how time seemed to stop when her father spoke to a stunned crowd. Steve stood in a place where he and Chris had shared so much joy and anticipation. Yet now, staring at a football field he once knew so well, he experienced misery and loss as never before. Sara said that when her father finished his brief plea for information, he just stood there, motionless. She hugged him and then they left quickly, an emotional meltdown imminent. Walking toward the car, Sara held her father's hand and asked for the keys. She drove both of them back to the Marriott.

A Once-in-a-Lifetime Friend

Neil Lorntson, Chris's friend since grade school, had played on many Eden Prairie football teams with Chris. A couple of months after Chris disappeared, Neil compiled a notebook with pictures titled "A Once in a Lifetime Friend." Neil wrote numerous stories about the experiences they shared. He described Chris as energetic, caring, confident, fun-loving, and extremely generous. When Neil had surgery and missed his entire senior year of baseball, Chris showed up at his house nearly every day during the month Neil couldn't walk. Neil wrote: "Chris sacrificed many of the last times he had in high school because he knew how bad I felt." Neil also wrote about high school football:

When Chris told me he was going to try out as an offensive line-man his senior year, I just couldn't picture it. He's not the biggest guy, weighing about 190. Most offensive linemen for E.P. were 250–275 pounds. It's not that I didn't believe in Chris, I just wondered if he could really make up for almost 100 pounds with his heart and dedication. Boy was I wrong. Chris proved he was tough enough to do it by pushing around guys twice his size all season long. He worked hard, played smart, and just competed with more heart than the guys he played against.

Neil decided not to play football his senior year; Chris didn't agree with his decision. He stormed into Neil's room at 6:30 on the morning of the first football practice of the year. He woke Neil up, told him he was going, picked him up out of bed, and proceeded to carry Neil out of his room and up the stairs. Neil didn't play, but he still laughs about his friend who had a bigger vision for him than he had for himself. Neil described what Chris meant to him: "Chris always believed in himself. However, to believe in other people more than they believe in them-selves as he did, is even more incredible to me."

More Missing Students

Other families joined our unfortunate lot. On November 6, 2002, a college student, Michael Noll, disappeared after leaving a bar in Eau Claire, Wisconsin. He had celebrated his twenty-second birthday that fateful night. Three days later, on November 9, at St. John's University in Collegeville, Minnesota, an hour northwest of Minneapolis, another young male college student disappeared. Josh Guimond left a card game with friends to walk a short distance to his dorm room. He was never seen again. Like Chris, he seemed to vanish into thin air between midnight and 1:00 a.m. Loesch and Enger raised serious concerns to law enforcement officers following these developments. Three young male college students disappeared from bars or a party late at night, all along the I-94 corridor, within a hundred-mile radius, in a ten-day period. We also learned that a college-age female, Erika Dalquist, vanished from a bar in Brainerd, Minnesota, on October 30, 2002, one day before Chris's disappearance.

USA Today headlines captured the disappearance of these four young adults, as did the *New York Times*. Four college-age young people within a 180-mile radius in an eleven-day period simply disappeared. How might these cases be connected? The public tuned in and kept asking questions. It seemed strange to many that law enforcement did not appear to share the public's concern.

The organized searches wound down, since all the areas between the bar and Chris's house had been combed two or three times. Many of Chris's friends remained loyal to him, and to us, by offering their assistance any time of day or night. Like us, they preferred to do something, anything, rather than wait. Few of us could concentrate on anything else. As victims of a tragedy, we experienced the bizarre phenomenon of looking at the rest of the world and realizing we no longer belonged. We had entered another realm, that of survivors. We were on the outside looking in—this new reality impacted many people for quite some time. Steve, Sara, and I still experience life from the outside looking in. That new reality took over our lives, and we wonder if that will ever change. It probably won't. A loss of this magnitude rearranges the puzzle pieces of life in a way that the picture never looks the same again. We now see life through a completely different set of eyes.

One Missing Person Alerts More Than 100,000 People

Steve and I continued to encourage Chris's friends to resume their daily lives as best they could. We let them know nothing would stop us from finding Chris; they could count on us to finish what we started. Yet in the midst of the greatest tragedy in most of their young lives, Chris's friends did not disappoint. Instead, they stepped up with spunk and ingenuity. We knew that thousands of people would attend the Gopher game on Saturday, November 9, and the Vikings game the following day, so we received permission to have people hold huge posters of Chris—thirty inches by forty inches—at several entrance points to the stadium for both games.

Tricia Lorntson, the older sister of Chris's friend, Neil, shared her moving experiences with us. As she stood faithfully holding a poster, hoping for a clue, strangers stopped to read the sign she held, or to speak with her. She told us: "Kind eyes and anxious faces showed me how many lives have been touched by this tragedy. So many people walked up to me to express their deepest sympathies and to tell me they prayed every day for Chris and his family."

Cold temperatures had set in that weekend. I remember how much my shoulders ached from holding up the heavy poster. We had many volunteers, so once again, our strong presence created awareness. During that weekend, more than 100,000 people likely saw at least one of us holding a poster, asking for information. Steve recalls his sheer desperation as his eyes sought to reach the eyes of strangers moving past, on their way to enjoy a sporting event. "Someone Knows Something," our plea for truth, had become more like a battle cry for Steve. As I watched his frantic behavior, I knew he would pass out from exhaustion before he would ever stop looking for our son. A couple of times I heard him tell strangers, "I'm the father; I have to find my son." My heart ached deeply watching him try to cope with the searing pain of our new reality.

A generous person from the crowd rushing into the stadium for the Vikings game handed one of Sara's friends, Jenny Guille, two free tickets. Jenny coaxed Sara into going to the game with her. Sara came to tell Steve and me she was going to watch the football game for some much-needed relief. We hugged her, encouraging her to find a small measure of fun. She stayed at the game only ten minutes—long enough to realize that watching a cheering crowd made her feel even worse. Sara said she wondered: *How can all of these people be so happy when my world is crashing down around me? I experience no joy, only panic and fear.* We returned to our hotel in Eden Prairie with empty hands and wounded hearts. As soldiers on a battlefield, we saw no end to the bottomless pit of missing.

Unyielding Grief

What now? We held another prayer vigil on Monday, November 11, this time at the Church of St. Therese of Deephaven, a western suburb of Minneapolis. Steve and I attended grade school and church at St.

Therese, when we were many years younger than Chris. Now here we stood, speaking to about two hundred people, thanking them for their efforts, pleading for information, and praying for Chris. I wanted to turn back the clock in order to change the events of the past twelve days. Sara and Steve shared my time warp fantasy.

We did just the opposite: we pushed forward. We spoke for Chris and the three other young adults who had gone missing in the past two weeks. The idea of a serial killer became a topic of concern to us and interest to the general public. Greta Van Susteren of FOXNews wanted to air our message again, this time with Michael Campion, superintendent of the Minnesota Bureau of Criminal Apprehension. We met in the studio in Minneapolis, and once again Steve and I had to tell the world we had no idea of our son's whereabouts. When I later reviewed the tape of this interview, I remember my shock at the faces of two old people I didn't recognize. The strain of the past several days had sucked the life right out of us. The clothes hung loosely on our weary bodies. Strained faces revealed the deepened wrinkles and vacant eyes of our unyielding grief.

Sara described her world in a message she left on the message board on November 15:

Today is day 15. I have probably eaten 1 meal a day, slept 3 hours a night, and cried infinitely over the past 2 weeks. My best friend was taken from me two weeks ago. Chris, you are my heart, soul, and blood. You are a big reason I've smiled for the past 21 years. You're my hero, counselor, personal comedian, best friend . . . We all love you, but I've known and loved you the longest . . . remember when we locked ourselves out of the house and had to sit on the front step till mom got home (boy was she mad). Remember when we left Coco alone for the first time and she dug herself out of her kennel and sat there waiting for us to come home? Coco and I need our third Musketeer to finish the pack. Remember pretending we were the crocodile hunter trying to find "dangerous animals"? Or, how about sitting on a log for hours hoping that Chucky the beaver would come out of his home . . . I also remember the petty fights. I wish to God I could take them all away because they don't mean a thing. I wish to God I would

Sara, Chris, and Coco wait for Chucky the beaver: "All we wanted to do was just catch a glimpse."

have come to the lacrosse game you played in Madison a few weeks ago. I wish to God I would have come to see you sooner. Most of all I hope God returns you to me, safe. I need you, I miss you, and mostly, I love you. Chris, I am pleading. Please come home to me, PLEASE. I don't want a life without you.

Two days later, Sara flew home to Cincinnati. Steve and I drove back home to Milwaukee. Two weeks of gut-wrenching searches with hundreds of brave volunteers ended in the darkest way: leaving without Chris. *Chris, where are you? And by the way, God, where are you?*

CHAPTER 5

Utterly Alone

November 17–19, 2002

*A hero is an ordinary individual who finds the strength to persevere
and endure in spite of overwhelming obstacles.*

CHRISTOPHER REEVE

The three of us returned home without any knowledge of the whereabouts of the fourth member of our family. In our hearts we believed Chris was the victim of a heinous crime. So many facts pointed to foul play. The surveillance tapes did not show him walking across the Hennepin Avenue Bridge or the Stone Arch Bridge, the most direct pathways if he had chosen to walk from the bar to his residence. A bloodhound produced two solid hits in the same spot in the lower level of a parking garage diagonally across the street from the Lone Tree Bar. Yet that was not the parking garage where Chris and his friends parked their car. As well, the owner of the Lone Tree had put a gag order on bar employees shortly after Chris disappeared. The menacing message on one of Chris's flyers posted only two blocks from the Lone Tree—"Loaded in Trunk . . . Paid for by dollars green"—supports these disturbing facts. Knowing that one of the last people to speak with Chris was a Minneapolis police officer in the bar, and that that person has never once attempted to speak with Steve and me, is also perplexing and extremely troubling. Moreover, the continuous resistance from the MPD to properly investigate our son's disappearance made no sense. Nor did we understand the cavalier attitude and behavior of several MPD officers we met.

Gratitude and Grief

Steve, Sara, and I looked like shadows of our former selves. Collectively we had lost well over fifty pounds. Our hollow eyes revealed crushed spirits. A devastating sense of failure threatened to swallow any residual ray of hope to which we clung. Sara sobbed during her entire plane ride from Minneapolis to her home in Cincinnati. It hurt us immensely to know our beautiful daughter must face the upcoming week alone. She had worked tirelessly to find her beloved brother, her only sibling. For Steve and me, the drive home to Milwaukee seemed like an eternity. Heavy, almost suffocating grief filled the car. We had given our all, and still, we had no answers. We had just experienced a parent's worst nightmare: a missing child. The absence of genuine concern or effort from those entrusted with public safety had dramatically intensified the pain of missing. This horror must be at the very edge of what a parent can bear.

I reflected on the blur of those two weeks. In addition to the debilitating grief, gratitude found its way into my heart and soul. The large number of people who stood by us, offering their time, intelligence, and resources, overwhelmed and humbled us. Family, friends, and strangers sacrificed their personal lives for Chris and our family. That commitment continued in the new search headquarters established at the YMCA on the Minneapolis campus of the University of Minnesota. We returned home to work responsibilities only because of our complete confidence and trust in the people who kept search headquarters open, promising to communicate at least daily with us.

Numerous strangers we will never meet demonstrated what is good and right in the world. What a blessing! One stranger in particular felt compelled to help. "W.T." sent us an e-mail after several days of joining searches and locating resources. At that point, Chuck Loesch and Don Enger, the private investigators we had hired, considered almost everyone a possible suspect, especially strangers. So W.T. decided to explain. While standing at a bus stop in Minneapolis three years earlier, he was stabbed several times, robbed of bags of Christmas gifts he had just purchased, and left for dead. A Good Samaritan saved W.T.'s life. In our situation and in countless others, he chose to give back rather than retreat in bitterness and fear. Over the years, W.T. has become one of our most valued, dependable, and brilliant team members. Due to his humility, he will remain anonymous. In addition to the thousands of hours he has contributed, he gave us the gift of friendship and trust. He continues to help in innumerable ways, and we treasure his selfless love. He has shown so many of us how to give unconditionally, how to contribute to creating a better world. W.T. expects nothing in return. We consider him a family member; he became the brother I never had.

Our connection with the UMN Men's Lacrosse team shines as another wonderful example of unconditional support for which we are eternally grateful. Christian Bailey and Ben Simms, the two remaining co-captains, had a daunting task. They lost a friend they respected and loved, yet still needed to figure out how to pull their team together and lead it to and through a successful lacrosse season. Ben and Chris had known each other since seventh grade. Christian met Chris during their freshman year at the University. Christian and Chris had had a silly argument earlier in the week, so they spoke on the phone that fateful Halloween day, to straighten things out. The last words Christian would ever hear from Chris—"Hey, I love ya, man"—are etched in Christian's memory forever.

A couple of days before we left Minneapolis to return home, Coach Lars gathered the lacrosse players together for a dinner to discuss the winter practices, the upcoming season, and the tragedy that had struck the team. In addition to losing a friend, leader, and mentor, the team had lost their starting goalie and co-captain Chris Jenkins. Chris's teammates had to deal with more than loss. They had to come to grips with the fact that someone their age, someone they knew and respected, could vanish with few clues left behind. Chris was smart and strong, both mentally and physically. If evil could befall him, it could happen to any one of them. At the same time, the players needed to focus on building their team by enhancing their skills and developing a winning attitude for the spring lacrosse season.

These wonderful young men touched our hearts at a time when we needed it most. They helped us, more than they will ever know, through the toughest days of our lives. Coach Lars invited us to the lacrosse team's dinner, which we gladly accepted. We wanted to thank all the guys for their fantastic support and positive spirit. Promising to dig until we found answers, we assured the team that Chris would not just disappear without a relentless fight from us. Eyes, ears, and hearts soaked up our words: "We love you for the effort you've shown in helping us search for Chris. You know how much he loved life. Go to class, play hard on the field, and live your life to the fullest. You know that is exactly what Chris would want you to do. Please be safe by walking in groups. You are not invincible. We will bring Chris home. In the meantime, here's his goalie stick. We want you to use it and take good care of it until Chris returns." Tears welled up and spilled over on their hopeful and determined faces. Without telling us, Coach Lars asked the guys to each write something to Chris that evening. We first learned of this in the fall of 2007 when Lars returned Chris's goalie stick to us. Those notes were stuffed into its hollow shaft, creating a time capsule. The notes will remain in place until we plan a special event with Chris's lacrosse brothers to open the time capsule, read the treasured messages, and celebrate Chris's life.

Fading

After leaving the dinner, my legs felt like Jell-o as Steve and I walked to the car. Exhaustion seemed to permeate every cell in our bodies; we felt broken. Our earlier display of strength served to uplift Chris's lacrosse brothers, and to demonstrate our belief in Chris and commitment to find him. Yet now, even Steve began to believe he might not see our son again. Those early weeks stole our previous joy and innocence in life. The veil of ignorance regarding safety, fairness, law enforcement, and justice, which had protected us from the harsh reality of violent crime, unraveled more and more with each passing day.

Dear neighbors in Wisconsin, Barb and Dave Baldwin, had taken care of our home, which we had so quickly vacated and forgotten. They raked leaves, put away lawn furniture, collected the mail, and discarded the smelly shrimp in the refrigerator that had never been tasted. We had prepared that shrimp in the last minutes of a life we would never know again.

We knocked on the Baldwins' front door. As Dave opened the door, I just stared. I stepped inside and hugged him. Choking on my words, I confessed: "We couldn't find our son." I saw Barb across the room. Her eyes filled with tears. Barb works as an ER nurse, so she knows about despair, about hanging on to hope as life ebbs away.

The Minneapolis CBS affiliate station, WCCO, wanted a follow-up story. We desperately needed to collect our thoughts, to come to terms with the chaos that now ruled our lives. Yet, what if this story aired, moving someone to speak up? We chose consistently to sacrifice our personal needs for a greater cause. A rock-solid purpose—to bring Chris home—drove our thoughts and behavior; we did not waver. So our first day back home, starting before the sun rose, a news camera and two reporters from WCCO followed us at home and at work.

At his office, Steve gathered as many fellow employees as possible in a conference room. He wisely acknowledged what had occurred and emphasized the need to carry on. He also offered to answer questions at any time. People don't know what to say or do. Steve hoped that by periodically meeting with co-workers, and breaking the uncomfortable silence, he could ease the awkward confusion and fear surrounding a tragedy. The news crew explained their purpose: to air a story of our first day home in hopes of someone coming forward with information. They stayed for a couple of hours, capturing Steve in his ordinary routine.

In my home office, I tried to go through mail, pay bills, and cope with hundreds of e-mails. I kept looking at the delete key, wondering if there might be a way to erase the past two weeks. Logically, it was ridiculous. Emotionally, I wrestled with how to assimilate what I never wanted to accept: Chris was gone. I knew I would not see him again; yet I still wanted so desperately to be wrong. Missing, loss, grief, betrayal: this slippery slope moved in with no warning, no time for preparation, no training of any kind. Step by step, we had to learn how to handle one of the worst tragedies a family will ever face.

Needing desperately to connect with Chris, I walked into the backyard amongst the trees to a fire pit he had built two months earlier when he came to visit and do yard work to earn money for college tuition. Sitting on a rock, staring at the ashes, I sobbed till my throat ached and my head pounded. I didn't have any tissues, so I just wiped my nose on the sleeve of my jacket. Eighteen days before, that would have seemed gross. Now, it was so trivial—even with news cameras recording my searing pain.

In the months to come, we realized so often that in addition to the many new roles we assumed, we also needed to help others learn how to relate to us. More than anything, people wanted us to be OK. We thanked them profusely for their concern, yet rarely satisfied them because we told the truth. Admitting that our lives had turned into a living hell, we assured others we would not stop until we found our son. Less than three weeks after Chris disappeared, one of my dearest friends told me I needed to accept that he was gone, cherish wonderful memories of him, and be grateful for the years he spent with us. I told her she didn't get it. What I would learn over and over in the years without Chris was that very few people would ever get it. How could they? We belonged to a club no one chooses to join, yet membership demands the highest possible price—enduring the ultimate tragedy of losing a child. No parent or adult sibling wants to even think about that possibility; it is too terrifying. Missing renders that loss infinitely more incomprehensible and horrifying. Consequently, the disconsolate situation left Steve, Sara, and me in a very lonely place. Some friends and family members simply faded away.

Pleading for Help on National News

In the afternoon of our first day back home, we received a call from ABC's *Good Morning America* to appear the following morning. A couple of hours later we flew to New York, where we spoke on *GMA* and *Hannity and Colmes* on FOXNews. Lisa Cheney and Brian Guimond, Josh Guimond's parents (Josh disappeared on November 9 from St. John's University), also joined us on *GMA*. We requested a multidisciplinary task force to investigate the disappearance of our sons and two other college-age young adults, missing in a ten-day period, within a 180-mile radius.

To date, no one in authority has stepped forward with enough concern or courage to resolve these suspicious disappearances and deaths. Yet over the past twelve years at least seventy young college men have vanished from campuses and nearby bars, even private parties, under strikingly similar circumstances. One by one, their bodies turn up in rivers and lakes. Who is killing our children? Denial is an easy way to avoid accountability. How many more will be murdered before proper investigative efforts are initiated?

Nineteen Days without Chris

On November 19, 2002, the same day we spoke on *GMA*, Chuck Loesch continued to follow up on pertinent facts, people, and places in and around the Lone Tree Bar. He walked through many areas of interest, including the parking ramp at Fifth Street and Hennepin Avenue, where ten days earlier he had observed Scrumpy the bloodhound pro- duce a solid hit at stall eighty-nine. He spoke with an employee of the parking ramp, who verified that Rob Rankin, owner of the Lone Tree Bar, did not have a parking stall there but that a couple of the bouncers did. Loesch also learned that one of the bouncers who worked at the Lone Tree, "Mike Ellington," parked his vehicle in that same parking facility Halloween night. The following day, Loesch gave this informa- tion to authorities.

We returned home from New York late in the afternoon on Novem- ber 19. There had been no communication from the MPD, which left us wondering what was being done for our son. We phoned Sergeant Jackson, who told us that Chris's disappearance was either suicide or an accident. Yet when we pressed for facts that would lead to either of these possibilities, we heard none. We maintained that homicide must be considered before it could be eliminated. That clear logic received no response.

With rising anger I asked, "What's next?" Sergeant Jackson re- sponded, "We're in a wait-and-see mode." "Wait and see what?" He an- swered, "For the body to show up, which could be a couple of months or in the spring." Steve and I couldn't believe what we were hearing. Basic investigative protocol had not been followed: tapes from only a few security cameras in downtown Minneapolis had been viewed; police search dogs were not released; MPD had only interviewed one person out of four who accompanied Chris to the bar on October 31; not one person in the bar was interviewed by the MPD—the list is long. How could this investigation be stalled when it had scarcely begun?

"Sergeant Jackson, if you're convinced Chris is in the river, why aren't you doing everything possible to find his body? Boats, divers, what do you need?" He told us no efforts were necessary. Perhaps we should have guessed that response by now. Several days earlier, a stranger who saw Steve and me on *Hannity and Colmes* sent an e-mail suggesting we contact a nonprofit Christian organization named ALERT (Air Land Emergency Resource Team) to help with the searches. We learned that ALERT is equipped to perform wilderness, underwater, and aerial searches for lost people. They only respond at the official request of a public official, however, and sadly Sergeant Jackson would not make that phone call. The majority of our requests did not cost the city of

Minneapolis one cent. What was going on here? In the past two weeks, our team had searched on foot, worked with a bloodhound we located, even viewed tapes from video cameras that volunteers collected. All of these efforts were accomplished with our team's planning and resources. What accountability exists in the city of Minneapolis when a responsible University of Minnesota student athlete disappears from a popular bar in the heart of the downtown entertainment district?

In desperation, I begged Sergeant Jackson to release the six cadaver dogs offered free of charge by Ramsey County Sheriff's Office. I reminded him that Sara had secured the release of the dogs from Ramsey County, but approval for that release had already been denied once by the MPD. Literally on my hands and knees on our kitchen floor, trying not to sob into the phone, I said, "Sergeant Jackson, I'm begging you from the heart of a mother. Please release those dogs so we can find our son." Silence. Then, "I won't do that."

Despair gripped me like a vice. Gazing up at Steve from the floor, I whispered in a strained voice, "We're on our own. We're utterly alone."

CHAPTER 6

Free-Falling

November 20–December 15, 2002

*Never leaving one of our own behind may not have been
the easy path; but for us it was the only path.*

SARA JENKINS

Steve voiced the gnawing agony we both felt: "If only we knew where the bottom is." Consciousness had become a living hell. The only relief came in the form of deep sleep. Sadly that state was rare indeed. The instant we experienced even a slight awakening, that uninvited companion— red alert—returned. Adrenaline pulsed through our bodies, fight/flight, irrelevant. A heightened state of anxiety stayed with us most of our waking hours for at least a year before it slowly loosened its deadly grip.

The position of the police was to wait for Chris's body to show up. This can't be happening. How does a case stall out before it gains enough momentum to move forward? Ashley Rice is the only one of four people who accompanied Chris to the bar Halloween night who has ever been interviewed by the MPD or the FBI. The designated driver, Casey Walter, voiced his frustration to us more than once. Since he was the last friend who spoke with Chris, he wanted to talk with someone in authority. To this day, no one from the MPD has ever questioned him or any employee who worked at the Lone Tree Bar on October 31, 2002. Wait and see is not a viable option for the family and friends of a missing loved one.

It didn't have to be this harsh; missing creates enough heartbreak. We knew that Mike Casey, an MPD officer, was one of the last people to have a conversation with Chris. Because Officer Casey never showed the courage or courtesy to speak with Steve and me, the unknown and consequent dread intensified dramatically.

For two solid weeks, Chris's family, friends, coaches, professors, and even strangers put up flyers, asked questions, and searched buildings, dumpsters, riverbanks. Officer Casey could have come to search headquarters, introduced himself, shaken our hands, and expressed concern that our son was missing. He could have given us details about the last known minutes of our son's life. That simple gesture of speaking with us, telling us what he knew, and offering support would have made all the difference. Through that act of courage and honesty, we could have established trust with the MPD. Officer Casey had the power to lessen some of the torture we lived. In his silence, he chose otherwise.

Sara

Since returning home to Cincinnati, how had our brave daughter, Sara, coped? In her words:

> In this desperate state of constant anxiety, I did everything I could to find some normalcy, to surround myself with love and comfort. Our adored family Border Collie, Coco Chanel, lived in Wisconsin with my parents when Chris disappeared. Chris and I absolutely adored her; she was a once in a lifetime dog—smart, sensitive, lovable, and extremely loyal. Due to her age—11 years—I just couldn't put her through any more major changes. So I bought my own Border Collie puppy, Bijou. I could love her, and distract my mind, even if only for a couple minutes, from the horror which now defined my life. I lived in terror, always on edge. Driving down the freeway, if I saw plastic bags, I'd wonder if my brother's body was in them. White cargo vans spooked me to the point I wouldn't park next to them. On the freeway, I'd slow down or speed up to get around them. It was almost as if I drove around Cincinnati looking for my brother's body. Crazy? Unless you've experienced losing a family member in the torturous state called "missing," it's impossible to comprehend the depth of the terror.

Speaking Out

We decided to hold a press conference in Minneapolis on November 27, the day before Thanksgiving. Steve and I wanted to request assistance and express disappointment in the lack of effort on the part of officials to investigate our son's disappearance. Steve determined that he could not miss any more days of work, so I went to Minneapolis alone to conduct the news conference with Loesch. We held the event at the YMCA, our new search headquarters on the Minneapolis campus. Crews came from all four local network TV stations and the two local newspapers to capture the latest buzz. The message I started with was the same plea we have today. "Someone Knows Something—dig deep within yourself and find the courage to do the right thing. Please step forward and tell us what you know or saw."

I proceeded with three key points: First, we asked for the creation of a local, state, and federal task force to conduct a full investigation into the disappearance of Chris and the other three missing young adults. The similarities in the cases were striking. As noted in a *USA Today* headline on November 22, 2002, "String of disappearances grabs experts' attention—4 young people vanished over 2 weeks around Minneapolis." The article went on to say that "there are no firm numbers on how many college students are reported missing each year. Missing persons' advocates say it's about a few dozen at most." Yet in one month there were four missing in ten days—all within a 180-mile radius—something is terribly wrong.

P.I. Chuck Loesch and Jan Jenkins ask officials for help.

Second, we expressed grave disappointment in the MPD for a host of reasons. While numerous resources were used (National Guard, helicopters, divers, police on horseback, scent dogs, and search boats) in the other three cases of missing college-age students in Brainerd and Collegeville, Minnesota, and Eau Claire, Wisconsin, all within the past month, Chris's case had stalled early in a "wait and see" mode. Adding insult to injury, we heard that some MPD officers had openly stated that Chris likely jumped into the Mississippi River of his own volition due to his bouts of depression. Not a shred of evidence in Chris's life supports that preposterous conclusion. In desperation, we requested a meeting with MPD Chief Robert Olson. The first date he offered—December 12—meant two more weeks of no action to find our son.

Third, we challenged members of the public who lived, worked, and played in downtown Minneapolis to seriously think about their safety. The city seemed more concerned about promoting new entertainment options in the downtown area than with alerting residents about the danger. I urged the public to hold elected officials accountable for safety in Minneapolis. I questioned the position of the Lone Tree Bar in appearing more interested in limiting its liability by issuing a gag order on employees, than in trying to help find Chris, their employee Rice's date on Halloween night.

Loesch briefly described two more reported abductions in the past week. He emphasized that with collective manpower, brainpower, and equipment, these mysteries could be solved. (Sadly, we learned in the following weeks that both instances proved to be hoaxes. Wasting a family's resources and emotions with pointless rabbit trails is a cruel trick conceived by sick minds.) I ended our brief presentation by stating: "Someone knows something. I beg you from the heart of a mother to step forward, and tell us what you know. Please help us find our beloved son, brother, and friend, Chris Jenkins."

Then I spoke to Chris: "Chris, Dad, Sara, Coco, and I miss you and love you so very much. Sara has a new puppy to show you, a female border collie she named Bijou. Hundreds of people who care about you are searching and praying. God is holding you. Be strong. We will bring you home, Chris."

On Our Own

When I returned home to Wisconsin from the press conference, Sara and Bijou greeted me. I was so excited to see Sara I hugged her and didn't want to let her go. I desperately wanted to take some of her pain away, but I knew she must walk her own path. Ultimately each of us who knew and loved Chris had to find his or her own way through this maze of confusion and disbelief.

We were on our own, yet a high-ranking member of the Bureau of Criminal Apprehension in Minneapolis told Steve and me that a week earlier he said to a friend, "If this was my son, I'd be wondering why every policeman in the state of Minnesota wasn't looking for him." If Chris were the son of a politician or member of law enforcement in Minnesota, would he have received a fair and thorough investigation from the beginning? If that had occurred, would it have been possible to solve this mystery shortly after his body was found, sparing his family and friends untold misery? If so, how many taxpayer dollars might have been saved? More important, if Chris had been murdered, how many lives would be saved by putting his killers behind bars?

Thanksgiving 2002

That Thanksgiving a seat at our table remained empty. Thanksgiving didn't exist for us, and raw grief replaced our usual gratitude. Fortunately, Coco and Bijou brought intermittent comic relief by chasing each other in the yard. Coco's annoyance with Bijou's energetic puppy advances produced much-needed laughter and smiles.

We had received more e-mails and voice mails than we could possibly manage, so we responded to those with concrete ideas of how to find Chris. We returned a call to Penny Bell of Milwaukee, Wisconsin, who offered the services of Keeping Tracks, her volunteer K-9 search/rescue/recovery team. Two hours after our conversation, Penny and her father, Harvey, sat at our kitchen table showing us a portfolio of missing person cases assisted by Penny's bloodhound, a humble hero named Hoover Von Vacuum. Flipping through the pages of the portfolio, we saw numerous testimonial letters and news articles praising Hoover's results. We noted that Keeping Tracks had worked with various fire

Hoover Von Vacuum offers hope.

departments and law enforcement agencies in twenty-eight counties throughout Wisconsin and one county in Washington State.

Penny's sincerity and offer of help represented the only sliver of hope we felt that Thanksgiving Day; we jumped at the chance to find Chris. Penny and Harvey explained that their team needed to rearrange work schedules and complete various preparations, so it would be two weeks before we could travel to Minneapolis to begin a bloodhound search. Thanking Penny and Harvey from the bottom of our hearts, we walked out to their vehicle to meet Hoover. Patting Hoover's head, we asked her to lead us to Chris. Sara, Steve, and I surely emitted anxiety, which we later learned is easily picked up by a bloodhound. No wonder Hoover seemed to know a search was imminent. As we waved good-bye, our spirits felt lighter.

We had something to be thankful for after all! Eating our Thanksgiving dinner of frozen pizza, we discussed the renewed hope offered by Keeping Tracks. We avoided stating the obvious: if Hoover did find Chris, she would find a lifeless body. To comfort ourselves, we watched old movies while hugging Coco and Bijou. It was so hard to say good-bye to Sara two days later, even though we knew she'd be with us soon on our first search with Keeping Tracks.

Sometime during those two weeks of preparation, we met Penny's assistant, Terry Kaminski, who had already worked extensively with Hoover. Terry's role was to document Hoover's behavior, including the exact path the hound took. Two additional assistants came to Minneapolis with Keeping Tracks: Randy Thrune (R.T.) and Jason Burhardt, both firemen from the New Berlin Fire Department, located in a suburb of Milwaukee. We felt blessed to have this qualified team graciously offer its services.

Leading with courage is a choice to love and serve. We always hoped someone in law enforcement in Minneapolis would care enough to undertake a serious investigation. By conducting ourselves in a respectful and professional manner, and sharing all the data we gathered, perhaps our efforts would inspire a leader to emerge. Maybe our work with Keeping Tracks would produce information and/or evidence to engage the MPD or the FBI.

Since Chris's disappearance four weeks earlier, we also had looked for a leader in an official capacity in Minnesota who would strongly support an investigation. We even contacted Governor Jesse Ventura's office. With his term almost finished, we thought Ventura could demonstrate integrity by assisting the community in finding Chris, which would reflect his passion as a Navy SEAL for "never leaving a comrade behind." Even though Steve spoke personally with Ventura's assistant more than once, we received no help from the governor's office.

Lack of Follow-up

Sergeant Jackson had told us earlier in November that he needed to interview Ashley Rice again regarding key issues. With Sergeant Egge, he went to her residence on November 9 to complete that process. When they arrived, all residents were present, as well as Rice's parents and the parents of some of her roommates. They were about to leave for the University of Minnesota Gopher football game. Jackson decided not to ruin their fun by detaining Rice or her roommates with questions, so he planned to return at a later date. These details are clearly documented in the official MPD report. Though we've asked several times if a follow-up interview occurred, it did not. Eventually, Captain Rich Stanek told us it was not necessary.

We knew about the Gopher football game that day. Chris's ticket sat on his desk, unused, a gift from his father. Along with many of Chris's friends, we held up missing posters just outside the stadium before the football game began.

The lack of follow-up tormented Steve. What if Rice had information regarding what happened Halloween night that could shed light on this mystery? Details that may seem innocuous to a witness could prove in-valuable in piecing together events impacting an investigation. I suggested to Steve that he contact Rice's father, requesting a father-to-father conversation. Rice's parents helped at search headquarters, so we had already met them. Deciding this idea had merit, Steve spoke with Larry Rice, only to be told Sergeant Jackson was tough on Ashley when he questioned her at search headquarters, so Larry would not commit. I listened to Steve beg for cooperation. After twenty minutes Steve was pacing and pounding the kitchen cupboard, yelling, "Hey, man, we know Chris is dead. Help us, for God's sake." Larry responded by asking Steve how he knew Chris was dead. Steve blurted out, "Of course he's dead; we knew our son. Chris did not disappear by choice. If Chris was abducted, he would fight relentlessly to save his life. He would have been

"*Dad, thanks for the ticket.
I missed the game; I was in heaven.*"

so difficult to control, he would surely be killed by now." Larry finally said he would have to speak with Ashley's mother, Cindy, adding that Ashley would soon be home for Christmas in Willmar, Minnesota. He promised to speak with his wife and Ashley, and call us back with their decision. Larry Rice never contacted us.

Hope

During the first week of December, preparations for the bloodhound search produced a flurry of activity. We needed supplies, permission to enter various buildings and bars and to mark Hoover's path with spray paint, as well as a clear understanding of local laws regarding private property and proper protocol for a bloodhound hit. We did everything possible to produce useful work so that the results would be accepted by law enforcement and in a court of law.

Although our background checks surfaced both strong admirers and harsh critics of experiences and results with Penny Bell of Keeping Tracks, why would a family not pursue a viable option when the resources in their own city were denied on several occasions? A search for a missing person is an emergency, yet it was now five weeks since Chris had disappeared from downtown Minneapolis, the city he lived in and loved, and no police search dogs had ever been released to look for him.

Since Hoover would be working in a busy downtown area with many intersections, obtaining traffic protection was another necessary precaution. Even with their acute scenting abilities, bloodhounds will often need to sniff around an intersection more than once because of environmental variations, including exhaust from vehicles and weather conditions.

Penny and her team would not accept money for their work. Believing an experienced bloodhound team had the greatest chance of finding Chris, our family covered all expenses for the entire crew. What a small price to pay for hope! During the searches in Minneapolis, most of us stayed at the Courtyard by Marriott in Eden Prairie, which generously covered the cost of our rooms.

Even though only a few people would assist in the dog search, we planned an informational session for our volunteers to thank them and share updates regarding our efforts in locating Chris. Early in the evening on December 7, 2002, more than fifty volunteers gathered in a large room graciously offered by the Holiday Inn Metrodome in Minneapolis, our former search headquarters. Wonderful friends prepared and served dinner. After dinner, each volunteer received a handout that included a description of the Keeping Tracks mission for Chris, a list of service opportunities, and key points regarding professionalism and standards of conduct for those involved in the hound search.

The Gentle Giant

We learned that Hoover was an American Kennel Club–registered man-trailing bloodhound that had already assisted in several cities in Wisconsin, including Oconomowoc, Sturgeon Bay, and La Crosse. Penny spoke briefly about basic bloodhound tracking behavior, warning that the breed tended toward willfulness. When the hound gets on a scent, instinct drives her to find the end of the trail. With approximately 250 million scent receptors in their nose (humans have about 5 million), bloodhounds are well equipped for their work. Even the folds of a hound's skin aid in holding scent particles.

Sara and Chris's dear friend Jeff Meixner, now a local law enforcement officer, volunteered to carry the scent bag, needed to periodically provide Hoover with Chris's scent. Jeff earned the title of "Stinky #1" that night. Once again, humor helped balance the mounting tension of what might be uncovered.

Penny carefully explained that for several weeks we had searched for Chris, the fun-loving college student. Now we must focus on finding *anything* connected to Chris. A hair in the crack of a sidewalk, a piece of fringe from his costume, a few skin cells on a wall or railing (skin cells are as unique as fingerprints), or possibly a drop of blood in the gutter—all would be potentially vital evidence for the MPD investigators.

Hoover's massive size belied her gentle nature. As Penny introduced her to all of us, the hound lifted her head, eyes searching the crowd with curiosity. Her long muzzle, drooping ears, and loose, wrinkled skin gave her a rather mournful, yet dignified expression. She appeared anxious to begin the search, so Steve, Sara, Grandpa Gene, and I patted her head through the bars of her crate. She seemed to connect deeply with us. *Will Hoover be the hero in locating Chris?* we wondered.

I looked into the eyes of many brave friends, who demonstrated that night what it meant to love someone. Gratitude, sorrow, and anxiety filled my soul. This remarkable display of courage by so many twenty-somethings and older adults touched me deeply. Steve, Sara, and I had to remain strong and vigilant; our attitude and behavior would set the pace, and these determined friends would surely follow.

Scenting

Penny began the first search by using the standard way to start a bloodhound. We went to Chris's residence, where Penny found perfect scent articles: sweaty lacrosse clothes and equipment. She chose Chris's lacrosse helmet and a navy blue bandana from inside the helmet, as well as a T-shirt from a pile of Chris's soiled laundry. Sealing these items in legal evidence bags, Penny continued with the standard scenting technique of bringing these articles outside and scenting the bloodhound. We then watched Hoover walk into Chris's residence, easily find his room on the third floor of the house, and stop directly in front of the same pile of unlaundered clothes. Not once did Hoover wander into any other room or area of the house. After exiting Chris's house through the back door, panic returned instantly when we saw his car. We stood for a moment under a streetlamp in the cold evening air, trying to hold ourselves together.

Complete details of the path Hoover took are well documented in Terry Kaminski's and Chuck Loesch's written reports. While many significant facts are noted here, some specific details are excluded because Chris's case is, once again, an open investigation.

The search resumed where Chris was last seen, a location commonly referred to as PLS (place last seen), which also represents a potential crime scene. Consequently, we scented Hoover outside in front of the Lone Tree Bar. Hoover proceeded into the bar (permission had been granted prior to our arrival), verifying that Chris had been in the establishment by exhibiting hits on numerous places, including the office door.

For whatever reason, family members were not allowed to enter the bar. I finally opened a door, stepped inside, and introduced myself to the bouncer, telling him we had permission to enter from Lisa Rankin, the bar owner's wife. The bouncer grabbed my entire face with his hand and pushed me backward. If Steve, Sara, and a couple of other people had not been standing behind me, I would have landed on my back with my head smacking the concrete sidewalk. Distraught, Steve called Lisa Rankin, who agreed to meet us in the Lone Tree Bar the following day.

Hoover and team exited the bar as we watched in wide-eyed amazement. A metal chain connected Hoover's harness to a belt around Penny's waist. Tethering the hound this way allows it to lead with no interference from the handler. Sergeant Nelson and other MPD officers provided traffic control that first night. Hoover's tracking clearly communicated that Chris had walked on city streets. Along her path, she rubbed her body on the wall of two different buildings, sniffed cracks in the sidewalk, licked the ground near a pillar, and dragged her jowls on the sidewalk outside a popular restaurant. Terry assured us these behaviors indicated clear hits. About 2:00 a.m., we ended our first bloodhound search in Minneapolis with Keeping Tracks.

The following day—Sunday, December 8—Jill Krause (the bar manager on duty Halloween night) and Lisa Rankin met with Don Enger, Chuck Loesch, Chris's uncle Don Thompson (an FBI Special Agent in Charge based in Richmond, Virginia), Steve, and me. Krause showed us where she had seen Chris in the bar. Hoover had already hit on those locations the previous night. In Loesch's notes recorded one month earlier, several other people who saw Chris in the bar Halloween night mentioned many of the same areas.

Krause's description of Chris, his conversation with Officer Casey, Casey's speaking with Norris, and Norris's escorting Chris out, then giving instructions not to let him back in, sent arrows through my heart. It was like watching a movie of the last known minutes of our son's life. Krause had just described our beloved Chris, whom we had not seen or held or heard in over a month. Our wonderful son, put on the street alone, without his wallet, cell phone, or house keys, by heartless bar employees who never gave him a chance to tell his friends what was happening. My throat ached with words I could not speak and tears flowed freely. With raw grief screaming inside me, I wanted to crawl out of my skin.

Later that day, just one block from the Lone Tree Bar, Hoover led us into an underground parking ramp where she worked until she stopped between stalls eighty-nine and ninety. She brushed her body against pillar eighty-nine, and then growled in that corner area. Before we started this search, Penny had told our family that Hoover would often go to the closest family member to point out the significance of a particular hit. She said it would likely be me, and if I weren't there, Hoover would go to Steve. Sure enough, after the solid hit on stall eighty-nine, Hoover walked straight up to me and stood still, pressing the side of her body against my leg. Our mouths dropped open as Steve, Sara, and I observed this behavior and tried to comprehend Hoover's amazing gift of tracking the invisible..

Next, based on a lead, we scented Hoover farther east on Hennepin Avenue in the direction of the Hennepin Avenue Bridge. She showed no interest whatsoever. So we returned to the pavement in front of the parking garage where Hoover had just had a hit, and scented her again. She pulled us right back into the garage, led us to the basement area, and started checking vehicles. One month earlier, Scrumpy had taken us from the Lone Tree Bar to that same garage two separate times, displaying solid hits both times, at stall eighty-nine. These behaviors exhibited by two different bloodhounds, one month apart, served as compelling evidence that a vehicle carrying Chris's scent had likely parked there on Halloween night, and possibly many times since. Casey Walter, the designated driver for Chris and their friends, told us he did *not* park in that underground garage on Halloween night. In fact, several of Chris's friends who were not with him that fateful night, have since assured us that they *never* parked in that unsavory garage, nor would they ever consider parking there.

The Lone Tree Bar in downtown Minneapolis is located west of the Mississippi River, about a mile and a half from Chris's house, which is east of the river. The following day we checked many locations between the Lone Tree and Chris's house, paying particular attention to areas along the Mississippi River. Hoover did not show the least bit of interest when walking across the Hennepin Avenue Bridge, which has many areas along the curb, sidewalk, and cement parapets where a scent could gather.

The following documentation, dated November 6, 2002, states that Chris was not seen walking on the Hennepin Avenue Bridge. Sergeant Paul J. Anderson, assistant supervisor of the Protection Services Unit at the Federal Reserve Bank of Minneapolis, wrote: "I have completed the review of the tapes from cameras 223 & 207. The tapes were reviewed from 11:00 p.m. October 31st 2002 to 4:00 a.m. November 1st 2002. There was no one observed on the tapes matching the description of Christopher Jenkins by dress or physical description." Keith Lange, supervisor of the Protection Services Unit, stated that he felt confident the cameras would have picked up Chris somewhere along the bridge if he had crossed it on foot. Several weeks earlier, Lange told Sergeant Jackson that Chris was not seen on the tapes. Although Jackson's entire theory is based on Chris's walking across the Hennepin Avenue Bridge, he did not request a copy of the tapes for viewing or for evidentiary purposes.

At one point, Hoover literally howled from her crate in the van when the van was under the northeast end of the Hennepin Avenue Bridge. This is the same area where Scrumpy walked right up to her shoulders in the Mississippi River four weeks earlier. Concerned by Hoover's behavior, Penny insisted on a short rest.

Starting again, we took Hoover north of the Hennepin Avenue Bridge on the east side of the river, near the footpath area—again, the dog showed no interest. When we scented her about two blocks farther north, at West Island Avenue, Hoover proceeded down a few stairs to a small dock, where she jumped into the river and then walked out onto the shoreline.

After a dinner break, we scented Hoover at the City Center, a couple of blocks from the Lone Tree, the location of another reported sighting of Chris on Halloween night. Hoover showed slight interest in two areas, then exited the City Center near Hennepin Avenue, heading back toward the parking structure where both bloodhounds had produced hits. In front of that parking structure, she went right into the street and started scenting the air, periodically checking the curb. Hoover's pace picked up as she turned, taking us east on Sixth Street. At Marquette Avenue she turned left, heading north. We had to jog to keep up with her. Witnessing the obvious change in Hoover's scenting behavior (picked up pace, sniffed air more, sniffed ground less), we asked if Chris's scent was now in a vehicle. When Penny answered yes, we silently prayed that Hoover would indeed lead us to Chris.

The MPD provided traffic control a couple of hours on some days of the search. Loesch assisted in his car, focusing primarily on protecting Hoover. Though we had many challenges while Hoover tracked in the streets, one of our volunteers, a friend and former neighbor named Phil Buchanan, offered us solid support and comic relief. Phil showed up for the hound searches wearing an orange headband and white gloves. When we had no traffic control, Phil hustled to the middle of the intersection and quite successfully managed the flow of traffic. "I'm a New Yorker. We get the job done," he said.

Shortly before midnight on December 9, we met MPD Sergeant Gerald Wallerich of the Second Precinct. He recognized Hoover because in 1999, Wallerich's brother Tom, a captain in the La Crosse, Wisconsin, Fire Department, witnessed Hoover and Penny take rescue workers to the exact location in the Mississippi River where the body of a male victim had been recovered six weeks earlier. Though purposefully led in the wrong direction by law enforcement to challenge her skills, Hoover proved her ability by leading everyone to the correct spot.

A few days later, during our second search with Hoover, Steve received a phone call from a reporter regarding the disappearance of another male college student. Chad Sharon, a freshman from Wisconsin on full scholarship at Notre Dame, vanished on December 13, 2002. Since Chad was the fifth young adult male missing in ten weeks from Minnesota or Wisconsin, Steve assured the reporter that either a serial killer was on the prowl, the green Martian theory deserved attention, or young adult males were simply vanishing into thin air! The reporter wanted to know if Steve thought these cases were related. Steve replied, "Coincidence can no longer account for the disappearances. Why doesn't anyone in law enforcement see this?"

On the last trip to Minneapolis in mid-December, Hoover ended her path by leading us north on Washington Avenue, where, with no hesitation, she sped up dramatically, taking the left lane onto the ramp of I-94 West. Although bloodhounds have successfully tracked a scent on a freeway, we realized that permission and expertise were necessary before continuing.

The following day, as we researched bloodhound capabilities, we found quite a bit of information about a heroic police bloodhound named Yogi. In 1993, near Denver, Colorado, Yogi followed Aleszandra "Alie" Berrelez's scent for approximately twelve and a half miles, which included tracking along C-470. On May 23, 1993, the *Rocky Mountain News* reported the following: "'I was totally dumbfounded that a dog could track a scent left from someone inside a moving car,' said Englewood Police Chief Dave Miller. Miller said the dog was able to track the scent from Alie's clothes that wafted from the car like pollen and settled on bushes and grass alongside C- 470." Since bloodhounds can provide an invaluable service in searches for missing people, even tracking a person in a vehicle, we are surprised they are not used routinely by law enforcement.

Inquiring through the proper channels, we discovered that law enforcement, understandably, must be in charge of searches involving tracking on a freeway. We received no assistance. In a conversation with Steve, Sergeant Jackson said the buzz at the MPD was that we made a spectacle of ourselves while searching with Hoover.

We had tried so hard to produce results worthy of consideration. Both Scrumpy and Hoover tracked Chris's scent, twice, to the same spot in the underground garage, and Hoover followed the scent through the streets of Minneapolis all the way to I-94 West. Though neither hound showed interest while sniffing along the sidewalk or curb when crossing the Hennepin Avenue Bridge, Scrumpy did lift his head and sniff the air partway across.

Not once did Hoover go down a one-way street the wrong way while tracking Chris's scent. Considering that much of her trailing occurred in a downtown area where at least 90 percent of the streets are one-way, this feat alone lends a high degree of credibility to the work Hoover accomplished.

Nonetheless, Sergeant Jackson would not consider even the possibility that Chris had been abducted. With heavy hearts, we realized our efforts were in vain. Worse yet, Chris was still nowhere in sight.

CHAPTER 7

Winter of the Soul

December 16, 2002—February 27, 2003

*Anyone can give up, it's the easiest thing in the world to do.
But to hold it together when everyone else would understand if
you fell apart, that's true strength.*

ERNEST HEMINGWAY

During one of the searches with Hoover the bloodhound in downtown Minneapolis, I gazed at the winter scenes with animated figures in department store windows. It was like peering through a looking glass into my childhood and seeing joy in a life that made sense. I remembered our annual family Christmas outing when Mom and Dad took us into Minneapolis. In eager anticipation, all six sisters would dress up, load into our nine-passenger station wagon, and head downtown to enjoy the holiday displays and dinner in a restaurant (a rare treat). Walking in awe through Dayton's Winter Wonderland, and shopping at the children's store in Santa Land right in the middle of that extravaganza, was the highlight of the evening. Steve and I had continued that same tradition with Sara and Chris.

Facing the Holidays

The tune of "Silent Night, Holy Night" rang in the streets and jarred me back to the frightful present. Under softly falling snow, I squeezed my eyes shut, covered my ears with my gloved hands, and rested my forehead against a shop window. I begged God to make our nightmare go away, but no such miracle occurred.

Back home in Wisconsin, the sights and sounds of Christmas filled the air. Twinkling lights and decorations on houses and trees, mangers in churches, and Christmas carols playing on the radio seemed to be reminding the world "'Tis the season to be jolly," but not for families like ours. We couldn't escape the unbearable thought of facing the holidays without Chris. Even a simple act like opening cards with holiday letters and family pictures reminded us our family was broken.

The day after we returned home, I learned my heart could break further. A huge box sat on the front porch. After reading the card from Sara and Chris, I couldn't even open the package. Although my birthday was in August, this gift had been back-ordered twice. The meltdown that ensued left me sobbing on the front porch on that cold December day. A gift from my daughter and son, purchased a few months earlier in a life long gone, now brutally reminded me of our profound loss. I had so many questions—*Chris, where are you? What happened? Who hurt you and caused so much pain?* Silence surrounded me.

Struggling to stand up, I wondered how I could possibly have any tears left. I walked into the house and called Steve, yet couldn't form words in between heaving sobs. An hour later when I spoke with Sara, she reminded me she had already told me to expect a large package. Of course I had forgotten. Sara and I both wept, not knowing how to cope in a world cruelly turned upside down. She said Chris kept bugging her for weeks to find out what had happened to the gift. He asked about it again, the last time she ever laughed with her brother—the morning of October 31, 2002. Wanting Chris's advice on an issue, Sara phoned him back, leaving a voice message to call her before he went out for the evening to celebrate Halloween. Her brother's call never came.

Somehow I pulled myself together the next day to review a sales course I had delivered numerous times for one of my clients, Ernst & Young. I had accepted the engagement a few weeks earlier, believing that serving others would also have a positive impact on me. My mission as a professional seminar leader, speaker, and executive coach is to help people feel good about who they are by encouraging them to discover and honor their strengths. An educator at heart, it's a privilege for me to help others learn, grow, and make positive changes in their lives.

Two days later I checked into the hotel in Chicago where the seminar would be held and learned that a respected colleague, Rick Nasal, would also be facilitating another sales course for Ernst & Young the following day. Rick and I had a chance to speak briefly after the sessions. A spiritual leader in his church, Rick easily shared his deep faith with others. With compassion and concern, he assured me that Chris lived in heaven and I would see him again. His words comforted me, yet we had had no confirmation of Chris's death. On the trip home I realized I still held on to that sliver of hope that Chris might be alive.

Determined to find something positive in life, I decided to bring out the Christmas gifts purchased on our vacation two weeks before Chris disappeared. There in the closet sat beautifully wrapped gifts for Sara and Chris. Not knowing how to deal with the gifts or my intense sorrow, I simply closed the closet door.

Instead, I dragged out boxes of Christmas items stored in the basement. One box contained several brand-new hand towels, each one decorated with one of Santa's reindeer. Every year, I sent small Christmas items or food to Sara and Chris early in December to cheer them up before finals and let them know how much we loved them. Smiling at two sets of silly-looking reindeer inspired me to think of a way to express gratitude. Chris's friends were still in college, trying to successfully complete a semester after six weeks of suffering profound and senseless loss. The idea of supporting these young adults by sending fun gifts energized me.

Santa's Workshop

Our neighbor Linda had just opened her holiday sale of wonderful handmade soaps, lip balms, and candles. Apparently, I became her best customer of the season! After buying more funky Christmas towels, I began assembling gifts, carefully choosing items for each individual. Our kitchen table looked like Santa's workshop as I created packages for at least two dozen students and many others who had stood by us during the worst six weeks we had ever endured. In addition to expressing gratitude, these gifts would let people know we were doing our best to stay strong and move forward in life.

The week before Christmas, Steve spoke many times with Chuck Loesch and Don Enger, our private investigators, trying to decide next steps. If the disappearances of Chris, Michael Noll, and Josh Guimond (all in similar circumstances in a ten-day period within a hundred-mile radius) were connected in any way, maybe St. John's held important clues to unraveling these mysteries. Guimond had disappeared from the St. John's campus in Collegeville, located about sixty miles north-west of Minneapolis. The end of Hoover's tracking led to I-94 West, the route to Collegeville. After much discussion, Loesch, Enger, and Steve decided the next search with Hoover would be at St. John's. Steve planned to leave two days after Christmas to meet them in Minneapolis to strategize and organize the search. I chose to stay in Wisconsin to spend as much time as possible with Sara and Bijou, who were arriving from Cincinnati to spend several days with us over the holidays.

A Semblance of Family

Wanting to create some semblance of family, I thought we should put up a tree and a few decorations, including the Christmas stockings. Steve reacted in anger and pain. "Christmas doesn't exist for us," he said. "We have nothing to celebrate. Why pretend we're happy? We're dying inside." I walked up to him, looked directly into his eyes, and replied, "Because we have a daughter named Sara. She deserves the best we can offer." Begrudgingly, he consented and carried the box containing our artificial tree into the family room. As he started pulling out the branches, he sank to the floor, grief stricken. Finally able to speak, he held up some strands of tinsel and reminded me what had happened the previous Christmas. Chris loved celebrations and had insisted on putting tinsel on the tree. It's such a mess to clean up, Steve kept telling him no. Chris ignored his dad and did it anyway. Now, a couple of strands of sparkling tinsel ignited memories of our son's positive and lively approach to life. My heart broke for Steve, the dad who gave up so much for his children. In a voice laden with sorrow, he whispered, "I didn't just lose a son. I lost my best friend."

What do you do with the stocking that says *Christopher*? We hung it up with the rest of our stockings, hoping against all reason that Chris would be home for the holidays. Somehow we managed to decorate a smaller tree and place the beautifully wrapped gifts from our vacation beneath it. As illogical as it seemed, maybe by pretending Chris would be there, he really would. Or perhaps I began to recognize that there could be grace in denial.

Sara and Bijou arrived on December 23. As excited as we were to see Sara, Coco was distraught at the arrival of Bijou. Once again, Bijou's

Steve is determined the border collies will like each other.

silly antics drove Coco crazy and brought much-needed laughter to our lives. My sister Carol and her family from Indianapolis stopped by on their drive to Minneapolis for the holidays. They brought fresh-baked cookies and other holiday treats. Their brief visit and gift of loving-kindness gave us a measure of comfort.

Our home in the country had dozens of windows. For the first time, we put electric candles in every window. Maybe these flickering lights would guide Chris home. I continually prayed for a miracle. Why not? Others experienced joyful miracles. On Christmas Eve, I walked to every single window in our home, gazing out, begging Chris to come home. I even imagined he would walk up to the front door and ring the bell. In my mind's eye, I saw him standing there on the porch in tattered clothing, unshaven, grinning in triumph from escaping his evil captors. On this holy night of the year, maybe, just maybe, if I believed strongly enough . . . After all, what is hope, and how do miracles occur?

Three days after Christmas we said good-bye to Steve as he left for Minnesota and another bloodhound search. A few days later I hugged

Sara and had to say good-bye again. I felt excruciating pain as I watched her car disappear into the cloudy morning. Every time Sara left, we wondered if we'd ever see her again. Life had taught us some tough lessons.

Wandering aimlessly through a quiet house, utterly alone, I felt absolute despair and confusion. Wanting to escape my loneliness, I stepped outside with Coco to walk. I just kept walking farther; the cold air and brisk exercise lessened my growing anxiety. Not able to make sense of our lives seemingly spinning out of control, I returned home and tried to restore order by cleaning the house. That didn't help either, so I decided to focus on next steps. We needed a long-term plan, so I began crafting "Operation Find Chris." In the process, I contacted the Jacob Wetterling Foundation and spoke with Nancy Sabin, the executive director. I asked her for a blueprint, a copy or an example, of how to conduct a long-term search for a missing young adult. When she told me it didn't exist, I couldn't believe my ears. I asked two more times before it began to sink in that we would have to blaze the trail.

Nancy assured me that to her knowledge, no one had ever attempted what we were trying to accomplish. Children under eighteen and females typically attract an all-out effort from law enforcement. Conventional wisdom said young adult men caused their own demise. Well, Chris was worth fighting for, and I knew we'd find a way.

Milestones

On January 10, 2003, Nathan Herr from Sheboygan, Wisconsin, disappeared. He became the sixth young male adult from Minnesota or Wisconsin, missing without a trace, in less than four months. The devastating news hit us hard, just a few days before Steve turned fifty-one.

Steve's birthday cards remained unopened in a pile of mail. A large envelope from the Boundary Waters Canoe Area in northern Minnesota caught Steve's eye. Steve and Chris had talked about taking a special fishing trip together for years. But maintaining a high GPA at the Carlson School of Management and playing collegiate lacrosse left little discretionary time for Chris. With Chris's college graduation only six months away, Steve began requesting brochures on various fly-in fishing excursions in northern Minnesota and Canada. His excitement grew when he decided to present this unique graduation gift to Chris over the holidays so that they could begin planning their adventure together. The surprise trip was easily forgotten in the fog of missing—until now.

I watched Steve literally fall to his knees, covering his face with both hands. He sobbed, huddled in a ball on the floor, just as I had a few weeks earlier when my birthday gift arrived. Steve and Chris had formed a significant father-son adult relationship over the previous year, sharing a special bond of mutual love and respect. Understanding the depth of his loss, I felt helpless, knowing I couldn't stop the unrelenting grief.

The first time I realized how much I had changed was late in January 2003, in the middle of interviewing with a potential new client, Walmart. In one of the interviews, I was asked to describe myself. For the first five minutes I spoke of the typical professional accomplishments expected in answering that type of question. Suddenly, I looked directly at the interviewers and said, "I don't feel like I'm telling you the truth. I did accomplish these milestones, yet that is not what defines me. I found out who I really am when my life changed forever on November first, 2002, the day our twenty-one-year-old son, Chris, disappeared. I dug deep, and found the courage and strength to move forward." When I finished the story, tears glistened in the eyes of everyone in the room. A week later, the interviewing team asked me to facilitate Walmart's premier leadership experience, the Walton Institute. I've been blessed with the opportunity to work with Walmart leaders since 2003. I use Chris's story, and the trust Walmart placed in me during the most difficult time of my life, as rich examples of courage in the workshops I lead.

Now, as I reflect on our long journey, I recognize that every time we chose to act with courage, we grew stronger and more confident. Sara's description of packing up Chris's room in Minneapolis late in January 2003 is an example of acting courageously in spite of unspeakable sorrow:

Few things will ever compare to clearing out Chris' room. Standing amongst his belongings, I hoped to feel near him. Instead, I felt the profound loss of a precious life cut short. I remember grabbing one of my brother's sweaters and holding it up to my nose. I closed my eyes and breathed in the unmistakable scent of

Chris's soap and cologne. Chris' scent, but he was not here, and would never be again. Twenty-one years, and all that was left were material things; most of them meaningless.

It was heartbreaking to touch Chris' fossil and rock collection he gathered as a young boy. My mother, father, and I spent countless hours at the Discovery Store in the Mall of America, picking out the perfect additions for Christmas, birthdays, etc. I remembered so vividly Chris' delight as he opened each new treasure. Now here they were, just objects, without the owner who cherished them.

On Chris' dresser lay a sheet of notebook paper with a list of local companies Chris had contacted for interviews—Cargill, Target, Medtronic, and others. Mom recognized the names, because she and Chris had worked on that together, shortly before he disappeared. I watched my mom crumple in grief as she held the list in her shaking hands.

Chris' close friends, Jonathan and Pete, came to help move

Chris's passion—his rock collection.

his furniture, which we gave them. We also offered them articles of clothing, and some of Chris' textbooks. Every box we filled with his possessions intensified the emptiness we felt inside.

As we packed, I found many clothes I had purchased for Chris the previous summer. He was in the best shape of his life—toned, strong, and slimmer. My recent job offer from Ford gave me a chance to treat him, which I loved doing. I even convinced Chris to get a suit since he'd be graduating soon and would need to look sharp in interviews. That suit represented his future; his hopes and dreams. Yet I was folding it and putting it into a cardboard box. All those dreams crushed, that future gone. I felt a vice gripping my heart and doubted a wound this deep could ever heal.

Coco came with us that intensely painful day. As soon as she entered Chris' room, she jumped up onto his futon, plopped down, and stared into the corner with paranoid and fearful eyes. We had never seen her so distraught. Inconsolable, she ignored us completely. I think Coco saw Chris, knew he had changed form, and somehow understood he could never play with her again. I sensed Chris' presence, yet ached with grief knowing his time on earth was over. How could I possibly live without him? Why did this happen to him? Why did this happen to us? Though I harbored much anger, and hated what evil people did to my brother, I wouldn't wish this upon them or their loved ones. No family deserves this.

A Snowman and Billboard for Chris

Early in February 2003, three of Chris's closest friends (who also were involved as junior detectives), Luke Fisher, Suzanne Cota, and Crystal Strohschein, built an eight-foot snowman and a four-by-five-foot billboard of snow. Inspired by ten inches of freshly fallen snow, they created these gigantic structures in the front yard of a house they rented, just off campus on Fourth Street Southeast, near the 35W freeway. People walking by stopped to assist them and join in the exhilaration of building symbols of hope to alert the public that Chris was still missing.

Another brilliant idea emerged when the trio realized the enormous snow sculptures were visible from the freeway. Luke maneuvered his

"We love you, Chris. We want you home."

car through snow-covered, icy roads to Walmart around 2:00 a.m., to purchase spray paint in maroon and gold, the University of Minnesota's colors. Suzanne and Crystal accompanied him because if the car got stuck, someone would have to get out and push. After spray-painting the snow sculptures, the dynamic threesome placed a huge "Missing" poster of Chris on the snowman; on the snow billboard they put "CJ#3" (the lacrosse number he had worn with such pride and passion) and a second poster proclaiming the search team's motto, "Someone Knows Something." They finished about an hour before sunrise. Suzanne sent us the following e-mail: "Seriously, this looks so cool. Jan, it is totally huge, colorful, and it is all devoted to Chris. So many people will see it as everything else around here is white. We need your help getting media attention on this!"

Recurring Tragedy

Every time another young male adult was reported missing in the Upper Midwest during the fall of 2002 and winter of 2003, we relived our personal tragedy. Just outside of Chicago, Illinois, Glen Leadley vanished on February 8, 2003. As had the other six young men, somehow he became separated from friends at the end of an evening of partying. Some people, including many in law enforcement, thought alcohol was the thief in the night—randomly stealing lives. Others, including most of the families of the victims, understood the undeniable similarities and believed a much more sinister force was likely at work. The young men ranged in age from eighteen to twenty-three, most were college students or recent college grads with high GPAs, and all disappeared near I-94. Handsome, athletic, responsible young men with no history of running away don't suddenly decide to take a road trip without telling anyone, or commit suicide because of nonexistent depression—at least not seven in less than five months, under similar circumstances, in roughly the same geographical area. Coincidence could not explain the shocking facts.

Nor could logic explain Steve's experience driving home from work a week before Sara's and Chris's birthdays. Under a dark sky, about thirty minutes after the sun set, Steve allowed himself to feel the agonizing grief he bottled up and hid during his work day:

A couple of miles from home on a dark secluded country road, Chris came to me for the first time. Every day I forced myself to turn on the stereo in my car so I could listen to the CDs Chris had put together of some of my favorite music. Eight months earlier, Chris had proudly presented them to me on Father's Day. They ranged from Rush, to the Allman Brothers, Albert King, Pink Floyd, the Grateful Dead, and my all-time favorite, Traffic's *The Low Spark of High Heel Boys*. As Pink Floyd's *Dark Side of the Moon* played in the background, I cried and begged Chris to lead me to him. "God, I miss you, Chris," I said aloud. Again, I asked Chris to give me any kind of sign he could hear me. Out of the corner of my right eye I saw a flash of light. Immediately taking my foot off the gas pedal, I started slowing down. There were no cars behind or coming toward me. Looking back to the right, I saw what appeared to be a slow moving shooting star. It was plummeting parallel with me, no more than forty yards to my right, when suddenly the light source fell into a cornfield. I stopped the car and walked to the shoulder of the road.

Standing in the evening silence, an incredible sense of calm came over me. A shooting star? No, I strongly believed it was Chris's spirit. He wanted me to know he was in a great place and we should be happy for him. Completely overwhelmed, I wondered how I could ever explain this.

Sara's Birthday

Similar to her father's decision to ignore his own birthday on January 17, Sara refused to even discuss her birthday. She simply said the only real celebration required the miracle of her brother's lively presence. On February 12, Sara would be twenty-five; five days later Chris would turn twenty-two. Sara and Chris had often celebrated their birthdays together; yet in February 2003, what possible joy could the Jenkins family find in that tradition?

Grandma Rose did not forget Sara's or Chris's birthday. Through her frequent contact with the Jacob Wetterling Foundation, she learned that Jacob had the same birthday as Chris—February 17. She desperately wanted to find her grandson, so she often thought about ways to keep Chris's disappearance in the public eye, hoping someone would step forward with information. She worked with Nancy Sabin at the foundation to schedule a birthday remembrance for Chris and Jacob in the Rotunda at the State Capitol in St. Paul. More than two hundred people came to honor Chris and Jacob, including the entire UMN Men's Lacrosse team. Charles Jennings, a lacrosse defenseman and very close friend of Chris's, had just returned from ten months in Australia. When Charles and I saw each other, we grinned widely. He walked up and lifted me in the air with a huge bear hug. We didn't say much; both of us were on the verge of a meltdown.

Chris had talked excitedly about the great defenseman who joined the team the previous year, but was unable to play because of a torn ligament. The upcoming spring season would be Charles and Chris's chance to play together, and they were both pumped. Yet the Gopher Men's Lacrosse team had already played two games of the 2003 season without the energetic senior goalie who had talked incessantly about leading the team to victory.

Steve, Sara, and I spoke. We expressed thanks for the outstanding support we had received, gave everyone an update on the investigation, and read a loving letter to Jacob from his mom, Patty Wetterling, who was unable to attend. When I spoke of Chris's many qualities, I added the name of one of his friends in the room who had shown each wonderful trait. I wanted to build the confidence of his friends so that they could move beyond the horror we had all experienced, and live fully. At

Chill time for Charles and Chris.

the end, we played "When I See You Smile" (a gift from our neighbor Phyllis, who was dying from cancer), and all of us held hands.

Ten days later, on the morning of February 27, I phoned my sister Nancy and said to her, sobbing, "I can't take it anymore." Unbeknownst to me, Steve started receiving calls from friends and colleagues living in Minneapolis around 4:00 p.m. that very day. A body had been found in the Mississippi River. By the time Steve got home, I had already heard the news. Even though this was the fourth time we had heard that a body was found in the river, this time felt different. This time I knew it was Chris. The call from Sergeant Jackson came at about 7:45 p.m.: "I'm sorry to inform you . . ."

Part II

Searching for Truth

Too often we take the stars for granted; we may not notice them for months. Then one crystal-clear night, a shooting star blazes across the sky and captures our full attention and our sense of wonder.

One star hangs in the heavens,
Another streaks across the sky,
A blaze of beauty,

Who can say which is greater—
The steady long-lived glimmer,
Or the shooting star?

For the young taken all too early,
Their starry path is the Christ light—
The star that never sets . . .
This is Chris.

ADAPTED BY DEBORAH WINGERT

CHAPTER 8

Chris Is Home

February 28–March 4, 2003

I have fought the good fight, I have finished the race,
I have kept the faith.

2 TIMOTHY 4:7

"We all sit here better people because of you." Christian Bailey spoke those words to a gathering of more than seventeen hundred who came to pay tribute to Christopher Mark Jenkins on March 4, 2003, at Pax Christi Catholic Church in Eden Prairie, Minnesota. Christian wrote the eulogy after listening to suggestions from Mike McTigue, Dave Wedemeyer, Adam Gamradt, Ben Simms, Charles Jennings, and Luke Fisher, all lacrosse teammates and close friends of Chris's. Imagine being a twenty-one-year-old man, asking close friends, "So guys, what should be included in our best friend's eulogy?"

Just how does one honor and say good-bye to a vibrant twenty-one-year-old? I packed a black suit every time we drove to Minneapolis to search for Chris because I never knew if I'd be attending my son's funeral. Now I knew, and this time I decided to wear purple. Chris's incredible life exuded color, humor, and love—the antithesis of black.

The discovery of Chris's body spread like wildfire throughout the media. We received a call from his close friend Chad Lunaas, a Marine stationed in Okinawa, Japan. Chad just saw the message scrolled across the bottom of the screen on CNN—"The body of college student Christopher Jenkins was pulled from the Mississippi River . . ." He voiced the stunning disbelief so many felt: "Tell me it isn't true."

Chris's Web site experienced so much activity after the news broke, it temporarily shut down. One of us checked the messages several hours before the memorial service, noting that a couple of people asked permission to attend the service. Thousands of people followed the story;

we understood Chris had become everyone's child. Steve posted a message welcoming anyone who wanted to attend the service and thanking those who had contributed to the search: "You helped create the wind that brought Chris home."

More than sixty pages of messages appeared on the Web site in a four-day period. The following excerpts summarize the thoughts and feelings of many who posted comments: "I can feel the love and spirit of Chris, though I never knew him"; "Chris didn't just leave this world, he blazed a trail of compassion and understanding"; "Chris was sent into this world to teach us how to love, live, and treat others; he led by example"; "Chris will live on inside those he touched; his impact far too great to ever forget"; "Jan, Steve, and Sara, thank you for sharing Chris with the rest of us. You all have truly and deeply changed our lives."

When Sara arrived at the Minneapolis–St. Paul airport on March 1, she saw the flashing lights of media cameras capturing shots of her, Chris's only sibling, coming home to bury her beloved brother. To her relief, several friends stood waiting, ready to support her. Sara decided to arrive a few days before the funeral, knowing she had to see her brother's body to say good-bye. She had already spoken with Sergeant Jackson, who advised her not to view Chris's body. Sara thanked him for his concern but insisted she needed to be the one to make that tough choice. Jackson told her Chris's body would undergo an autopsy and he didn't know when she could see her brother's physical remains. Sara asked to be notified when that procedure was completed, and Jackson agreed.

Forever Changed

In a conversation with her dad a couple of days later, Sara heard that Chris's body had already been cremated. No one had called her. She cradled her face in her hands and cried. "No, tell me that didn't happen. No matter what his body looked like, I needed to see him. I needed to see his fingers and toes. I needed to know he was really gone. I needed to know he really existed in the first place.

"This blow rocked me to the core. I'm struggling to keep my life going when I feel so broken on the inside. I feel so lost, so painfully lost. I don't know who I am anymore. The Sara I used to be is gone. I'm not even a sister anymore, just forever changed, forever lost."

News of the discovery of Chris's body prompted dozens of calls from reporters in Milwaukee, Minneapolis, and national networks, including the Associated Press. We decided to hold a news conference to answer questions at my parents' farm home near Watertown, Minnesota, about forty miles west of Minneapolis.

Shortly after Steve and I arrived, more than two dozen reporters and cameramen crowded into my parents' living room, eager to capture our family's reaction to this tragic ending of our four-month search. One of the most touching comments we heard came from a reporter speaking to my mom, Grandma Rose, that evening: "Our job is to remain objective, even in heartbreaking situations like this one. What is so extraordinary about this tragedy is the deep, enduring love these parents have for their son."

Chris's Loving Embrace

The night of March 3 Steve and I tossed and turned in a troubled sleep. I remember glancing at the alarm clock—4:00 a.m. I wandered downstairs and saw Steve, deep in thought, working on my parents' computer. When I asked what he was doing, he simply held up his hand. A half hour later, he found me huddled in the corner of the sofa with a cup of tea. Visibly shaken, he told me Chris had come to him in a dream, a dream so real, he felt Chris's warm embrace. Steve said he needed to write exactly what Chris told him before he forgot. That clear message from Chris became Steve's eulogy to his son at the memorial service later that day.

We held the visitation at Pax Christi from 4:00 to 6:00 p.m., just prior to the memorial service. Local news stations kept calling, wanting to film inside the church. We really struggled with that decision. In fairness to all who had hoped, prayed, and helped alongside us for the past four months, we settled on one station live with feeders to the other three stations in the church parking lot. Needing to get away from funeral preparations and focus on the difficult task ahead, Steve spent the entire afternoon at the church. As Chris's father, he felt an enormous responsibility to set the stage mentally and physically.

Knowing this day would be impossibly difficult for Chris's friends, we thought of ways they could help honor their fallen leader. Hopefully, their involvement would give them a sense of purpose and distract them, even if only for a few minutes, from the dread they felt. We asked several of Chris's friends to greet people as they arrived at each of the three entrances to the church. Other friends helped Sara arrange pictures and other memorabilia she had gathered on tables in the church foyer.

Steve and I distinctly remember comforting people as they hugged us. We helped many hold it together. Since Steve and I lived in Wisconsin, many people had not seen us in a year or more. Steve welcomed people near the main entrance, moving them as quickly as possible inside. A line of people rapidly formed to speak with me. Dozens of people were still waiting when the funeral director, Paul Huber of Huber Funeral Homes, gently nudged me for the third time: "Jan, we need to get started."

My sister Deborah had supplied numerous calming herbs for my ravaged nervous system, and so far, so good. Yet after hundreds of hugs and tears from many people, I needed to freshen up and clear my mind for the toughest moments of my life. In a few minutes, Sara, Steve, and I would walk down that aisle, take our seats in the front row, and know that hundreds of people watched, counting on us to stay strong. Each of us had prepared eulogies honoring Chris's remarkable legacy.

Walking into the Family Room at Pax Christi to restore myself, I smiled in surprise when I saw dear relatives from out of town—Patty Nyilas, Veda Lascody, Craig Lascody, and Sherry Greenan. After hugging them tightly, I gently asked them to do me a favor by taking their seat in the church to assure Paul Huber of our intent to begin the service. As I entered the large adjoining bathroom, there stood two of my sisters—Carol and Mary. They hurried, knowing the service must begin. I told them not to worry, it couldn't start without me, and I planned to take a few minutes to compose myself.

Cherishing Chris and the Gifts He Shared

Three priests presided over Chris's memorial service, with Father Tim Power, pastor at Pax Christi, leading the way. "We've come here to cry," acknowledged Father Tim. "We're also here to celebrate . . . But, most importantly, we're here to be faithful."

I stood between Sara and Steve. Sara and I held on to each other tightly. When we all sang "On Eagle's Wings," the tears flowed. Hugging our beautiful daughter, I wanted so desperately to take away her crushing pain.

Christian Bailey gave the first eulogy: "No matter how you knew him—Chris, Christopher, Jenks, or Schmenkins—he always left you feeling like you mattered. He had the ability to melt your insecurities away and make you feel welcome. He lived passionately; confident, but never cocky. Chris stood up for what he believed in; most importantly—his family and friends. He never lived his life for other people, but he always included everyone in his life.

"His smile went from ear to ear and his blue eyes sparkled when he filled a room with laughter. He thought even ordinary events should be celebrated, finding joy in the people and experiences in his life. Chris loved telling stories, often creating ten-minute narrations, complete with sound effects and a sound track. The last time we hung out together, we listened to a band at a local bar. Jenks laughed and danced until the place closed. Then he danced the whole way home.

"Chris's ability to work hard and persevere was without equal. On the lacrosse field Jenks always stepped it up a notch. He was a great

"Bailey ain't heavy; he's my brother."

player and a tremendous team leader. A two-time team captain and team vice president, he is currently the reigning MVP goalie in the Upper Midwest. His awards include All-American on the field and Academic All-American in the classroom. Chris demonstrated a total team commitment; only his family and school came first. He made himself into the player he became, always working hard at practice, lifting weights, and exercising. He set the standard by never taking credit, yet he was always willing to share the blame. Chris constantly pushed his teammates toward success, wanting everyone to succeed on and off the field.

"As the quintessential jokester, Chris was never afraid to be the butt of his own jokes. He wore a Spiderman costume made for a twelve-year-old (backwards to boot—a mistake?) to our lacrosse banquet, a full-body one-piece snowsuit to practice one warm spring day, used pillows as a chest protector when a thief stole his gear, and he always wore his big goalie cup on the outside of his shorts. You never knew what he would do next! He saved the life of a cat named Marley, and did more good in his twenty-one years than most would do if they lived one hundred years. Although he was stolen from us too soon, I consider myself lucky to have known him.

"Jenks exemplified all that is right in this world . . . he took the path less traveled . . . Quick to make you laugh, genuine even in jest, Jenks, we mourn our loss with heavy hearts . . . We will celebrate the gifts you have given us so generously. It was an honor to have known you and a blessing to be your friend. We are going to miss you, Jenks, but we will *never, ever forget.*"

Next our private investigator, Chuck Loesch, delivered a heartfelt speech. He cared deeply, sacrificing so much, giving his all, in the search for Chris.

Father and Son

Then Steve shared Chris's message: "In a dream-filled sleep, I saw a brilliant light approaching me, the intensity of the sun, but I didn't need to squint. Suddenly, I clearly saw Chris. As he reached out and embraced me, I was overcome with his intense love and pure joy. Chris's determination to speak to me and everyone at Pax Christi celebrating his life, inspired me to share with you as best I can, Chris's innermost thoughts.

"'Dad, let me start by telling you, Mom, Sara, and Coco that I love you with an intensity I have never felt before in my life. I want to speak to each and every person here today in remembrance of me. Dear family, friends, and the many strangers who came to our aid in a time of need, I wish to express my thoughts to you on four topics: sorrow, immeasurable appreciation, dire concern, and most of all hope.

"'Sorrow: I am so sorry for the overwhelming sadness, hurt, agony, anger, and helplessness you have all felt the past four months and five days. I wish things could be different, but they are not.

"'I have immeasurable, eternal appreciation for everyone here today, and for those all over the world, who carried me in their hearts. I could not believe the overwhelming outpouring of help, physically and financially, in your search for me. My wishes are to create the Chris Jenkins Memorial Fund. I know in my heart of hearts that Dad, Mom, and Sara will advise the board of trustees to grow the fund, and make the important decisions to support those things I was passionate about in life, so my memory goes on forever. But my eternal appreciation goes way beyond personal and financial involvement. I have been humbled by the overwhelming individual prayers, Mass dedications, rosaries, prayer vigils, personal thoughts, and song. All of your coordinated power in scripture has transferred my soul to such intense luminous energy, all these people up here are asking, "Who is this brightest bulb on the tree? CJ3's lumens are even more intense than JC!" That's OK. I have a bet with Jesus that I may be outshining him for some time but I asked him not to take it personally. So you all have executed your jobs to a level that far, far exceeded my expectations and I am truly grateful.

"'I have a dire concern I want to express, especially to my cousins and close friends. My concern is for your personal safety and well-being. Downtown streets are not safe. If you are going to any establishments, first, go in numbers. And please be sure if you leave the establishment willingly, or not willingly, absolutely demand the buddy system. We are not as invincible as we think we are.

"'And finally, hope. I have come to realize that with eternal life, human life is truly short-lived. Whether you listen to someone who left

Chris at twelve o'clock; then, clockwise, FBI Bob, Aunt Linda, and cousins Christie, Sean, Blake, Jeffry, Katie, and sis Sara. Not pictured: Eric Stein.

this earth at the age of twenty-one—me—or someone turning eighty on April first—Grandpa Lee—you will hear that life matters. Grandpa Lee will tell you that years melt into decades, and before you know it, you will be asking yourself if you have lived your best life. Now that I'm shining brightly in eternal paradise (the jealous guy next to me has to wear sunglasses), I hope you can focus your prayer on those around you. Look to the left, right, in front, and in back of you; pray for those people. I hope you lead your life with God. Trust me, when your time comes to join me, I will be honored to be your personal tour guide. Hey, dudes, I love you. Jenks, signing off for now.'"

Steve concluded by saying: "Chris, we were so privileged to call you our son, brother, and friend. We will do our best to share your message of hope with the world. Love Dad, Mom, Sara, and Coco.

"P.S. The door to my dream world will remain unlocked forever. Come back soon, let's talk for a spell."

Sara—Surviving Sibling

Sara walked up to the microphone, wearing Chris's UMN lacrosse jersey with his number—3. She took us on Chris's road trip with his close friend Luke Fisher from the previous summer by reading pages of his journal: "'4:04 pm Jenks expressing himself: The world is in my head. We have been blessed with beautiful scenery and great times . . . Anywho, we are down 3 lacrosse balls for our trip. I launched a pass right over Luke's head and it went over a huge cliff and into the Badlands. We are en route to the Black Hills, where we hope to find a campsite.

"'Sunday, August 25th 11:48 am. Sunday morning, I am looking at the legendary Mt. Rushmore. We came in to the Black Hills at 8:00 pm last night, and ended up camping at the Center Lake Campground in Custer State Park. Despite setting up our tent in an hour-long mountain downpour, it was rather relaxing to finally have a camp set up that we could call our own. Once the rain stopped, we built a campfire and prepared a feast consisting of meat, potatoes, carrots, and onions, YUMMY. The Black Hills are BEAUTIFUL, very mountainous and covered with various types of conifers and roaming bands of buffalo or "boofalo," as I like to call them. I am rather intrigued by these massive animals, and I actually had the pleasure of having three run-ins with them that are worth telling you about. I told Luke that one of my goals on this trip was to touch a boofalo. As dumb as that might sound to you, I was rather excited about it. While traveling in Custer Park, I spied a boofalo only 10 yards from the road. We parked the car and I anxiously hopped out. This was a massive boofalo and my excitement and sense of fearlessness turned into anxiety. I decided to put my fear behind me and I slowly approached the wild beast. When I got within 4 feet of the bull, we both simultaneously scared the bejeebees out of each other, and ran in opposite directions. My first attempt at touching a wild boofalo had failed.

"'We spotted our second boofalo about 10 miles down the road and were excited because it was a baby boofalo. I got out of the car and headed towards the baby, out in the middle of a field 60 yards in front of me. The baby was acting very strange, and when I got closer, I figured out the tragedy. The baby's mother was lying dead on the ground and the baby was literally crying while ramming his head into his mother in an attempt to wake her. I was devastated, knowing I could do nothing for him. Deciding this was not the right time to fulfill my goal of touching a boofalo, I said a quick prayer for him, and headed back to the car with a bad feeling inside.

"'Though my 2nd attempt failed, I had a 3rd encounter with a boofalo. My third attempt was by far the most intense, and I knew I would never forget it for the rest of my life. We pulled onto the side of the road where the King Kong of boofalo was grazing 5 yards off the road. I slowly approached the mammoth boofalo. He greeted me with an enraged look—showing the whites of his eyes. This is where I should have turned back. With adrenaline rushing through my veins, I was ready to run at any moment if things got a little "out of my league." I was only 3 feet away when the boofalo's back legs tensed up and he lunged and attempted to thrust his massive head and horns into me. I immediately ran back to the car and decided I was not going to mess with any more boofalo. Attempt #3, FAILED. Mission has been cancelled.

"'Loving Life—Jenks signing out . . .'"

Mother to Son

In celebration of Chris's life, I'll share just a couple of classic Chris stories from the tribute I read at the memorial service: "Chris, your first season of football brought us so many laughs. Two teams of five-year-olds, without a clue how to play, ran up and down the field, simply enjoying the perfect fall day. As you ran down the field in your little Viking football gear, at one point you looked up and saw your Grandma Rose and me. A huge smile spread across your face as you came running up to us on the sidelines, waving and yelling, 'Hi Mom, hi Grandma!' Amidst enough laughter to produce tears, Grandma Rose and I told you the game continued and you needed to go join your team. You kept waving and smiling, then suddenly stopped. 'Well, OK then,' you yelled, as you ran back, and promptly joined the wrong team.

"Your high school math teacher told us another story of how you brightened everyone's day. One hot, humid day in the spring when the air conditioning broke down, many people in class started sweating, almost sticking to their chairs. In situations like this, you usually figured out a way to turn a cranky atmosphere into one with humor and

"Practicing my moves before the first game."

fun. This time you decided to run up to the floor fan, pick it up, and start singing into it, 'You've got that lovin' feelin' . . .' Singing into a fan sounds like talking after breathing into a helium balloon—hilarious. Apparently your classmates wanted to be in your math class the following year.

"Sara and Dad helped you become an incredible man. Sara loved you from the day you arrived. She adored holding and kissing you. About a year ago, Sara bought you a complete stereo system for your car. You climbed out your bedroom window onto the roof, literally shouting from the rooftop, 'My sister Sara is the best sister in the whole world.'

"Two of your outstanding traits—kindness and taking care of others—came easily to you. You learned from a master of both—your dad. He leads with kindness and generosity in his personal and professional life.

"Sara, Dad, and I don't know how to live without you. We don't understand why we had to lose you so soon, so young, so full of dreams and hope. God must need you for a really big job in heaven. In your honor we'll continue life's journey as best we can, knowing you want us to savor every moment we have on earth. You are in our hearts and smiles—now, forever, and always. We'll see you later."

A Few Treasures

In a Catholic Mass, gifts are brought to the altar before communion is consecrated and served. Some of Chris's friends carried up his lacrosse helmet and goalie stick, his harmonica, a rosary from his Grandma Jenkins, and a brand-new Eden Prairie football jersey with Chris's number—70—kindly presented to us just prior to the service by Mike Grant, Eden Prairie's head football coach.

Blake Koness played "Here I Am, Lord," as the communion song on his viola. Just twelve years old at the time, he played brilliantly for his cousin Chris. In describing his thoughts and feelings that day, perhaps Blake summed up the out-of-body experience many of us felt: "I never imagined we would be here. It seemed unreal, like we played roles in a depressing movie. Yet I also felt a strength emanating from our family as we all sat together in the front of the church. I sensed an empowering feeling of community—this tragedy occurred, and we feel heartbroken, but we are all here, together. After the service, my parents, sister, and I just started hugging each other, sharing this awesome family embrace for a minute or so. I remain very thankful we experienced that small opportunity to grow as a family in the midst of sadness."

When people return home, and the noise dies down, all of us are left with our thoughts. Chris's ashes sat in a box covered with a maroon cloth. My sister Mary gathered the bouquets of flowers, and Chris's ashes, to take them to her home temporarily for safekeeping. She voiced what our family held in our hearts: "You are home now, Chris. No one can hurt you anymore."

CHAPTER 9

Someone Knows Something

March 5–April 30, 2003

I can be changed by what happens to me. I refuse to be reduced by it.
MAYA ANGELOU

The morning after the memorial service we met with the chief medical examiner, Dr. Garry Peterson, assistant chief medical examiners Dr. Baker and Dr. Berg, and the deputy medical examiner, Dr. Rivera. To our surprise, two Hennepin County attorneys, Peter Cahill and Michael Miller, also came to the meeting. MPD Sergeant Jackson, lead investigator on Chris's case, attended this meeting, but he did not go to the recovery scene, nor did he participate in the autopsy. Chuck Loesch, Sara, Steve, and I listened carefully, while observing very unusual behavior that concerns us to this day. For the first twenty minutes of the meeting, Dr. Peterson stared at the table with both of his hands shaking so hard he couldn't hold a pen. During that time he did not make eye contact with anyone. Scowling, Sergeant Jackson sat at one end of the table, with crossed arms and his back partially turned toward the group. The presence of two attorneys, Peterson's anxiety, and Jackson's attitude as evidenced in their nonverbal behavior made us wonder what the heck was going on.

We asked about Chris's body position and Peterson did say Chris was found on his back, with arms and hands crossed in front. His slip-on shoes were on his feet. There was no bruising, yet Chris played two full days of lacrosse in the position of goalie with only a chest protector five days before he disappeared. Frustrated with receiving no answers, I asked how Chris could have ended up like that if he had jumped or fallen off a bridge. We'll never forget the response as long as we live: "Maybe he jumped in the river to save a duck." Raised eyebrows from Sara, Steve, and me may have prompted the next statement: "The river does strange things." We felt that something much stranger than the river was occurring right in front of our eyes.

Dr. Peterson stated that Chris's death resulted from one of three things: accident, suicide, or homicide. After we left the meeting, Sergeant Jackson showed us where a biker allegedly had seen Chris walking on the Hennepin Avenue Bridge. The biker had to approach the MPD three times before someone thought he was credible. In an angry voice, Sergeant Jackson stated, "By the way, it's one of two things: suicide or accident." He told us to get rid of the notion of someone kidnapping Chris and driving him down to the river, and to forget the I-94 connection among the missing men. Four agencies had met (Sheboygan and Eau Claire, Wisconsin, and St. Cloud and Minneapolis, Minnesota) and found no commonalities. I responded, "Well, that may be, but there are at least twenty-two young men missing in less than five years in a relatively small geographical area. The similarities in the profiles of these young men and the fact that their bodies show up in water with no explanation, surely demands consideration from someone in law enforcement."

With heavy hearts and broken spirits, Sara, Steve, and I drove a few blocks to the Third Avenue Bridge. After parking the car, we walked over the bridge until we stood directly above the location where Chris's body was spotted. Holding four roses—three red ones representing each of us, and one white one representing Chris—we prayed and told him how helpless and sorry we felt about his tragic death. Promising him we would seek justice for this heinous crime, we kissed the white rose and tossed it, then watched as it drifted down to the water. After tossing the three red roses, one at a time, we put our arms around each other's shoulders, watching the roses floating in the frigid water. The harsh realization of the finality of our life as a family of four felt unbearable. Huddled together on the bridge with an icy wind whipping around us, we saw all four roses eventually join together, right by the log jam where Chris's body was found. We'll be together again, someday.

"Look in the River"

"He's dead. Look in the river." Father Tim called to give us this message. Shortly after the funeral, he received a phone call from a distraught woman. She described a startling event that occurred in November 2002. Along with her son and his friend, "Sharlene" had just watched the first Holidazzle parade of the season. Holidazzle, a parade of floats and huge cartoon characters, starts the day after Thanksgiving. It winds through downtown Minneapolis several nights a week until Christmas. As they waited for a bus to return home, her son had pointed to one of Chris's early "Missing" flyers taped up on a light post at the corner where all three stood. The message on the flyer, artistically printed in black marker, alarmed them: "He's dead. Look in the river." After calming her son and his friend, Sharlene had carefully studied the handwriting until the bus arrived.

We immediately contacted our key volunteer and friend, W.T., asking him to see if the flyer was still on the light post, even though three and a half months had passed since Sharlene and the boys had seen it. W.T. checked; unfortunately, it was gone. But we did speak with Sharlene, who gave us a detailed description of the handwriting. She specializes in graphic design, and therefore certain characteristics of the letters remained quite clear in her mind. She apologized for not contacting someone sooner; she had heard on the news that Chris committed suicide. When she saw televised coverage of the funeral, she realized the importance of the handwritten message and the need to report what she saw. That flyer was only a few blocks from the one found shortly after Chris disappeared; that one had read, "Loaded into Trunk . . . Paid for by dollars green." Both flyers with their handwritten messages were within a few blocks of the Lone Tree Bar.

Though I spoke with Sergeant Jackson about the mysterious writing on yet another one of Chris's flyers, he saw no value whatsoever in the message. His response frustrated us since we believed the facts continued to point to foul play, and nothing supported suicide or accident. While speaking with Jackson, I reiterated that Steve and I remained very troubled by the missing items from Chris's room that might contain information, notably, his journal and PDA. Whoever had them might not have considered that valuable information could be there. I asked Jackson if he would check with Ashley Rice, who had gone into Chris's room the day after he disappeared. Jackson told me Rice had taken a trip with her mother out of the country. He agreed to contact her when she returned to inquire if she had either of those articles, or might know who had them. A few months later, we learned from Jackson that he did speak with Rice, and she said she did not have them. We wondered who else might have Chris's belongings. As of this writing, those two items, potentially containing key data, have not shown up.

In the midst of the cold, cloudy month of March, we desperately needed a psychological lift. Our son would never come home again, and we had few solid clues about his tragic death. We continued to believe strongly that homicide must be considered before it could be eliminated. The circumstances around Chris's disappearance, coupled with the lack of basic investigative protocol, left us with many questions. We challenged the nonsense each step of the way.

One night after dinner, Steve and I realized that neither of us had picked up our mail, so I threw on a coat and walked down to the mailbox. After opening a letter from Dr. Robert H. Bruininks, president of the University of Minnesota, I read several lines and teared up. I handed it to Steve; his reaction was about the same as mine. "Chris was an outstanding student in the Carlson School of Management and a talented athlete . . . The faculty of the Carlson School of Management, and Dean Benveniste have recommended that the Bachelor of Science degree in Business, with a major in Marketing, which Chris would have been awarded this spring, be given to him posthumously. I strongly concur . . . The outpouring of concern expressed by people throughout the University and the Twin Cities, and the hundreds and hundreds of hours his fellow students, lacrosse teammates, and University staff gave to the search for Chris, reflect an enormous and widespread love and respect for your son. I hope that knowing how deeply he touched people, and how painfully he is missed, can be of some solace to you in the months ahead. I hope, too, it will be at least some small comfort to know he will live on in the hearts of many people for years to come."

Amidst tears, I told Steve this news brought honor to Chris and served as a powerful testament to his character. As grateful and excited as we were about this unexpected tribute to Chris, the reality of the magnitude of our loss hit again with merciless force. We could not begin to imagine spending the rest of our life without our enthusiastic and loving son. At this point, we had no clue that the happiest moments of life in the future would also be extremely painful. The soul remembers a wound this deep for all time.

Fortunately, Sara found a cruise departing from Miami in less than two weeks. For a brief week, we could soak up the sun in an attempt to breathe new life into our weary bodies. Along with Sara and her friend Jenny, we physically left the Midwest winter of frightful memories far behind.

Sign of the Sundog

One of the stops on the cruise, Grand Cayman, holds a very special place in our family's life. Three years earlier, our entire family and Chris's first love, Crystal Piram, celebrated the millennium on the island. Sara and I found last-minute, very inexpensive tickets. Once on the island, Chris wanted to rent a jeep in the worst way, so he devised a plan. He convinced Steve and me to attend the infamous timeshare pitch. By doing so, we received a free rental vehicle. Chris's plan far exceeded his goal: we ended up buying a timeshare! One of the strongest selling points came from Chris. He kept reminding us that as he and Sara became more involved in their own lives, scheduling time together as a family would prove more challenging. I can still hear him: "Mom, just think, we'll be together every year right here. Sara and I will even bring our families someday."

Sadly, Chris never made it back to Grand Cayman. In 2001 and 2002, he played on the UMN Men's Lacrosse team, whose season coincides with our interval at the timeshare. A starting goalie and dedicated co-captain, Chris would never let his team down by missing a week. He did create a truly sacred family tradition that we've been able to enjoy every year in the middle of winter.

So in March 2003, as soon as the cruise ship docked in Grand Cayman, we rented a car and took Sara and Jenny to a small, gorgeous beach named Rum Point. The two young ladies basked in the sun for a couple of hours while Steve and I did some shopping. Shortly after the girls settled in, Jenny looked up at the sky and pointed to an amazing sundog (a halo edged with rainbow colors around the sun). Not thinking much about it, the girls simply enjoyed the beautiful morning.

"A rite of passage—my son offers me a Cuban cigar."

Around noon Steve and I picked up the girls and drove a short distance to a secluded area on the shoreline named Starfish Point. Three years earlier at that exact spot, Steve and Chris had strolled in the shallow water enjoying their Cuban cigars and Heinekens when they happened upon huge red starfish. Chris hopped around excitedly as he discovered one starfish after another. His childlike enthusiasm created so much laughter and love in our family.

Cherishing that delightful experience father and son shared in 2000, we chose Starfish Point as the location to throw some of Chris's ashes. As soon as we got out of the car, Sara pointed to the sundog. I felt strongly that somehow this atmospheric optical phenomenon appeared as a sign from Chris. Sara, of course, thought I was crazy.

Sara, Steve, and I each took some of Chris's ashes and walked into the water. Lost in our own thoughts and prayers, we tossed the ashes when the spirit moved us. Sara threw hers first, when out of nowhere, a small gust of wind blew the ashes back, covering her in white powder. With a smile on her face, Sara yelled, "Chris, you always had to have the last laugh!" Then she dunked underwater to wash off. I was last to throw the ashes (I didn't want to let go), and as I walked out of the water, the rainbow around the sun opened as brilliant rays of light poured out.

Our grief defies understanding.

Spellbound, we stared at the celestial beauty—our eyes didn't blink or water from staring at the intense light. As we gathered our belongings, we noticed that the entire halo had started dissipating; in a few brief minutes, it was gone completely. Though it had been visible for at least three hours, now the sundog seemed to follow our actions. All of us felt Chris's presence in this extraordinary marvel from the heavens.

Over the years, we've asked many people on Grand Cayman if they've ever witnessed this solar halo. They've all said no. After researching this topic, we've learned that sundogs typically appear when the sun is low, that is, at sunrise and sunset. They seem more common on cold, clear days. Whether the incident appeared as a sign from Chris or not, we believed it did. *Belief makes all the difference.*

Golden Gopher Men's Lacrosse—Spring 2003

Men's collegiate lacrosse had started in February, and we felt such heartache for Chris's teammates. Before the team could say good-bye to Chris, their friend, co-captain, respected leader, and starting goalie, their lacrosse season was in full swing. Although Steve and I planned to attend at least one of the games, just thinking of lacrosse brought waves of grief. Looking at a lacrosse field—any lacrosse field—I could only see and hear Chris: between the pipes, defending the goal, shouting directions to his team: "right side! top center! back left!"—noting the location of the ball in reference to the goal. It was no surprise that Chris was extremely hoarse after every game; in sports, he always seemed to end up in the middle of the action, one way or another.

As remaining co-captains for the Golden Gopher men's lacrosse team, Ben Simms and Christian Bailey needed to create a unified and motivated team in Chris's absence. Christian said he felt numb; he saw himself as the behind-the-scenes leader, watching out for everyone, taking care of paperwork and other club needs. He didn't see himself as a vocal leader and didn't feel ready to become one, because in his heart, he knew that role belonged to Chris. Christian noted that everyone looked up to Chris, wanted to play well for him, and would follow his lead. Ben's leadership role played out on the field as a player and a coach. Reinventing themselves after the senseless loss of a friend and teammate so full of life and promise required time, and digging for courage to persevere. Yet Chris's team, the team he loved, had no time to adjust to this new reality.

Ben and Christian decided not to elect another captain, yet they continued talking about ways to honor Chris. Just before the start of a lacrosse game, the captains of both teams meet at midfield, facing each other, to listen to the ground rules and shake hands. To honor Chris, Christian and Ben started every game meeting the captains of their opponent midfield for this pregame tradition by leaving the place between them open, making room for Chris's spirit. While they didn't discuss the significance of this open space with others, they remained very conscious of Chris's place on the team and in their hearts.

We greatly admire Ben and Christian for leading the Gophers all the way to the Upper Midwest Lacrosse League championship game that year, with the winner advancing to the nationals. The Duluth Bulldogs beat the Minnesota Gophers in overtime to win the tournament. Since Duluth was ranked eleventh nationally, well above the Gophers, the Gophers clearly played their hearts out to stick with Duluth the entire game, forcing overtime against a much stronger opponent.

Defining Moments

What happened at the awards ceremony created a defining moment for many. The prior season, 2002, Chris received the MVP Goalie Award for the tournament. Now, in 2003, Sam Litman of the Duluth Bulldogs won that same award. Standing next to Gopher Coach Chris Larson, Sam waited patiently for the applause to quiet. Then he thanked the league for the award and the goalie stick. He told the crowd he was extremely honored to receive the award, yet could not keep it. Turning to Coach Larson, he handed him the award, noting, "I'm returning this award to the Gophers in honor of Chris, because I wouldn't be the goalie I am today without playing lacrosse with and against Chris Jenkins. Chris made me a better goalie." At once, everyone stood and started clapping. As the clapping continued, tears flowed freely, even from the players.

Moments like this remind us that life is precious and fragile; they remind us what matters most. For Christian, Sam's words hit hard. Sitting on the field on that glorious spring day, Christian realized his college lacrosse career had just ended, and in spite of all he accomplished and hoped for, Chris still wasn't coming home, ever.

Spring 2003 proved to be the season of defining moments on a number of levels. We received the following note in April from our friend of forty years, Tim Katzman, director of corporate communications for the San Diego Padres: "Last month, I took on the challenge of climbing Mt. Kilimanjaro. There were more than a few instances along the way when I doubted my training, my equipment and my resolve. When I happened on one of these weaker moments—and there were many— my thoughts turned more than once to your son, Chris. Despite having met him on only a couple of occasions, I could not help but be impressed by his perseverance, quick wit, sensitivity and intelligence. To meet him—if only briefly—was to be enriched by him.

"I made it a point to bring back something from that nearly 20,000 foot summit to acknowledge and celebrate your son's life. I collected the piece of volcanic rock you find enclosed. Up in that rarified air on the roof of Africa, I felt Chris' presence, spirit, and light. Surrounded by towering glaciers and bracing winds, I once again saw your son bounding across the University of San Diego lacrosse field, unbridled in his enthusiasm, keen on leading his team to another score."

In the same letter, Tim summed up our intent to celebrate Chris's life while still in the throes of unearthing the events and individuals who robbed Chris of life: "You have both been tireless in your efforts to seek the truth and apprise friends and supporters of key facts throughout this ordeal. That in itself speaks volumes about the manner in which you never lost your focus or hope. Understanding Chris touched so many with his engaging personality, essential goodness, and his ongoing concern for others, shall continue to bolster your resolve."

CHAPTER 10

The Bravest Lions in Oz

May–July 2003

As we are liberated from our own fear,
our presence automatically liberates others.

NELSON MANDELA

Steve, Sara, and I are the bravest lions in Oz? Well, that's what Grandma Rose says, so it must be true! Actually, if we had found a magical place like Oz, I'm confident we would have traveled there long ago. Overwhelming grief caused us to fantasize—for brief moments—an escape from our current reality. Yet we knew escape did not solve problems. So we chose to forge ahead in our quest for truth, even though that path hid innumerable twists, turns, and stalls along the way.

Unanswered Questions

By choosing action over paralysis or escape, we avoided, to some degree, the helplessness of a victim mentality. We learned that the decision to act courageously required ongoing commitment. When we faltered, connecting with our purpose strengthened our resolve. Seeing a picture of Chris and looking deeply into his eyes, or hearing the hurt in Sara's voice, put me back on track to stay the course. Facing life without Chris presented tough challenges, but we did not have the luxury of dealing with that loss in choosing to solve his senseless death.

The decision to investigate demanded fully committing ourselves and our resources. We understood we were on our own, since law enforcement had determined, only days after Chris disappeared, that suicide or accident explained the mystery. We needed courage to challenge that nonsensical conclusion as well as many other ridiculous assumptions. We believed that Chris did *not* choose to disappear; that the cryptic notes written on his flyers *might* contain important clues; that people in the Lone Tree Bar, where he was last seen, *should* be questioned; that bloodhounds *can* follow a scent after a week, *and* in a downtown area. Above all, we held firm to our conviction that because of Chris's highly suspicious disappearance and subsequent death, homicide *must* be considered before it can be eliminated. Furthermore, two MPD officers were introduced to Chris at the Lone Tree. Many witnesses saw one of those officers flirting with Chris's date throughout the evening. Although we have asked on numerous occasions, the two officers have never been seriously questioned. Clearly, the entire situation created a conflict of interest, yet no internal affairs investigation occurred, *and* the MPD resisted FBI and BCA involvement. This stonewalling does not pass the smell test.

Early in May, one of our worst fears came to pass when we learned from a Hennepin County medical examiner that Chris's blood alcohol content (BAC) measured .12, fairly low for someone who had been drinking during the evening, knowing a friend was the designated driver. Through research, we learned that BAC actually increases as a body decomposes owing to bacteria attacking sugar enzymes. Since Chris was missing for four months, his BAC would have been less than .12 when he died. Sara and I feared the same thing: was Chris held for a period of time, which would have allowed his BAC to decrease? We agonized over the suffering he surely endured and hoped to learn more at our second meeting with the medical examiners later in May.

Facing Adversity Strengthens Courage

While we did not realize it at the time, whenever we bravely faced adversity, our courage strengthened. In May 2003, we had the opportunity to expose a string of mysterious deaths by filming with FX Networks for a new fall series, *American P.I.* Mary Bess Walker, representing FX and producer Gavin Polone (producer of *Panic Room*) contacted Loesch, explaining FX's idea of focusing on private investigators around the country working on old, unsolved cases. Once Chuck Loesch told her about the Chris Jenkins case he was currently involved with, Mary Bess wanted more details. Ultimately, FX producers decided to use Chris Jenkins's and Josh Guimond's cases for the premier episode of their series. Not only did both represent current, dynamic investigations, they also were part of an emerging bigger picture.

From September 2002 to March 2003, seven young men in the Upper Midwest alone had vanished in the early hours of the morning; and one by one, their bodies kept showing up in bodies of water. Within a five-hundred-mile radius, two disappeared from Minnesota, two from Wisconsin, two from Chicago, and one from northwestern Indiana. Once we realized these sobering statistics, we researched further and discovered that at least two dozen young men in the preceding decade, mostly from Minnesota to New York, had met the same fate under strikingly similar situations.

It took every ounce of courage we could muster to reenact the experience of losing our son. Yet we thought increased public awareness would put pressure on law enforcement to consider the bigger picture in these senseless tragedies. We also believed we must take action to prevent this from happening to another innocent young man and his family.

Filming began on May 13, 2003, in St. Cloud, Minnesota and ended on May 21 in Minneapolis. Loesch filmed every day, joined during the week by Guimond's family, Penny Bell and her bloodhound Hoover Von Vacuum, and last of all by Steve, Sara, and me. "Excruciating" does not begin to describe the pain a family endures in repeating, in detail, the circumstances leading up to their child's/sibling's disappearance and death. In fact, after the first day of filming, a severe migraine forced me to stay in bed the next day, missing an entire day of filming.

So I missed watching Hoover display her genius. Penny wanted to give Hoover closure after the exhausting search for Chris in previous months. Steve watched as Penny tethered Hoover at the east end of the Third Avenue Bridge. Without being given an article of Chris's to "scent," the dog started across the bridge, stopping directly above the area where walkers spotted Chris's body. The tree that likely stopped Chris's body from going over the dam was still there. Hoover howled loudly, rolled, and went straight to Steve, touching her body against his leg. Steve teared up, hugged the dog, and marveled again at her amazing ability to track the invisible. Perhaps the greatest benefit of using bloodhounds is that they work independently of half-truths, self-serving motivations, and political games.

While filming in St. Cloud, Josh's grandfather walked up to me and asked what I thought about the woman who reported seeing Chris's body floating in the water. The only sighting we knew of came from my conversation with Sergeant Jackson regarding the man who inquired about the reward. So I listened carefully as Josh's grandfather explained that a woman who worked at Qwest in Minneapolis also reported a sighting. Since she parked her car in the St. Anthony Main municipal parking lot on the east side of the Third Avenue Bridge, and worked on the west side of the bridge, she walked across the bridge twice a day. Qwest had recognized her for demonstrating brave citizenship. Josh's grandpa agreed to send me her name and phone number.

We left St. Cloud and drove to my parents' farm in Watertown, where we stayed during this trip. On the drive, we tried to block our thoughts and emotions from the difficult filming, in order to prepare ourselves for Chris's graduation the following day. I wonder if having the courage to grieve means walking through the pain—whether that entails honoring the departed loved one, or mourning the loss. Many situations involve honoring and mourning at the same time. If the heartbreaking filming we had undertaken helped prevent even one death, then we had created something good from our agonizing loss; and by doing so, we honored Chris.

Graduation Day

All three of us completely underestimated the difficulty of standing on Northrop Mall on the campus of the University of Minnesota, watching the excitement of graduates with their families. Four years earlier we had stood on this mall with Chris after his high school graduation ceremony. Today, May 21, at Chris's college graduation, we stood holding a box of ashes—the ashes of the son and brother we loved so dearly for almost twenty-two years. I wanted to scream at the cruelty of our loss or, better yet, simply vanish into thin air. Steve's and Sara's faces projected similar emotions. Instead of caving, we sucked it up, as we had done for months. This time we composed ourselves for the final shoots with FX Networks. We had agreed to allow them to film us on campus prior to the ceremony.

"My buddy Chris—a once in a lifetime friend," says Neil Lorntson. Eden Prairie High School graduation, 1999.

After the filming, we promptly joined my parents and my sisters Nancy and Carol in the front row in Northrop Auditorium, which was already filled with joyous families. It seemed fitting that Nancy and Carol, who also graduated from the Carlson School of Management many years earlier, honored Chris and supported us by attending.

The ceremony started by welcoming Carlson graduates and their families and friends. Then the dean praised Chris's character and accomplishments as a university student and athlete, and offered sincere condolences regarding his tragic death. Sara walked up onstage to accept her brother's degree. I remember how proud I was of her courage and love for her brother. When she held Chris's degree high above her head, the entire auditorium stood and clapped. As the clapping began to subside, Sara looked toward heaven and blew her brother a kiss. Steve and I could no longer contain our tears.

Chris whispers from heaven, "Sara, thanks for standing up for me."

We held the box with Chris's ashes in our laps. Before coming to Minneapolis that week, we discussed whether to bring the ashes. What prepares parents to honor their murdered son at his college graduation? Who talks about the experience even if they have walked this path? Our choices to dignify Chris's life, and investigate his death, compelled us to blaze our own trail, guided by grace, intuition, and intense love for our son.

Due to the large number of graduates, the ceremony lasted about three and a half hours. Warm weather and thousands of people caused the auditorium to become hot and humid. Several professors sat in chairs on the stage, and we could see sweat beading up on their faces. Two of Chris's close friends, Adam Gamradt and Christian Bailey, sat directly behind us. At one point Christian leaned forward and said in a low voice, "Those professors look wilted. I think they could use a good watering." I laughed out loud. The spunk and humor of young adults are so refreshing. I sensed Christian just wanted to lighten things up, something we could always count on Chris to pull off, especially when situations grew tense.

Following the ceremony, the school held a celebration on its West Bank campus. Alan Fine, senior lecturer at Carlson, searched the crowd for our family. Fine taught three classes Chris attended during his junior and senior years at Carlson. Fine was relieved to find us, because he wanted us to know he did not believe Chris had committed suicide. He told us he called the MPD twice to tell them that, for numerous reasons, Chris did not fit a suicidal profile.

When Chris disappeared, he was in Fine's entrepreneurial studies class. Fine explained that entrepreneurship is the discipline and pursuit of implementing plans to fulfill one's personal dream. This mind-set of passion, purpose, and a positive expectation for the future is the antithesis of the thoughts of someone who would commit suicide. Fine described Chris as a vibrant young man with a tremendous zest for life: "Chris was so excited about his future and his business plan to change sports in America through a chain of lacrosse stores! I suggested to him that his store should really be a combination store for many alternative sports. He disagreed, confident that one day the sport of lacrosse would be so popular, his stores would serve the needs of thousands of players, and enjoy healthy profits. We spoke many times about his business plan, as well as his life and future. Chris often expressed pride and gratitude regarding his leadership role on the UMN Men's Lacrosse team. In my opinion, Chris exhibited no tendencies indicating depression; quite the contrary. I recall Chris as an attentive student who stood out from the crowd as an energetic person, poised to make a positive difference in the world." We thanked Alan profusely, agreeing with his fact-based account of Chris's character, while assuring him we did not believe for one minute that Chris committed suicide.

Alan promised to mail us the marketing plan component of Chris's business plan submitted in October 2002, just two weeks before he disappeared. He remarked, "You will see Chris's enthusiasm for his dream— the lacrosse store he wanted to create. He proudly called it 'America's First Sport' and chose 'Lacrosse 'N USA' as the store name."

A few minutes later, we spoke with a graduate, Chris Flynn, a friend of Chris's since high school. Flynn echoed Dr. Fine's perception of Chris's passion for life and lacrosse: "Prior to Chris's disappearance, I sat next to him in several classes. Walking into a class after Halloween, I always looked, hoping to see Chris. It's easy to forget the topics of the lectures, but I vividly remember the laughter Chris brought to a class. We both enjoyed our entrepreneurial studies course, which required us to develop a business plan. Few people, including me, seriously intended to start a business in the near future. Chris was different, though.

Passionate about opening a store to fully supply lacrosse players with gear, he worked diligently to develop a solid business plan. Even during lectures, he read lacrosse books for ideas and constantly doodled notes, creating his dream."

Remembering Goodness

Later that evening we held a party at the Town Hall Brewery to share a toast to Chris with his wonderful friends and several other volunteers who stayed by our side during the darkest days. Not wanting Chris's memorial service to be the last time we saw those amazing people, we decided to host a gathering to thank them, reminisce about happier times, and wish them well. Those remarkable people helped us remember that goodness is more widespread than evil.

During the party, Chris's first love, Crystal, shared a dream with me she had about a week before Chris's body was found. In the dream, Chris assured Crystal, "Don't worry. They're going to find me soon." I had heard a similar story from another friend of Chris's just a month earlier. Both young ladies felt comforted by their dream, yet they found it hard to believe it when the "dream came true." Death ends a life, not a relationship. When a dynamic young person like Chris simply vanishes and shows up dead in a river four months later, loved ones struggle for answers. Maybe in that struggle, our relationship with Chris took on a new form. So many of us tried to make sense out of the void, the black hole of loss with no answers. Steve, Sara, and I remained open to possible connections with Chris, and felt so grateful that some of his friends shared their experiences of Chris with us.

Chris became the first person from the Carlson School, the business college at the University of Minnesota, to be awarded a degree posthumously. Several weeks later, Sara recorded her thoughts regarding Chris's graduation. She praised her brother, declaring that no one deserved that honor more than he did: "As a leader and hard worker, Chris would have accomplished such great things. He proved his ability to succeed and live with great enthusiasm; a balance most people ignore or can't achieve. Our dear friend W.T. heard some students talking a couple days after graduation in a restaurant near campus. They complained that a dead kid received his diploma and they had to work for theirs. Chris had one semester left to complete his undergraduate degree in four years. W.T. walked up to them and said, 'Chill out, it's not like you're competing for jobs with him.' Unfortunately they aren't; but if they were, who would have been hired? Chris did not entertain negative thoughts. He gave credit to others and accepted blame even when he wasn't involved. Chris pushed full speed ahead, loving life the whole way. I miss my brother so much; the pain is indescribable."

May and June are traditionally the months of graduations, award ceremonies, and new beginnings. We desperately missed Chris. Our family accepted and held the diploma, the awards, but we couldn't hold the person who earned them. Chris wasn't here to receive what he worked so hard to achieve. Mother's and Father's Day also fall in May and June. Are we Chris's mom, dad, and sister, or is the past tense "was" or "were" the new, more accurate terminology? How do we answer the toughest question: "How many children do you have?" We live a new life, without a clue how to navigate this foreign territory. A gaping wound inside has replaced the joy we felt in Chris's presence.

UMN Lacrosse Awards: Chris's Number Is Retired

Chris's lacrosse team invited us and my parents, Grandma Rose and Grandpa Gene, to their award dinner and celebration. My parents accepted Chris's UMN Lacrosse Team Awards for the 2003 season: peer-appointed team captain and a varsity letter. Then Coach Lars presented Chris's maroon-and-gold jersey, professionally framed, to Steve and me. We held up Chris's #3 Gopher jersey, worn by Chris with boundless energy and pride, for three and a half years at the university. Chris's spirit and passion for lacrosse came to life, shining boldly through the glass. Lars announced that the team had decided to retire Chris's number—3—to signify his contribution to men's lacrosse and to honor the remarkable life Chris led. Every time I opened my mouth to thank them, I started sobbing. I did not feel quite so foolish or alone when I looked around and saw many people in tears, even tough lacrosse players who greatly respected our son. Maybe by sharing my emotions, they found the courage to grieve their loss by letting go of some of that raw pain through tears. Honoring and mourning, strong human emotions, dovetailed in a powerful tribute to a young man who taught all of us so much about loving each other.

Loesch's Investigation Heats Up

Before returning home to Wisconsin, we met with the medical examiners. Steely resolve helped us hold it together, but as Chris's parents, these meetings ripped our guts out. So, to be certain we heard and understood all the information we received, we asked Loesch to accompany us. That meeting produced many more concerns and questions than answers. Though we praised the work completed by the Hennepin County Medical Examiner's Office, we left disappointed and frustrated. Chris's death certificate would read: Cause of Death—unknown, apparent drowning; Manner of Death—undetermined.

No bruising had been found in the autopsy, yet Chris played two days of lacrosse as goalie with only a chest protector for padding five days before disappearing. He was found floating on his back with arms crossed on his chest, clothes neatly in place, both oversized slip-on shoes still on his feet, all of which was inconsistent with falling or jumping off the Hennepin Avenue Bridge. Most drowning victims lose one or both shoes, even shoes tied with laces. Even the lack of obvious trauma to Chris's body seemed to eliminate, to a degree, the possibility of coming off that bridge and drowning. If he did enter the Mississippi River from the Hennepin Avenue Bridge, Chris's body would likely have made contact with the steel I-beam located exterior to the bridge wall. Surely his shirt would not be tucked into drawstring pants, nor would shoes have remained on his feet.

As Steve and I discussed the situation over the next several days, we concluded that water destroyed evidence, even visible marks like bruising. Why hadn't we heard that possibility from the medical examiners? We started searching for additional evidence gathered at the recovery scene since it represented a *potential* crime scene. Our disbelief in the responses we received from Hennepin County had only just begun.

Chuck Loesch remained troubled by the incongruities between how Chris's body showed up (the position of his body, the fact that his clothing and shoes were in place, the lack of internal or external physical damage), and the MPD's theory that Chris might have jumped or fallen off the Hennepin Avenue Bridge. Based on how Chris's body presented itself, Loesch believed the Iron Bridge, a low bridge connecting Nicollet Island with the eastern shoreline of the river, presented a possible answer. So he conducted an analysis to determine river flow from objects entering the river from that bridge.

Loesch obtained an orange dummy (similar to one that would be thrown to a dog) to release on the east side of the Iron Bridge, and he watched as it drifted underneath the Third Avenue Bridge. The dummy then took a sharp eastward turn before the Horseshoe Dam, ending on the shoreline southeast of the Third Avenue Bridge. Next, Loesch released the dummy from the west side of the Iron Bridge, observing its course until it stopped near the Xcel Energy Hydropower Plant—again, east of where Chris's body stopped. This initial testing showed that objects coming off the Iron Bridge eventually ended up on the eastern shoreline of the river or at the Xcel plant, not near the Horseshoe Dam, where Chris's body was first seen.

To verify his initial findings, Loesch drove to the Xcel site, where he met and spoke with Marlowe Peterson, who worked for Xcel, and Charles Nguyen, an information technology professional working for the University of Minnesota at the St. Anthony Falls Laboratory. Based on his experience, Peterson confirmed Loesch's observation that objects flowing underneath the Iron Bridge would most certainly end up by the Xcel plant, not at the Horseshoe Dam. Nguyen suggested that Loesch meet with Dr. Omid Mohseni, associate director for applied research and engineering at the St. Anthony Falls Laboratory, to discuss conducting river current experiments with life-size dummies to help determine where Chris's body entered the river.

The Witness Who Saw Chris's Body Floating with Trees

After receiving contact information from Josh Guimond's grandfather, I phoned Lynn Diederich to thank her for reporting her sighting of Chris's body. She told me she enjoyed looking at the river every morning and evening on her walk across the Third Avenue Bridge. Anxiety gripped me when Lynn said Chris's body had appeared to be wedged between two trees or large branches in the area of a sandbar just south of the bridge. Because she makes an effort to notice the river scenery twice a day, Lynn felt certain Chris's body was not in that location the day before she saw it. Still being carried by the river current, his body had not yet reached its final resting place. Lynn did speak with the MPD and was told not to expect a call back from homicide. No one from MPD homicide ever followed up with her, yet our son's body had been recovered four months before. Every cell in my body screamed that something was very, very wrong with the picture.

A phone call to express gratitude had turned into the discovery of more data raising serious red flags. We remain so grateful to Lynn Diederich for speaking up about what she saw and how she responded. She agreed to speak with Loesch, who followed up by phoning her on June 29, 2003. Diederich told Loesch she had called 911 and given the following description of the body she saw in the river: in calm part of river—just south of Third Avenue Bridge, lying on back between two trees forming a "V," flowing with river current—head first downstream between trees, white face, arms and hands crossed on chest, one leg straight and one leg slightly bent—both legs clearly visible just below the surface; clothed in long pants, shirt, shoes. Lynn also stated that the river bottom can be seen from the bridge on a clear day in the area where she first saw Chris's body. Recalling her observation of that sand-bar as she gazed at Chris's body in the river strengthened her conviction regarding where she stood and what she observed. Loesch documented her statements from the phone conversation regarding what she saw, who she called, and how she followed up. Diederich and Loesch then agreed to meet at the Third Avenue Bridge early in August.

Now Loesch had real data with which to push forward. Further convinced that the recovery scene held valuable clues, he located re-covery scene video footage obtained with professional-grade camera equipment, from sources within the news-gathering business. Through careful viewing and analysis, Loesch identified individuals at the scene who later gave him information that put missing pieces in the puzzle of what happened to Chris Jenkins.

CHAPTER 11

Jenkstock

August 2003

I'll lean on you and you lean on me and we'll be okay.
DAVE MATTHEWS BAND

Build it and they will come—and they came! Our yard looked like a tent village. Jenkstock started as an idea to host a small group of Chris's friends for the weekend. When Chris visited us during the summer of 2002 to earn money for college tuition by landscaping, he built a bonfire pit amongst the trees in our backyard. Chris adored bonfires, so Steve thought bringing Chris's friends together around a bonfire would create a meaningful way to say good-bye to Chris. I liked Steve's plan, but I told him I had no intention of ever saying good-bye to Chris. The best I could do was say au revoir (roughly, "till I see you again"). Believing I will connect with Chris in the afterlife helps me stay sane.

Steve also wanted to make Chris's ashes available to anyone who wanted to put some on the fire. Sara, Steve, and I knew Chris would not want his ashes sitting in a box somewhere for years to come. Chris found his greatest pleasure in life simply by hanging out, "chilling" with his friends and family. As Maggie Schultz wrote on Chris's Web site, "Chris didn't ask for much; he just wanted to be with those he loved."

Chris lived full tilt, savoring everything along the way, yet thoughts of him now conjured up grief and anger. We struggled with how to serve as lead investigators and celebrate our son's life at the same time. Though we often felt ourselves hanging on to the edge of a cliff by our fingernails, for this weekend we resolved to boost these young adults who had a full, glorious life ahead of them. We wanted to provide an opportunity for ourselves and others to focus on Chris's wonderful life rather than his shocking death.

The word spread and soon we realized dozens of people planned to

123

spend the weekend at our home in "Scony" (Chris's nickname for Wisconsin). Filled with enthusiasm, I named the event Jenkstock: a party to remember and share the good times with Chris, connect, and help each other make sense of his inconceivable and mysterious death.

On the second weekend in August, we would welcome about seventy young adults driving five and a half hours from the Twin Cities and flying in from the East Coast. We decided the best way to feed dozens of hungry people, mostly guys, would be a pig roast. We invited our neighbors and Deputy Matt Prochaska (who came to our home to verify our identity to the MPD on the first night Chris was missing) to the pig roast on Saturday evening. Although we had lived in Rochester, Wisconsin, for only a year when Chris disappeared, the neighbors in our small subdivision in the country supported us during the worst days. They brought food, donated to the Find Chris Jenkins Fund, and took care of our property numerous times. Our loving pet Coco found her way into the Baldwins' hearts, our next-door neighbors, so we often left her with them rather than drag her through the inevitable trauma of dozens of trips to Minneapolis.

Sharing Chris

Grandma Rose and Grandpa Gene arrived first, on Friday night. During the previous week, I washed almost all of Chris's clothes and arranged them in piles of like items for his friends to choose. I did not wash the clothes we kept because we could still smell Chris on them. His smell—something tangible to connect with our living son—something so ordinary became more precious than gold.

First, I put clothes in boxes for my five sisters and their families. Mom helped me make some of those decisions. As I filled our dining room with stacks of Chris's clothes, memories flooded in. I saw the tie I bought for Chris shortly before he vanished, the jacket Steve bought with Chris when he came to Scony, the blanket Grandma Rose made for him his first year in college, and the shirts Sara bought in Cincinnati. Sitting on the floor, holding my face in my hands, I wept. "Oh Mom, what am I doing? This tears me apart." Grabbing a pile of clothing, I held on as if hugging Chris. Pictures, clothes—that was all I could hug. No more dancing eyes and silly smiles; no more Chris throwing me over his shoulder and twirling or running around; no more giant bear hugs. I was struck with the pain of understanding that sometimes there just isn't any more.

Looking at my mom's grief-stricken face, I remembered what my brother-in-law Pat Koness said about Mom when she heard Chris's body had been found: "It was probably the most poignant part of the whole sordid series of events. When we received your call that day, we were caught off guard. I recall your mom on the phone as we all fell silent. Your mom was sitting on the floor with the phone, just listening. As we watched her, she gave up the phone, to who I don't recall, then put her face into her hands and began weeping. It was perhaps the saddest thing I ever saw. I realized this was the first time I actually witnessed someone's heart breaking."

Mom ached for her own loss of the grandson she adored, and for me, Sara, and Steve. Since Sara and Chris were born (first grandchildren for my parents), Mom stated several times, "I just don't know what I'd do if I ever lost a child or grandchild." How I wish to God she had never found out.

Here They Come!

Crystal and Christian arrived very late Friday night to be available if we needed help. I stood in the driveway gazing at the stars as I waited for them to arrive. On a clear night in the country, the stars shine so brightly. These twinkling stars looked like Chris's dancing eyes—so full of promise and hope for the future. I remembered looking at a starry sky about a year earlier, as I sat on the front lawn, petting Coco, waiting enthusiastically for Chris to drive up. Seeing car lights shining at the end of our road, I anxiously ran down to the bottom of the drive waving, knowing Christian and Crystal had arrived safely.

The following day, carloads of young adults started arriving around noon. By five o'clock that afternoon, both our front and back yard resembled a campground. Excitement filled the air. Players tossed lacrosse balls back and forth, horns honked with each new car full of friends, and the roasted pig arrived on a huge rotisserie grill, still cooking. A keg of beer sat in the backyard, available to those who handed us their car or van keys. We told them no one could drive if they drank beer, and since we lived in the country, the biggest excitement for miles around was occurring at our house anyway! They teased us, just like Chris and Sara did when we enforced a rule, and tossed their keys into a huge cardboard box. Grandpa Gene, keeper of the keys, hid the box. Perfect! Grandpa Gene is a nice, quiet man; no one would have argued with him anyway.

Late in the afternoon, a group of people that included Jared Keepman, Bethany Mosley, Steve, and Grandpa Gene, headed into the Baldwins' woods to choose a tree. The explorers pushed their way through the thick woods, ultimately selecting "the perfect tree." They struggled more than anticipated just in digging it up, much less hauling it back to our front yard. Next, they had to dig a hole before lowering the tree into it and filling the hole with dirt. With the tree securely in place, Steve brought out the box of Chris's ashes and offered them to the laborers to place at the base of the tree. Jared later wrote: "I had never held or been around a person's ashes. I must admit it was a bit awkward at first, but in planting the tree and holding Chris's ashes in my hands, I had an incredible feeling of ease—a continued confirmation he was in a better place, reminding me he was OK, and looking forward to reconnecting with all of us."

When speaking with small groups of Chris's friends throughout the day, I urged them to choose articles of clothing from the many piles in our dining room. Assuring them that Chris would not want his possessions to sit in boxes in a closet, I told them to choose something meaningful to them. Slowly, more and more people looked at the clothes and chose one or more items. By the following day, I heard frequent and funny comments coming from the dining room: "Hey, those are *my* shorts. Chris never returned them!" "I remember when he bought that shirt online. I helped him pick it out." "That was my favorite sweatshirt of Chris's—can I really have it?" Through their excitement and honesty, we learned more about our son and knew that our decision to offer his clothes to friends was the right one.

Deputy Prochaska delighted us by coming to the pig roast with his wife, Maggie. When we introduced him to Chris's friends, he received a hearty round of applause. I proposed a toast: "To Deputy Matt Prochaska—a cop with heart." Everyone cheered again. Some of the guys even tried to teach him how to throw and catch a ball with a la-

Jenkstock—we come together as family.

crosse stick. The guys also spent a great deal of time teaching our young neighbor, Cody Nannemann, how to play the game. They promised him a spot on the Gopher Men's Lacrosse team if he kept practicing and improving. Seven-year-old Cody loved lacrosse and all the attention from university players. He tried to convince his parents for the next several weeks to move to Minneapolis so that he could become a star lacrosse player.

Coach Larson came with his wife, Vicky, and their son, Casey. They felt close to Chris; he even babysat Casey. Steve and I had watched Lars lead with courage by loving and serving many of us. While experiencing tremendous personal grief, he remained at search headquarters for two weeks as the point person for all the maps, searches, distribution of vans, and other details. We felt so fortunate that Lars had coached our son in lacrosse and in life. He held us up, never lost faith in Chris, and dignified Chris's life and death through his actions.

As dusk approached, Steve reminded people to set up their tents before dark. A few listened and strategically positioned their tents in the yard. Several who had only brought sleeping bags spread them around the first floor of our home. I told them to just push the furniture against the walls to make room. Smiling, I watched the silly antics involved in staking out territories. These kids reminded me so much of Chris. Their energy, humor, and genuine kindness warmed my soul. I easily understood why Chris loved them; I did too. It was also easy to open our home and our hearts to these awesome kids who loved our son, and walked side by side with us during the grueling searches.

I vividly remember Maggie Schultz and Tanya Bradach struggling to set up their new tent in the front yard. We hugged, laughed, and cried. Tanya and Maggie shared with me how much Chris cheered them up when they felt burdened. Tanya added, "I still feel Chris is here to harass me whenever I get in a bad mood. He never allowed me to be in 'a mood' as he called it." I thanked Maggie for the e-mail she sent eight days after Chris disappeared. She hadn't been able to write her thoughts on the message board, since it was temporarily down because of the high volume of incoming messages. Maggie wrote: "Chris, if I was the best writer in the world, I could not begin to explain what you meant to us. You were the smile that inspired our lives, the energy that gave us strength, the person we could all rely on. No matter how bad things got, we all knew you were there; you were the hope that would help us through."

Flames and Ashes

We waited until dark to gather around the pit Chris built in our back-yard. With a small fire ablaze, Steve gave an update on our investigation and answered questions. Then he opened the box of Chris's ashes and offered them to the group. Several people backed up, looking be-wildered. After the first person took some ashes, said a few words, and threw them on the fire, a few more stepped forward. While some spoke out loud to Chris, others held their thoughts in their hearts. I started crying. I remember that P.J. 85 (he liked to include his lacrosse number) hugged me, probably so that I would not fall over. P.J. had transferred to the University of Minnesota from the East Coast a year earlier. After joining the lacrosse team, P.J. met Chris, who heartily welcomed him to the team and to Minnesota. P.J. attributed his easy transition and successful year to Chris's compassionate leadership.

Chris's warmth and exuberance extended to all these kids. Kris McMillan and so many others told us Chris made them feel important:

"He made me feel like I was the most important person in the room whenever I saw him." We heard that phrase many times, almost the exact wording. Sara praised her brother, telling us after Jenkstock, "I never realized the impact Chris left on his friends and strangers alike. He used his many rare gifts to help others. What an amazing man, true friend, awesome brother, and kind-hearted son. I have become even more proud of my brother after his death, though I miss him immensely. Only when our souls are rejoined will I be whole again."

Tears, hugs, "I love ya, Jenks," and a few smiles traveled amongst us as we stood around the fire, supporting each other in honoring Chris— our fallen hero who gave so much of himself. Those who wanted to throw ashes completed their farewell to a dear friend. After listening to what people said about Chris, I realized how much they depended

Holding Chris in our hands and hearts.

on him, and highly respected him as a strong leader. I agreed with Christian when he said his teammates would have followed Chris into fire. In a way, they just had.

Slowly, groups moved from our small fire pit to the Baldwins' next door, where a massive twenty-foot pyramid of wood waited to become a Jurassic Park–size bonfire in their backyard. Dave Baldwin and Steve had chopped down five enormous dead trees the previous week, splitting the wood into logs. After piling up logs and branches, they still had more than three cords of wood off to the side, ready to keep the fire going for the whole evening. Charles and Christian had finished sawing the remaining logs before the evening festivities. I think they wanted to supply enough firewood to create a bonfire worthy of *The Guinness Book of World Records*. They succeeded. The fire blazed so high and bright, it looked like daylight for hours to come in the Baldwins' backyard. Throughout the evening, stoking the fire with wood became a team effort as people came together bravely sharing thoughts and feelings of grappling with pain, ambiguity, and hope.

Sitting on lawn chairs, blankets, large rocks, or sprawling on the ground around the massive pyramid of fire, we laughed, cried, and tried to make sense of our incomprehensible loss. The mystery of Chris's death was yet to unravel, but one sentiment rang loud and clear—most believed Chris was murdered. Though we heard lots of frustration, confusion, and questioning, we heard even more about how Chris had positively changed their lives. In addition to personal growth, people talked about walking in large groups, never leaving anyone downtown alone, keeping track of each other in bars, and appreciating those they loved. They gave Chris credit for showing them how to live fully and enthusiastically.

Stories of Chris sprang to life. I shared a glimpse of a young Chris from a post to the message board soon after his memorial service: "Moving to Minnesota from New York with my family in the winter of 1988, I can't help but remember our son's 8th birthday the following summer. I just gave my son a brand-new 20-inch bike with all of the fancy trimmings. We invited Chris and some other kids to help us celebrate the day. We lived in a house just behind and up the hill from the Jenkinses. Everyone, of course wanted to ride the newest bike in the neighborhood; Chris was no exception. The kids waited patiently for their turn, riding in the backyard with minimal excitement. Then it was Chris' turn. He decided to go down the hill towards his house. It must have been halfway down the hill, when he noticed the brakes had failed. Chris continued the ride, passed his house, went across the street, passed the neighbor's house, and almost into Purgatory Creek. We were all worried standing on top of the hill. However, you could tell Chris didn't want to stop the ride. Once he finally stopped, he gave out a big hoorah of satisfaction, and became the hero of the celebration. My wife and I could tell right at that moment he was going to give life a ride of excitement and he was to glow when it was all done. He gave a new meaning to the expression, 'Living life to its fullest.' Thanks for welcoming us to Minnesota's way of life." After hearing that story, many agreed that Chris continued that joyful ride through life to the day his life was taken.

Around midnight I went into the kitchen to replenish the food trays and found Nicole and Adam sautéing vegetables and slicing cheese. They told me they were vegetarians and had just got hungry. How cool that they felt comfortable enough to help themselves. When people arrived, we told them to act like part of the family because that was how we saw them. We felt so honored that they did just that. Enjoying the company of Chris's friends brought us closer to him, even though at times our hearts ached, knowing he could not be here in the way we wanted.

The stories continued, we kept throwing logs on the fire, and in the wee hours of the morning, people headed to their tents or sleeping bags whenever they felt ready. Dream neighbor Barb Baldwin helped with anything needing attention. With Barb's extensive background as an ER nurse, we knew that if any accidents occurred, we were in good hands. Steve and I did not sleep much; we wanted to be available to these kids, who truly had become our own. We also wanted to be certain everyone stayed safe, had enough food, and knew how much they meant to us.

The following morning we picked up doughnuts from the local bakery, fruit trays and juice from the grocery store, and served a simple breakfast. Grandma Rose had brought her huge coffeemaker, and it percolated for hours as she made fresh coffee and refilled cups. Coffee was not the only thing waking up groggy campers. The sun filled parts of the yard woke up many, literally baking people out of their tents. Some of the strategies of tent placement from the night before no longer made sense in the morning heat.

By noon, almost everyone had left for home. Hugs, kisses, and thank-yous abounded. Steve and I choked up more than once saying good-bye. Each good-bye felt like another farewell to Chris. Whatever the future holds, we had provided an uplifting opportunity to share happy memories of Chris. Jenkstock unfolded without a wrinkle, creating a truly magical experience.

A few days later, a letter arrived from Tanya: "By spreading some of Jenks' ashes, I was able to hug him one last time and tell him I will always cherish how he changed my life. I believe that all seventeen of those shooting stars I saw last week were Jenks' way of telling me he was safe and OK now, and he would always be there. Thanks for letting us have some of Jenks' things, it must have been difficult to let them go. You guys will be in my heart forever."

Maggie wrote: "I will always hold on to those memories from lacrosse in the backyard, to the big bonfire, my favorite sweatshirt of Chris', and the ashes. Your strength is amazing and I love you so much more for it."

Adam summed up Jenkstock with these words: "By observing the deep bonds his family shared, I gained a better insight as to who Chris was and what drove him to learn, to lead, and to love. His ability to move people was still on display, reflected in the faces at once smiling and sad. Seeing the impact he had on his family and friends was truly inspiring."

Chris lives on in the hearts, smiles, and laughter of those who love him.

CHAPTER 12

"Look, Mom, It's Not Hard to See"

September 2003

I never met your son. From everything I've heard,
he was a remarkable young man. Who he was and
what must have happened are so disparate.

DR. ROBERT SEYBOLD

Chuck Loesch sent us a DVD of the footage taken at the recovery scene along with copies of digital photos he pulled from that footage. As Steve and I watched the first ten minutes of the DVD, I sat on the opposite end of the sofa from Steve, trying to conceal my tears with a pillow. My actions did not matter; during those ten minutes, Steve lived in the world of his son's recovery. As he watched, his eyes widened and he started shaking his fist and yelling at the screen, "Stop staring at my son, get him out of the water!" My agony for Steve exceeded my own pain.

We saw an aerial view of Chris's body before recovery efforts began. Our son, the human being we brought into the world, loved beyond measure, lay in the cold waters of the flowing Mississippi River. Floating on his back, his upper torso encased in thick ice, he appeared tangled in the branches of a tree stopped at the Horseshoe Dam. No ice covered his legs, which were floating slightly apart, clearly visible just below the surface of the water.

From this distant view, Chris drew me in. As our hearts connected, I sensed him saying, *Look, Mom, it's not hard to see.* Deep inside, I knew that scene held answers to our son's death.

Almost three hours lapsed from the start of the recovery footage shortly after walkers spotted Chris's body, until his body lay in the water along the shoreline, ready to be lifted out and transported. A significant amount of ice must have melted or broken off during recovery because now we could clearly see his arms and hands crossed on his chest. A few yards away, we saw the body bag.

About a month later, I spent a weekend with Sara in Cincinnati. We watched the same DVD of the recovery scene. A few minutes into the footage, the identical message seemed to almost bounce off the walls: *Look, Mom, it's not hard to see.* I started patting the sofa we sat on, whispering, "Chris, you're here, where are you?" Sara teased me, though she clearly understood something magical and critically important was occurring. Any sliver of doubt about Chris's death vanished. My connection with Chris confirmed in my bones what I believed all along: Chris died at the hands of others.

Loesch on the Move

Key information discovered that summer kept Chuck Loesch busy indeed. The recovery footage and the witness's description of her sighting of Chris's body rendered clues and raised serious questions about what happened to Chris on Halloween night 2002. Loesch systematically followed up, relentless in his quest to uncover the facts.

As planned, Loesch met with Lynn Diederich and her friend Cindy Danley on August 5, 2003, at the Third Avenue Bridge. They walked to the spot where Lynn first saw Chris's body floating with and behind large tree branches. She pointed to a sandbar just south of the Third Avenue Bridge, confident for two key reasons that she had seen Chris's body in that exact location. First, Lynn remembered looking at his body wedged in tree branches, noting the underlying sandbar. Second, she walked a few feet past a specific lookout area on the bridge, past the dam, when she stopped directly above Chris's body to observe the unusual scene. Continuing across the bridge to phone 911, she suddenly decided to return to that same spot to reconfirm what she saw.

After studying the scene a second time, Lynn said she phoned 911, then her husband, and finally, her friend Cindy. Sharing the same details on each phone call, Lynn described the body tangled in trees, her location on the bridge, and her subsequent actions. When Loesch asked if she spoke with the police, she said yes, at about 6:00 p.m. that same evening, she received a call from the MPD. The officer asked for her name, address, phone number, and the time and description of what

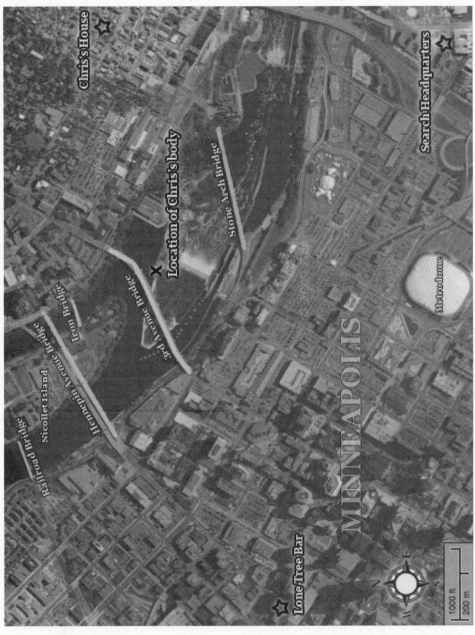

To drive from the bar to Chris's residence is 1.6 miles and six minutes' drive time, or thirty-two minutes' walk time.

she saw. Then he gave her his name, badge number, and the case number, adding that homicide might contact her, but he doubted it.

Loesch, Lynn, and Cindy finished their discussion of key facts and then proceeded to a nearby restaurant on Nicollet Island, where Loesch recorded statements from both women. Cindy noted that she also looked at the river every day, as did many walkers and bicyclists who crossed the Third Avenue Bridge. She seemed as certain as Lynn that the body and trees could not have been there for long, because of heavy traffic from early morning till late at night on the bridge. Both women agreed Chris's body was not in that spot the day before.

The location of Chris's body when Lynn first saw it remains highly significant. Based on her repeated, identical descriptions of that setting, his body had not yet reached its final resting place. Of equal importance is the positioning of his hands and arms. More than once, Lynn referred to Chris's arms and hands crossed on his chest as looking unusual; it reminded her of someone posed in a casket.

Loesch thanked the women for coming to the bridge to describe their recollection of events on February 27, 2003. On the drive back to his office, he contacted a professional to transcribe the statements. Then he phoned us with an update, and a few weeks later we received a copy of the conversations.

The Significance of Where Chris Entered the Mississippi River

The recovery footage and witness description of Chris's body in the water convinced Loesch he needed to seek more information to ascertain where Chris's body entered the river. The idea that he had gone into the river north of the Hennepin Avenue Bridge pointed to foul play. Why would Chris go north of that bridge when his residence was in the opposite direction? Particularly since October 31, 2002, was a cold and extremely windy night, and Chris only wore a thin nylon costume, no jacket.

To get from the Lone Tree Bar to his residence, Chris had to cross the Mississippi River. Three bridges provided the most direct route, from north to south: Hennepin Avenue, Third Avenue, and Stone Arch. Closed-circuit TV footage from the Hennepin Avenue and Stone Arch bridges did not show anyone crossing who resembled Chris, either late the night he disappeared or early the next day. Since the Mississippi River did not ice over in the area of those three bridges during the fall and winter Chris was missing, if he had gone into the river near the Third Avenue Bridge, river currents would have carried him farther downstream. Yet Chris's body was found just a few yards south of the Third Avenue Bridge.

Pondering these questions, Loesch followed up with information technology specialist Charles Nguyen's suggestion to contact his colleague at the St. Anthony Falls Laboratory, Dr. Omid Mohseni, associate director for applied research and engineering at the laboratory. Loesch prepared a list of detailed questions on river and weather patterns, and then met with Dr. Mohseni on August 7. They reviewed recovery footage and the ten digital photos created from significant parts of the footage. Their discussion included the tree stopped at the Horseshoe Dam because Chris's body appeared to be iced into that tree. If they could determine the origin of that tree, perhaps important clues would emerge, leading to where Chris entered the water, or to the location of his body in the river during the four months he was missing. They discussed at length the possibility of building a model of the river to answer the key questions. Dr. Mohseni agreed to estimate costs of different types of models and contact Loesch in a few days.

Less than a week later, Dr. Mohseni phoned Loesch to explain that river currents around the Third Avenue Bridge posed several challenges to obtaining accurate results. Because of that, it would be necessary to build a complex model, resulting in significant expense. Over the next several weeks, Steve discussed numerous possibilities with Dr. Mohseni and Loesch, including enlisting volunteer help to build the model.

Dr. Mohseni suggested an easier and relatively inexpensive solution— satellite photos. If available, the photos might show Chris's body and the tree, perhaps along the shoreline of the river. During the month of August, Dr. Mohseni and others contacted satellite companies seeking available photos, particularly ones taken on February 27, 2003 (the day Chris's body was recovered), and a few days prior.

Loesch and our trusted volunteer W.T. also searched for satellite photos. After speaking with cartographers while conducting research at the UMN libraries, W.T. realized aerial photographs might be more readily available than satellite photos. He remained optimistic since commercial and residential development along the river continued strong late in 2002 and throughout 2003. While it seemed a long shot, the possibility of finding a photograph of Chris wedged or frozen into a tree gave W.T. renewed energy.

Late in August, Dr. Mohseni phoned Loesch to report that he had not located any satellite photos close to February 27. He was able to find photos from mid-January 2003 of the area north of I-694 and extending south, beyond the downtown Minneapolis area. A key discovery yielded through an examination of the photos was that ice buildup on the river started about one mile north of the Hennepin Avenue Bridge, around 27th Avenue and Lowry, and continued north, while little ice formed on the river south of that area.

Dr. Mohseni also mentioned that river currents had actually decreased during the four months Chris was missing, only increasing again at the end of February 2003. The decrease in river flow from November 2002 to February 2003 supported the buildup of thick ice covering Chris's upper torso. Likewise, the week before Chris's body was found, temperatures had risen, causing snow and ice to melt. As the river rose and the current strengthened, frozen objects in the river and along shorelines broke free and began moving downstream. (See Notes for detailed information on river flow and air temperatures.)

Armed with new data from the recovery footage, information from engineers and researchers at the Xcel Energy Hydropower Plant and St. Anthony Falls Laboratory, and the witness's description of sighting Chris's body, Loesch knew the recovery scene held answers. Speaking with those who recovered Chris's body seemed the next logical step. Through skillful investigation, Loesch learned that two men had recovered Chris's body: one from the Minneapolis Fire Department and the other from the Hennepin County Sheriff's Office Water Patrol. Before meeting with either of these men, Loesch carefully reviewed all the data recently gathered. He determined that the facts seemed to eliminate some areas in the river as possible locations where Chris entered the Mississippi.

The Most Logical Point of Entry

Dr. Mohseni and Nguyen from St. Anthony Falls Laboratory, and Marlowe Peterson of Xcel Energy, confirmed that because of river currents, anything entering the river on the northern or eastern shoreline of Nicollet Island, or east of Nicollet Island, flows to the Xcel Energy Hydropower Plant, not toward the Horseshoe Dam. Since the Iron Bridge connects the eastern shoreline of Nicollet Island with the east side of the river, Chris's having entered the river from the Iron Bridge or traveling underneath it did not seem feasible. To end up at the Horseshoe Dam, just south of the Third Avenue Bridge where he was found, logic dictates that Chris's body entered the Mississippi River west of Nicollet Island, most likely north of the Hennepin Avenue Bridge.

If Chris had gone off the Hennepin Avenue Bridge, or entered the river in the vicinity of that same bridge, his shirt would not be tucked in and slip-on shoes would not have remained on his feet, nor would he be floating on his back with arms and hands crossed on his chest. When a person drowns and is submerged for a period of time, unless he is held down by cement or something in nature (weeds, branches, debris), gases will form internally and eventually raise him to the surface. How could Chris's body have been submerged, floated to the surface in extremely cold water, and formed several inches of ice in the six-minute float between the Hennepin Avenue Bridge and the Horseshoe Dam? In fact, at river level, even solar radiation is a factor *preventing* ice formation.

To further appreciate the significance of the thick ice on Chris's upper torso, it is important to understand that the winter of 2002–3 was relatively mild. The area of the Mississippi River between downtown Minneapolis and the University campus did not freeze over, even though the average mean low temperature was below 32 degrees Fahrenheit after November 11, 2002.

If Chris's body had frozen along the western shoreline of Nicollet Island, between the Hennepin Avenue and Third Avenue bridges, he would have been seen, since part of his face and right hand were exposed. Both bridges and Nicollet Island are heavily traveled every day, even in winter, by walkers, bicyclists, and cars. In addition, many joggers run along the river's eastern shoreline in the area between the Hennepin Avenue Bridge and the Stone Arch Bridge (the next bridge south of the Third Avenue Bridge). Several restaurants and bars are located along that stretch, resulting in countless pedestrians day and night. Even photographers frequent this area to capture pictures of the river surrounding Nicollet Island and the Minneapolis skyline.

In November 2002, numerous search teams combed Nicollet Island

and the surrounding areas. Then in December, when small amounts of ice formed along the shorelines of Nicollet Island, several of us poked through that ice with thick sticks and logs. The only area we might have missed is the northernmost section of the western shoreline of Nicollet Island, north of the Railroad Bridge (the next bridge north of the Hennepin Avenue Bridge). Traveling on foot is difficult and dangerous on that steep, heavily wooded stretch of riverbank. Consequently, this was one of the areas we believed the National Guard should check. Since the MPD would not request the services of the National Guard, a thorough search of the northern section of the western shoreline of Nicollet Island did not occur.

Over the years, every expert examining Chris's case (Dr. Mohseni; University professor and head of the Department of Forest Resources, Dr. Alan Ek; Deputy Sheriff Walt "Butch" Hendrick and Andrea Zaferes, president-founder and vice president, respectively, of Lifeguard Systems, Inc.; forensic pathologist Dr. Michael Baden, who is co-director of the New York State Police Medicolegal Investigation Unit; and others) agreed Chris's body must have been in a shaded area for an extended period of time with little river current to form the extensive amounts of ice covering his upper torso. Recovery scene photos clearly show that the left side of his face and his right hand (partially covering his clenched left fist) were exposed to the elements for an extended period of time, the appearance resembling freezer burn.

The only area between the Hennepin Avenue Bridge and the Third Avenue Bridge where several inches of ice formed early in 2003 was at the southern tip of Nicollet Island. With all of the walkers, joggers, restaurant and bar patrons, someone would have seen his body. It seemed highly unlikely that his body lay unseen in that area all or part of the winter, formed inches of ice, and floated a couple of minutes from the southern tip of Nicollet Island to his final resting place.

CHAPTER 13

One Year Later

October–November 2003

What you leave behind is not what is engraved in stone monuments,
but what is woven into the lives of others.

PERICLES

Leaves turned brilliant colors, cooler temperatures brought sweaters out of closets, bonfires and football games marked weekends of fun; our family loved autumn. Jumping into piles of raked leaves, venturing out on long bike rides, carving pumpkins and roasting the seeds, dipping apples into melted caramel—we savored the joys of the season. Starting when Chris was only six months old, we made our annual family trek to the Minnesota Landscape Arboretum. Sara and Chris loved the bog trail, waterfall, maze of evergreen trees, woods, and colorful flowers and shrubs. Our tradition included a picnic lunch spread out on a blanket on the grass. Lying on the blanket, gazing at the sky, life seemed peaceful. Chris's disappearance on October 31, 2002, changed all of that, even the memories.

Fall returned with familiar sights, smells, and events, but waves of anxiety and dread replaced the anticipation and joy of previous years. We gave away all the Halloween masks, costumes, decorations, even the cookie cutters. The mere sight of pumpkins produced a surge of nauseating adrenaline. We abandoned carts in grocery store aisles, avoided farmers' markets and retail stores, walked away from conversations about Halloween parties. Surely those who tell us to cherish the memories have not endured the trauma of a missing and murdered son or daughter. Memories of fall are tainted with Chris's blood.

Chris's friends experienced similar angst during the fall of 2003. Mike McTigue, a lacrosse teammate and close friend, wrote a song as

*Family time—
creating memories.*

*Surrounded by the
sounds of nature.*

"Hey, Mom, who's gonna fall first?"

he struggled through the pain of harsh memories and profound loss (the complete lyrics can be found at www.FootprintsOfCourage.com):

> I took a drive by myself one day about a year after Chris
>   disappeared . . .
> . . . Sat by the banks of the Root River
> Saw the leaves all changing color
> Right about then I began to wonder . . .
>
> In a sense, I've gotten older
> Innocence, I'm still a youngster
> In a sense, life should be cookin'
> In a sense . . .
>
> I'm still lookin'
>
> In the bushes
> In the river
> It's gettin' clearer . . .
>
> Gonna have to find him in the mirror

Two Rings and a Braided Necklace

Since none of us saw Chris's body, Steve chose to view Chris's clothing as a way to connect with his son's final hours. He also wanted to see the condition of the clothes to satisfy his need for answers. Sergeant Jackson agreed to Steve's request and accompanied him to the MPD Property Inventory warehouse. Covered with mud and algae from the river, the clothes showed no marked damage. Before they left, Jackson gave Steve a few personal items of Chris's—two rings and a braided necklace, both worn by Chris on the last day of his life.

When Steve told me about receiving Chris's jewelry, he reminded me that Chris had made the necklace from nylon used to form the pocket of a lacrosse stick. Chris loved the necklace so much, he made a few for his friends. I could not bear looking at Chris's jewelry. Determined to restore each piece, Steve spent months removing algae and decay, eventually resorting to bleach. After dozens of careful cleaning routines, Steve showed me the three pieces of jewelry.

Lost in thought, I held our precious treasures for several minutes. My eyes zeroed in on the turquoise ring. The bleach had faded the turquoise color to a grayish light blue resembling a pair of washed-out jeans. The faded turquoise color troubled Steve because we had already decided to give that ring to Sara. For some reason, we felt Chris wanted her to have it.

On a visit to Cincinnati in the fall of 2003, Sara picked us up at the airport and we went straight to a restaurant for dinner. When I handed Sara the ring, her eyes filled with tears and she whispered, "I miss him so much." Steve and I nodded in silent empathy. Suddenly, she asked, "Hey, what happened to the color?" After we explained, she set it on the table, and the three of us enjoyed a leisurely dinner.

Just before leaving, Sara picked up the ring. Wide-eyed, she exclaimed, "Look!" To see more clearly, we held the ring next to a lighted candle on our table. Sure enough, the turquoise color had returned. Steve remained skeptical. As he paid the bill, Sara and I ran outside to hold the ring under a streetlamp in front of the restaurant.

Every time we passed a light on the drive to Sara's house, I held up the ring, trying to see the color. After arriving at her home, Sara and I ran up to her bathroom to look at the ring under a bright light—it was still turquoise. Cradling the ring in my cupped hands, I sensed Chris's presence. "Sara, Chris wants you to have his ring. He is reassuring you, 'Sara, I will always be with you.'" She dropped to the floor sobbing, "Oh, Mom, I feel the same thing."

Before going to bed, Steve put the ring on the cold kitchen countertop. He believed the turquoise color would disappear by morning, reasoning that temperature had caused the color change. Steve looked perplexed the next day as he examined the ring—it was clearly turquoise. He stood shaking his head. Sara and I just smiled.

Looking for Clues

With new information from the recovery scene, we had questions regarding the autopsy and subsequent testing. In a conversation with me on October 8, 2003, Dr. Baker of the Hennepin County Medical Examiner's Office clarified that the items listed on the autopsy report under "additional procedures" had not been done. Specimens, tissue samples, and other samples had been retained for potential future needs. Apparently the MPD still did not consider Chris's death suspicious, since only blood alcohol and a few drug tests had ever been requested. Medical examiners found no marks on Chris's body to indicate foul play, so they also requested no further testing.

The autopsy report indicated that no bruising had been found. Since we knew Chris had bruising on his thighs and forearms from playing lacrosse for an entire weekend just five days before he disappeared, I questioned Dr. Baker. He verified that we had correctly interpreted the report in regards to bruising. Sara, Steve, and I surmised that water and time destroy important evidence.

Dr. Baker confirmed that he had examined very few bodies that had been in water as long as Chris's; most bodies found in water showed up within a week or two. He said it was most unusual that Chris's body was found four months later, especially since the water temperature in the river remained quite cold in late February. The other medical examiners involved in the autopsy concurred: submerged bodies do not typically surface in cold water.

Dr. Baker listened well and responded with clear answers to my questions. When I asked for photos taken at the recovery scene, he clarified that providing such pictures was not the role of medical examiners. Dr. Baker treated Chris and our family with respect and compassion, making a positive difference during many dark days.

Following our conversation, I signed a general release form and a release of liability form in order to receive a CD of the autopsy photos. I faxed back the signed forms to the medical examiner's office. Although we did not intend to review the autopsy photos ourselves, it seemed wise to retain the CD for future investigative work.

The video footage showed someone from Hennepin County taking pictures. Believing that recovery scene photos held key information, Steve contacted MPD Sergeant Jackson after I spoke with Dr. Baker. First, Jackson told Steve we had no right to the pictures, then he said there weren't any, and finally he told Steve to call the medical examiners. Steve explained that we had already spoken with them, and they had no recovery scene photos. A heated argument ensued, ending with Jackson giving Steve the name of the MPD person in charge of fingerprints and photographs.

A week later, Steve received a return call from the man in charge of that department. He told Steve the MPD had taken no close-up shots of Chris's body at the recovery scene. By carefully reviewing the video footage, Loesch identified the photographer as someone from the Hennepin County Sheriff's Office. Eventually, we found photos at the Sheriff's Office Crime Laboratory and paid to get copies of them. It appeared that Sergeant Jackson had not looked at those photos, nor were they put in Chris's file. With dogged determination, we pushed forward, firmly believing we were the only detectives working to solve the mystery of our son's death.

Our growing suspicions of a possible cover-up caused us to request Chris's clothes, shoes, and other items. In a conversation with Sergeant Jackson, Steve got permission for Chuck Loesch to pick up the sealed evidence bags on October 9, 2003. Jackson did not tell Steve we would be breaking the chain of custody, nor did he explain the consequences of that action. Although we did not know it at the time, breaking the chain of custody casts doubt on potential forensic evidence that may be used in the future to prosecute a suspect.

Operation Find the Truth

Acting on advice from the Jacob Wetterling Foundation, we decided to take advantage of the one-year anniversary of Chris's disappearance by asking the public for information regarding his death. We launched Operation Find the Truth by dedicating the month of October to speaking out in the media and planning other activities to raise public awareness. Early in October, I sent an e-mail to volunteers outlining scheduled events throughout the month.

My sister Linda Sweet flew in from San Francisco to run in the annual Twin City Marathon the first weekend in October. A few months before disappearing, Chris had started a running program with suggestions from Aunt Linda. They had briefly discussed running a race together. Wanting to fulfill a goal of Chris's, Linda ran the marathon for him. A couple of his friends, Suzanne and Crystal (whom we called "junior detectives"), joined Linda for a mile or two, encouraging her to keep going. Linda said she felt as if Chris ran the entire marathon with her. Crossing the finish line she started to cry. One of the volunteers asked if she was OK. How do you explain those tears?

Welcoming volunteers on October 11 at the YMCA, our former search headquarters on the University campus, produced heartfelt hugs and tears. Our brief organizational meeting kicked off the weekend events of putting up new flyers and hosting a press conference. We distributed new "Someone Knows Something" flyers and slicks (which stick to glass and are easy to remove) highlighting the increased reward money: "Up to $175,000 for information leading to the arrest and conviction of those responsible in the death of Christopher Jenkins." The wording gave us latitude to give an award commensurate with the value of the tip. If a solid lead came in, we would find a way to raise the money.

After organizing "flyer teams," we asked everyone to exercise good judgment by respecting people and property when putting up flyers in Minneapolis and on campus. As teams left with flyers, tape, and slicks, we encouraged them to return by 2:00 p.m. for food.

Gathering in a room at the YMCA, we held a press conference for local media focused on new announcements, recent developments in Chris's case, and recognition. We thanked the media, including *Inside*

Edition, a syndicated TV news program, for attending and keeping our pleas for information alive. Announcements mentioned:

- Reward up to $175,000
- New Web site: www.rememberchrisjenkins.com
- The FX Network's new *American P.I.* series featuring the disappearances of Chris Jenkins and Josh Guimond in the first episode on October 24, 2003: "Suspicious Drownings in the Upper Midwest"

We continued with our most important development in Chris's case, namely, the discovery of data to help determine where he had entered the Mississippi River. We introduced Dr. Omid Mohseni, who described his preliminary findings based on weather and river patterns gathered from the Army Corps of Engineers, and video footage of the recovery scene.

With deep gratitude, we recognized Hennepin County personnel involved in the search for Chris and recovery of his body, Hennepin County medical examiners, our P.I. Chuck Loesch, dedicated volunteers, and the Jacob Wetterling Foundation. We also praised staff at the University of Minnesota from St. Anthony Falls Laboratory, the Department of Forest Resources, and Counseling and Consulting Services.

A Potential Suspect

Last, we introduced Pat Brown, an investigative criminal profiler who had approached us shortly after Chris disappeared. Brown, CEO of the Sexual Homicide Exchange, then based in Minneapolis, had studied serial killers extensively and published a book titled *Killing for Sport*. Brown told us she had learned of a suspicious man named Richard Lily (one of his numerous aliases) when Detective Mike Harvey of St. Charles, Missouri, had contacted her prior to Chris's disappearance. Though Harvey had recently arrested and prosecuted Lily for felony assault after following him for three years (Lily's previous arrests included terroristic threats and male prostitution), Harvey requested Brown's analysis of Lily's potential for acting out his violent ideation and desire to drown men. Through our own efforts, we later learned that Lily was arrested in Minneapolis in August 2002 by the MPD. After the arrest, Lily had threatened to go on a killing spree by drowning healthy young men if the MPD did not get the FBI to profile him.

Brown connected with Lily on a Web site, Men Under Water, where men contact each other to role-play drowning their victims. Posing as a fifteen-year-old boy, Brown exchanged numerous e-mails with Lily in a chat room on the Web site. Lily wrote scenarios of himself as the offender and Brown as the victim. His "drownings" of her in various bodies of water contained a sexual component. Brown reported back to Detective Harvey that Lily exhibited psychopathic behaviors and certainly had obsessive ideations about drowning young men. She considered Lily someone to keep an eye on.

Though Lily later stated in an interview with Colleen Henry of TMJ-TV in Milwaukee that he never committed murder, he *had* traveled up and down the I-94 corridor. A confessed admirer of serial killer Jeffrey Dahmer, Lily described to Colleen Henry his fantasy of going across the country befriending athletic men between the ages of eighteen and twenty-three. He spoke of completing his fantasy by drowning, suffocating, or burning his victims—his three favorite methods of murder.

Brown believed Lily should at least be questioned regarding Chris's death, and possibly the deaths of five other young men in the Upper Midwest. All six men disappeared in close proximity to I-94 in the fall and winter of 2002–3, and eventually all but one of their bodies showed up in water. One of the six young men, Josh Guimond, is still missing.

We spoke with Detective Harvey, who told us he contacted Sergeant Jackson and Lieutenant Carlson at the MPD numerous times in October 2003, before reaching them. When Harvey eventually reached one of them, he explained his grave concerns regarding Lily's potential involvement in Chris's death and perhaps others. He offered the wealth of information he had gathered, including video recordings. Harvey was told there was no crime to investigate in the death of Christopher Jenkins; therefore, there was no reason to speak with him.

Homicide must be considered before it can be eliminated, especially in a highly suspicious death with no evidence to support suicide or accident. Jackson's and Carlson's lack of interest in Harvey's work both stunned and frustrated us. Digging for facts, we discovered that Lily lived on Nicollet Island late in 2001 and early in 2002. In 2002, Steve and I begged Jackson to follow up with Lily shortly after Chris disappeared. We asked again early in 2003. Sergeant Jackson, the lead detective in Chris's case, told us it was not necessary.

Operation Find the Truth: October 18–19, 2003

Faithful volunteers arrived an hour before the Gopher football game on October 18. We met them outside the Metrodome to distribute huge posters (four feet by three feet) with Chris's picture, tip line, and reward money. Members of our team stood all around the circular Metrodome; anyone attending the game likely saw at least one poster. The comment we heard most often from strangers did not surprise us: "I knew something stunk from the very beginning." What did surprise us was how often we heard similar comments, and still do.

Shortly before the game began, we joined the University's president, Dr. Robert Bruininks, and his staff. A few weeks earlier, he had invited Sara, Steve, and me to join them at the football game. We gratefully accepted his offer and thoroughly enjoyed getting to know him and his staff. Though we looked for a leader in law enforcement over the past year without success, the leader we found guided the University of Minnesota—President Bruininks. He seemed to enjoy a strong relationship with his staff, clearly bringing forth the best in those around him.

Halloween 2003

Several of Chris's teammates and friends wanted to hold posters outside the Lone Tree Bar, hoping someone would come forward with information. Sara, Steve, and I could not bear the thought of returning to Minneapolis, especially to the Lone Tree Bar, on the anniversary of Chris's disappearance. Loesch and one of his associates agreed to oversee the event on October 31, 2003. I sent an e-mail and spoke with many of Chris's friends, emphasizing our guiding principles: Please honor yourselves and Chris by taking the high road, stay together for safety, and support each other. This is about seeking truth, not stirring up trouble.

Local media interviewed a few of the students, mentioned the reward money, and asked the public for help. While many leads came in, none brought substantial results. Grateful to the students who bravely stood up for their friend Chris, and to the media for keeping Chris's story alive, we hoped eventually someone would talk.

After Halloween 2003, we did receive numerous e-mails with stories of people being attacked on the streets of Minneapolis and pushed out of bars without belongings or friends. Seeking to clarify details, we followed up by contacting the authors of several e-mails and speaking with them. Some were parents whose son was beaten by cops and left in a parking lot; a few had had a drug slipped into their drink; others found themselves suddenly surrounded by a gang on the street. The victims were businessmen and -women in their twenties and thirties (one group reported that they were all over six feet tall), as well as college students—alone or in groups. Many times, people were not robbed but rather beaten for sport. In each situation, innocent people suffered unprovoked attacks.

CHAPTER 14

A Lonely Path

December 2003–May 2004

Should you shield the canyons from the windstorms,
you would not see the beauty of their carvings.

ELISABETH KÜBLER-ROSS

One week before Christmas, Steve was terminated. Yet as vice president of new business development, he had successfully led his team in achieving 40 percent growth in a declining industry (down 30 percent). While sales performance is easy to measure, the sting of this blow could not be measured—we had missed living close to Chris the last year of his life by moving to Wisconsin to accept a new job opportunity.

The job termination paled in comparison to what we learned twelve hours later: our precious border collie, Coco Chanel, had an inoperable tumor on her liver. Sara flew to Wisconsin to say good-bye to her adored pet. Looking at Steve and me, she cried, "Well, you guys have managed to lose two children in one year." Almost thirteen years old, Coco did indeed qualify as one of our children.

Sara and I took Coco on her last walk. We let her sit on the deck for a few minutes, enjoying nature. When I opened the sliding glass door to let her in, she walked right by me. She also ignored Sara, who was coaxing her up on the sofa. Coco walked straight to a picture of Chris on the fireplace, plopped down, and just stared at him. Somehow, she knew that in a couple of hours, her suffering would be over.

When we returned home from the vet without Coco, Steve, Sara, and I qualified as complete train wrecks. Our faithful companion Coco had remained by our side during the traumatic year following Chris's disappearance. Her unconditional love had comforted us and brought smiles to our faces. Significant loss seemed unending. The decision we made a year earlier, to support each other no matter what, held us together.

We gathered Coco's bedding, food, and toys, placing these treasured items by Chris's set of weights in our basement. Coco had simply adored Chris. One year earlier, when we brought his weights and bench to our home, she sniffed around them for several minutes. Although Chris had not used those weights in at least three months at that time, Coco smelled his scent. Completely distraught, she had searched for Chris by running frantically around the basement. We wondered if Coco would join Chris for the holidays. Now two Christmas stockings evoked tears of shock and profound loss.

Fortunately, we had already planned to spend Christmas with my sister Linda and her husband, "FBI Bob," in San Francisco. We could hardly wait to get out of the Midwest. We did not care if we ever returned.

Christmas 2003—Jamie Lightner

A few days after Christmas, Sara's handsome new boyfriend, Jamie Lightner, joined us in San Francisco. Steve and I had met Jamie in mid-December when he and Sara drove to Wisconsin for a weekend visit. Four years older than Sara and somewhat reserved, he seemed comfortable in his own skin. Jamie had served as a police officer in West Chester, a suburb of Cincinnati, for ten years. Impressed by his confidence, I could not imagine being a cop and stepping into our lives.

Sara and Jamie enjoy the beauty and each other.

Linda and Bob opened their home and hearts by including us in their family Christmas celebration. We felt so grateful. At the same time, we instinctively knew our family Christmas had changed forever. We were learning that previously joyful events produced the deep grief of incomprehensible loss.

Before returning home to the Midwest, Steve, Sara, Jamie, and I decided to spend two days exploring the coastline and towns from the San Francisco Bay area to Monterey. The four of us drove south on the Pacific Coast Highway, marveling at nature's majesty. We stopped several times to climb up on huge boulders on the Pacific shoreline. Though Sara, Steve, and I had previously enjoyed the beauty of the Pacific Ocean, we had never seen it so turbulent, with waves cresting higher than twenty feet. Standing on a boulder with the spray of crashing waves hitting him, Jamie phoned his father, Ron. It touched me that Jamie chose to share the awe of his first experience of the magnificent Pacific Ocean with his dad.

Dr. Baden, Nationally Known Forensic Pathologist

After appreciating the splendors of nature along the West Coast, we spent the last day of our Christmas getaway with Linda and Bob. That evening Sara and I happened to see Michael Baden, nationally known forensic pathologist, on the FOXNews program *On the Record with Greta Van Susteren*. Dr. Baden stated that when bodies are found in water with moderate to severe decomposition and nothing else makes sense, the likely cause of death is strangulation or suffocation. Our jaws dropped open as Sara and I stared at each other, scarcely believing what we had just heard. Dr. Baden was describing a situation like Chris's. We decided we must speak with him upon returning home.

Steve did contact Dr. Baden, who confirmed that, yes, we had heard correctly. Steve described the recovery scene, seeking Baden's opinion regarding aspects of the situation we found most unusual. Baden concurred with our concerns: drowning victims are rarely discovered faceup, slip-on shoes still on their feet, their shirts tucked into drawstring pants. Three details in particular caught Baden's attention: Chris's arms crossed on his chest, torso encased in ice, low blood alcohol content (BAC), and the fact that Chris's personal effects had been given to his family. Baden had never heard of crossed arms on a drowning victim. He noted that a blood alcohol level of .12 was low for a body Chris's size having undergone four months of decomposition. Decomposition actually raises blood alcohol level, and we knew Chris had consumed alcohol Halloween night. Based on all these facts, Dr. Baden believed Chris's death was indeed suspicious. He questioned why we had Chris's personal effects, telling us those items are typically kept by police departments for many years, particularly in unresolved cases.

What percentage of the total BAC can be attributed to endogenous production after death (i.e., production caused by factors within the body)? We researched that question to help us determine the approximate time of Chris's death. Since Chris drank alcohol Halloween night, if he walked home after being escorted out of the bar and somehow ended up in the river, his BAC would correlate with the amount of alcohol he consumed that evening.

Although we found several articles related to postmortem forces in the body increasing blood alcohol level, one in the *Journal of Forensic Sciences*, "Alcohol in Decomposed Bodies: Postmortem Synthesis and Distribution" (see Notes), presented quantitative outcomes. A retrospective study of 286 autopsied medical examiner cases showed the following results: "We conclude that for the majority of cases in which endogenous blood production of alcohol occurs the concentration in blood may be as high as 0.15%." These findings concur with Dr. Baden's comments that with a BAC of .12, due to Chris's body size and four months of decomposition, Chris may have had very little if any alcohol in his blood when he died. So the possibility of Chris's being abducted and not murdered right away must be considered. This data also coincides with Hoover's path through downtown Minneapolis, which indicated Chris's scent was in a vehicle and the vehicle stopped for a period of time at another location before continuing onto the ramp leading to I-94. The facts continued to point toward foul play, and abduction.

Steve shared Dr. Baden's opinions with W.T., who had diligently continued searching for satellite or aerial photos. W.T.'s persistence and optimism led him to Bordner Aerials, Inc., located in Bloomington, a suburb of the Twin Cities. He spoke with the owners and explained the purpose of his quest. Knowing they had taken aerial photos when the new Guthrie Theater was being built on the riverbank, the owners dropped everything to check their archives. A two-hour search produced photos of the Mississippi River from just north of the Hennepin Avenue Bridge to slightly south of the Horseshoe Dam: one taken in January 2003 and the other taken in March 2003. W.T. contacted Chuck Loesch, who immediately drove to Bordner Aerials, Inc. Satisfied the photos would help unravel the mystery, Loesch requested poster-size copies of each.

The Hennepin County Sheriff's Office Crime Laboratory

After obtaining the photos taken by the Sheriff's Office Crime Laboratory, we also found a brief written report regarding the recovery scene completed by the same agency. Three key points in that report confirmed troubling facts we had already discovered: there was substantial ice on the body, the shoes remaining on the feet had a lug-type sole and no laces on the top, and the body had undergone considerable decomposition—especially the head, face, and hands.

Unfortunately, since the recovery scene was not considered a potential crime scene, we noted the following on the report: evidence retained: no; inventory: no; and latent fingerprints recovered: no. Worse yet, we learned by speaking with the two men who recovered Chris's body that no one from the MPD had ever contacted them for information regarding the recovery. Several years later, the chief of the MPD told us that communication between those who recover a body and the investigator on the case is standard procedure. If that is standard procedure, why wasn't it followed in Chris's case? Undeterred by the MPD's hard-line position of suicide or accident, we continued to push, as we had from the beginning, for basic investigative work in the highly suspicious death of our son.

Loesch compiled several questions after carefully reviewing photos and the report from the Sheriff's Office Crime Lab, photos of the river from Bordner Aerials, and video footage of the recovery scene from local media. He reread his notes from interviews with Lynn Diederich, who spotted Chris's body from the Third Avenue Bridge, and Dr. Mohseni, research engineer and authority on river currents and patterns. Based on the data, Loesch believed Chris's body likely entered the river somewhere north of the Hennepin Avenue Bridge.

Rescue Teams—Minneapolis Fire Department and Sheriff's Office Water Patrol

The meeting between Loesch and a few members of the Minneapolis Fire rescue crew responsible for recovering Chris's body proved invaluable in clarifying exact details of the recovery efforts. The firemen reported to Loesch that when they arrived on the Third Avenue Bridge between 3:30 and 4:00 p.m., they viewed the recovery scene with binoculars from the bridge. Their main concern stemmed from the extensive amount of ice on Chris's upper body because it appeared his body was iced into a large tree branch. They felt additional risk existed since his body would need to be separated from the tree while in close proximity to the Horseshoe Dam.

The concern prompted fire rescue personnel to equip the two men in the Zodiac (one from Minneapolis Fire rescue crews and the other from the Hennepin County Sheriff's Water Patrol) with a gas-powered chain saw and an electric circular saw. These two men launched the Zodiac about 6:30 p.m. with both saws aboard. As they approached, a strong odor of decomposition indicated that Chris's body had been on the surface, thawing out, for quite some time.

Nearing the body, the fireman observed that Chris's upper torso lay partially on top of tree logs and branches, with a long, curved branch crossing the top of his body. Due to the large amount of ice, he decided to remove the branch from Chris's upper chest to assess the situation before attempting the recovery. Much to his surprise, the branch lifted rather easily. From that vantage point, he realized Chris's body was lodged, more than iced, into the branches, so no saws were needed. After attaching a rope to Chris's right leg, he easily removed Chris's body from the logs. How does a body become wedged into a tree while floating in a river? It seemed more likely that someone placed Chris in that position.

Further discussion with other firemen at University Fire Station number 19 led to a consensus on two issues: ice melt and the location where the body entered the river. When comparing the recovery photos taken at 3:45 p.m. to those taken near the shoreline at 6:45 p.m., a significant decrease in ice is evident. Outside air temperature, removal of the body from the tree, and subsequent towing of the body from the edge of the dam to the shoreline, all contributed to the ice melt. Due to the thick ice shown in the initial photos, some individuals wondered if Chris's body might have come from much farther upriver where large amounts of ice formed that winter. A few firemen also mentioned Boom Island Park, just north of Nicollet Island. A boat launch on the northern side of the park provides easy access to the river, where one could easily dispose of a body without being noticed.

University Experts Examine the Data

Numerous authorities from various fields sought data to unravel Chris's mysterious and unexplained death. Knowing that a University student— a member of their community—had met a tragic death, Dr. Ek and Dr. Mohseni graciously offered their time and talent to help our family find answers. With the assistance of graduate students, they looked for satellite and aerial photos, checked weather records, and considered vegetation along the river. Through discussions of the data they gathered, including information from the recovery scene, Dr. Ek thought Chris's body might have entered the river north of the Hennepin Avenue Bridge, possibly a few miles upriver. If so, when ice along the shoreline melted and water levels rose, then Chris's body, tangled amidst logs and branches in a block of ice, broke away from the shore and floated downstream.

Dr. Ek determined that the large tree hung up at the Horseshoe Dam was a cottonwood or possibly an elm. He did not believe it came from Nicollet Island, as the island is well maintained and there are few, if any, such large pieces of dead wood there. The tree showed lots of wear and tear, indicating that it likely came from a considerable distance upstream. Did Chris's body connect with it somewhere in the river or at the Horseshoe Dam?

To answer that question, Loesch conducted an intensive review of all data, photos, video footage of the recovery, and the aerial photo taken in January. After seeking opinions of other emergency rescue and recovery personnel, and making numerous comparisons of photos, he determined that the tree hung up at the Horseshoe Dam did indeed appear in the January photo. However, Chris's body, lodged in logs and tree branches encased in ice, did not. So Chris's body, amidst logs and branches, likely floated into the large tree, which was already stopped at the Horseshoe Dam. That large tree and surrounding debris prevented Chris's body from going over the falls.

One fact is certain: Chris's upper torso had to be exposed, above the surface, for an extended period of time for thick ice to form. Ice forms on the surface of water, not below; and Chris's legs floated slightly below the surface of the water, *clearly visible* from the bridge. If he had been near the Horseshoe Dam for any length of time, dozens of people would quickly have seen him. So where was Chris's body the four months he was missing?

With feedback from qualified experts in many disciplines, including the two men who recovered Chris's body, we felt confident we were asking insightful questions and moving in the right direction. Yet intelligent, handsome, and athletic college-aged men in the Midwest and elsewhere (primarily northern states from Minnesota to New York) continued to disappear. Most were found in water, and a few are still missing. Of course we wanted answers in Chris's case, but we also wanted to raise awareness to ultimately stop this consistent pattern of presumed drownings. Fortunately, the FX Network *American P.I.* series, which described this pattern, aired numerous times during autumn 2003 and winter 2004. Many friends and family members of the victims hoped federal law enforcement would take action. As of this writing, however, that has not happened, and the number of bodies of young adult men found in water during winter months under suspicious circumstances continues to climb.

Sara's Gift

People ask about the parents. Who asks how siblings are managing? Surviving siblings have a tough, lonely path to walk. Suddenly, the brother or sister they've shared their childhood with can never be a part of their adult future. From our experience, surviving siblings almost always suffer painful guilt, often believing he or she should have died instead. We watched Sara continuously block her overwhelming sorrow just so that she could function. She was dating a young man when Chris disappeared. That friend disappeared from her life immediately after the discovery of Chris's body. It takes courage and effort to deal with grieving people. We've learned through our own experiences and speaking with other parents of missing and murdered children, some friends and family members decide not to exert the effort.

Jamie became a friend to Sara. Rather than running away when he learned about Chris, he tried to bring happiness to Sara's life. In February 2004, he invited us to a surprise birthday party for her. Delighted, we flew to Cincinnati to celebrate Sara and, we hoped, lift her up. Even her birthday created an emotional hurdle; Chris's birthday came five days later.

Before leaving home, we tried to secure a meeting with the newly appointed Minneapolis police chief, Bill McManus, who still resided in Dayton, Ohio, only forty miles from Cincinnati. Determined to start with a clean slate, we phoned his assistant in Dayton, saying we would like to help McManus succeed by giving him a heads-up regarding Chris's politically charged case. Although we were unable to speak with McManus, or get a meeting, we welcomed the possibility of creating an effective relationship with the MPD in 2004.

The Greatest Joys Evoke the Deepest Sorrow

A few weeks later during our annual March trip to Grand Cayman, Jamie proposed to Sara on the dance floor in front of a roomful of people. He arranged the surprise with the evening's entertainer, "Barefoot Man," a local legend, who strums his guitar and sings humorous and irreverent ballads one night a week at the Royal Reef.

Bob and Linda came as our guests for the week. How fantastic it was that they could share in Sara's happiness. While we celebrated heartily throughout the evening, as we walked along the sand back to our room, Linda pulled me aside, asking, "How can you stand it?" I mumbled, "I can't" as the tears flowed. At such a special time, Chris's absence permeated the unspoken longing—he should have been with us. After sobbing our hearts out, Linda and I walked back to the room to find Sara crying as well.

Just a week after we returned home to Wisconsin, Steve left for his new job in Minneapolis. Thinking about living in the Twin Cities without Chris seemed so harsh; yet we did have a huge support network there. Reluctant to voice my thoughts, I suspected we had a personal job

"I just upstaged the Barefoot Man," muses Jamie.

to finish in Minneapolis—justice for our son. Grateful to witness Steve's excitement regarding his new position, I decided to find the good in our upcoming relocation.

A Bloodhound Picks Up Scent Eighteen Months Later

In April 2004, we heard that a bloodhound named Calamity Jane had found the remains of Erika Dalquist, who disappeared from a bar in Brainerd, Minnesota, eighteen months earlier, just one day before Chris vanished. Although the circumstances of Erika's disappearance were not similar to the repeated patterns of the missing young men, our hearts understood her parents' anguish; we had experienced the emotions of that double-edged sword. A child is home, but the family chain is broken and dreams are shattered.

Sergeant Jackson had told us hounds could not pick up a scent in a downtown area, or after one week. We did not understand the blatant resistance to the work of two different bloodhounds, six weeks apart,

who both had many of the same hits on Chris's scent in the underground garage, the bar, and the river. One hound, Scrumpy, followed
Chris's scent only one week after he disappeared.

The Chris Jenkins Spirit Award

Chris's close friend Luke Fisher helped coach the Eden Prairie High
School Boys Varsity Lacrosse team in the spring of 2004. In June 2004,
Luke and Steve attended the team's banquet to present a special award.
The Eden Prairie Lacrosse Association created the Chris Jenkins Spirit
Award in the spring of 2003, the season Chris would have helped coach
the team. Each year, the head coaches select the player who best embod-
ies the spirit and character of Chris. The inscription on the trophy reads:

> His laughter would draw you near, his character would awe you,
> his compassion would keep you by his side, and his determina-
> tion would captivate you. He is sorely missed.

Although the award honors Chris, it also acknowledges his contribution to men's lacrosse in the state of Minnesota. Along with several
other Eden Prairie football players, Chris started a boy's lacrosse team
in 1998, his junior year. In 1998, only seven varsity boys' lacrosse teams
existed in the Twin Cities area. I distinctly remember Todd Lukens
and several other guys showing up at our front door. Todd said no one
wanted to play goalie (the only pad worn is a chest protector, and the
hard lacrosse ball comes at speeds of 70–90 mph), so all of them planned
to talk Chris into playing the goalie position. It didn't take much; Chris
jumped at the chance. They took Chris out to a parking lot, put up a
net, and blasted him with shots. That afternoon a goalie and dedicated
lacrosse player was born.

Father's Day, 2004

Steve and I closed on our home in Minnesota in mid-June. Sara flew into
Minneapolis to see our new house and join us at a high school graduation
party for Sean Davis. Sara and Chris babysat Sean and Trevor Davis, our

next-door neighbors in Eden Prairie. Sean's mother, Mary, had put her life on hold for months to help us the previous year.

The following weekend Steve drove to Wisconsin to gather some necessities to take back to our home in Minnesota. We rented a small U-Haul trailer and loaded it with furniture, cooking supplies, a bed, a television, and most of Steve's clothes. Since our Wisconsin house had not yet sold, I stayed several more weeks to complete necessary tasks in the house and yard.

Steve returned to Minnesota on Sunday morning, Father's Day. Earlier in the week, he received a heartfelt e-mail from one of Chris's close friends, who tried to soften the blow of another Father's Day without Chris. In a voice choked with emotion, Steve read it to me: "No one loved his father more than Chris. I always envied the relationship Steve and Chris shared. But I think they still share it and always will. Not many people our age could say, 'My dad is really cool.' But Steve Jenkins pulled it off. Steve J. is one cool dad. Happy Father's Day, Steve."

In the front seat of his SUV, Steve had water, sandwiches, and the six CDs Chris had burned for him for Father's Day in 2002. The passenger seat remained empty except for one cherished item. On that Father's Day, I watched as Steve drove off with the ashes of the son he adored, in a box covered with maroon cloth, and Chris's signature blue bandana, on the passenger seat next to him.

CHAPTER 15

A New Beginning—Case Closed

June–September 2004

The world is a dangerous place. Not because of the people who are evil,
but because of the people who don't do anything about it.

ALBERT EINSTEIN

Who was responsible or accountable for investigating Chris's highly suspicious disappearance and death in Minneapolis? Nineteen months after Chris disappeared, Sara, Steve, and I did not even have the satisfaction of knowing the MPD had questioned key people. They interviewed only one of the four students who went with Chris to the Lone Tree Bar on Halloween night. To our knowledge, no one present in the bar that fateful night—managers, security personnel, bouncers, servers, not even the owner—was ever questioned by the MPD. Colleagues advised Don Enger, who assisted Chuck Loesch with interviews in the first few critical days, to walk away from the Jenkins case; Loesch was considered a marked man in Minneapolis.

Yet through those initial interviews with people in the bar on October 31, 2002, Enger and Loesch established a valid baseline of what happened that night. Baseline refers to the first round of questioning, which, if conducted in a strategic and competent manner, generally elicits the highest degree of truth from people who saw the victim. Hence, only one credible baseline can exist, rendering the information invaluable.

A New Chief

In an interview with the *Minneapolis Star Tribune* early in 2004, newly appointed MPD Chief Bill McManus stated, "People want to be treated properly and with honesty. I've always done that. Be honest with people and never tell them what you can't do for them." Hearing integrity in those words, we decided to wipe the slate clean and give McManus a fair chance. Still wanting to make someone in law enforcement a hero by offering all the data we had gathered, we requested a meeting with the new chief. In May 2004, we sent a letter to Chief McManus, congratulating and welcoming him to Minneapolis. Since McManus had emphasized the value of family and strong leadership during the selection process for a new chief, we asked him to help us dignify our son's life by allowing us to present pertinent and eye-opening facts surrounding Chris's disappearance and recovery of his body. Based on the findings of two professors at the University of Minnesota, the men who recovered Chris's body, and Dr. Baden, we assured McManus we had discovered facts that shed new light on Chris's case.

On June 18, 2004, Steve, Sara, Loesch, and I met with Chief McManus and the head of homicide, Captain Stanek. We congratulated the chief on the recent birth of his third child, another son. Smiling, he showed us pictures of his three children. Admiring his young family, the familiar lump returned to my throat. We no longer carried family pictures to proudly share with others; it hurt too much. Looking directly at McManus, I said, "We'd like nothing better than to see you succeed in your new role as chief, and we hope to develop a positive working relationship with your department. Are you willing to help us renew our faith in the MPD?" When he assured us he wanted to understand what happened in Chris's case, I replied, "Please listen with your eyes, ears, and heart."

After stating our goal—a fair and thorough investigation into the disappearance and death of Chris Jenkins—we briefly described Loesch's experience and his involvement in the case. Loesch proceeded by presenting the critical information gathered from work with Enger, Dr. Mohseni, Dr. Ek, Dr. Baden, the Hennepin County Sheriff's Office Water Patrol, and the Minneapolis Fire Department. Highlighting what happened in the bar Halloween night and the subsequent two weeks, Loesch emphasized many issues demanding follow-up. With our poster-size maps of the river, he described his work with the orange dummy, conversations with river experts, and with Lynn Diederich, who saw Chris's body before it reached its final resting place. Again, he stressed the need for further investigative work on numerous specific points.

Conflict of Interest

We explained our belief that the entire situation represented a conflict of interest for numerous reasons. First, the Lone Tree Bar is a cop bar—cops get free food and drink there. Second, MPD Officers Casey and Grant were at the last known location of the victim, Chris Jenkins. In fact, Chris's date, Ashley Rice, introduced Chris to both men, yet neither made the effort to lend support or understanding by coming to search headquarters, or by ever speaking with Steve and me. To our knowledge, no one seriously questioned Officers Casey and Grant. Third, as her Halloween costume Rice had worn the official shirt, patch, and badge of Officer Casey—allegedly one of the last people to speak with Chris alive. Following the after-hours staff meeting at the Lone Tree Bar to address the problem of intoxicated employees, Officer Casey took Rice home. No internal affairs investigation occurred; we checked.

Steve continued: "Due to these concerns, and the reality that the MPD did not question several people who saw Chris Halloween night, we began to suspect a possible cover-up. So we requested and secured the evidence bags, which remain in our possession. No one has opened or contaminated them in any way.

"Exams of fingernails and clothing never took place. Yet Chris's uncle, FBI SAC (Special Agent in Charge) Don Thompson, told us that standard procedure in Richmond, Virginia, included hair/fiber extraction and exam of clothing; as well as an exam of fingernail clippings for the presence of biological material suitable for DNA testing. As director of the FBI Lab in Quantico in the mid-1990s, Thompson had extensive experience in forensics. Both Thompson and Dr. Baden, another forensic professional, told us that finding DNA under fingernails was a long shot after four months in water, but certainly worth the effort, especially if skin from an assailant was present on one or more of the clippings. Since Chris's left hand was clenched, we thought there might be a better chance of obtaining DNA from those fingernails."

At the end of our meeting, Chief McManus stated, "The Chris Jenkins case is a top priority for our department." We left with the understanding that McManus would follow up with Steve, and Stanek would review the case and communicate next steps to us. Once out of the police department, Sara, Steve, and I literally skipped with glee the whole way to the car. We did it! After nineteen long months, Chris's case had hit the radar screen at the MPD; the chief had definitely used the words "top priority." Committed to a new beginning, we did not allow ourselves to doubt the message or the messenger. Trust cannot teeter on the fence—it exists or it doesn't.

Two days later I sent an e-mail to Chief McManus and Captain Stanek, thanking them profusely and outlining our request: (1) a fair and thorough investigation, perhaps conducted by the Bureau of Criminal Apprehension (BCA) and the MPD Cold Case Squad; (2) interrogations with everyone who saw Chris on Halloween night, as well as the owner and employees of the Lone Tree Bar (Chris's last known location); and (3) forensic exams. I wrote: "We remain hopeful justice will finally be served. We are counting on you to do the right thing."

Grandma Rose sent Chief McManus a laudatory e-mail on July 1, 2004:

> I am so grateful to you for meeting with Jan, Steve, and Sara . . . You have a new son and you must know the treasure you have been given. Chris was a special treasure to our entire family. He was our firecracker on July 4th, our bunny at Easter, and Santa at Christmas. Our whole family loved his easy manner and giving nature . . . I prayed you would become our next police chief . . . Always be honest and have integrity and you will never go wrong. I am seventy-four years old and I know a bit about life . . . With a grateful heart . . .

Permission Granted:
The BCA Will Review Chris's Case

In a follow-up conversation with Steve, Stanek scheduled another meeting with us, promising a full disclosure of the case. Then Stanek added, "What little there is of it."

So Steve, Loesch, and I arrived at the MPD on July 19 to meet with Captain Stanek and Lieutenant Carlson. With everyone present, I asked if the purpose of the meeting was still a full disclosure of the case. After everyone agreed to that understanding, Stanek turned to Loesch and demanded, "So, what have you got?" Loesch had brought a copy of his case notes; he did not come prepared to deliver a presentation. Yet several times during the meeting, he tried to give his case notes to Stanek and Carlson; neither would take them. Carlson and Stanek did apologize for the way the MPD had treated our family, and for the fact that no investigation occurred for several days. Carlson stated: "We basically did nothing the first six days."

After praising the beat cops for their support, we proceeded with our three requests, already communicated in our meeting the preceding month. When we asked about forensic testing Carlson told us, "That would not be a good use of taxpayer money," adding, "There are no suspects for comparison." His answer did not make sense to us, so we asked, "How can suspects be determined when key interviews have not occurred?"

We also spoke of the opening of the BCA's state-of-the-art crime lab in St. Paul at the end of 2003. Michael Campion, Minnesota BCA superintendent, told the *Pioneer Press* that the BCA's new DNA lab had been built with specialized DNA testing in mind, adding, "If there's a delay in getting forensic work, that's justice delayed."

If a full case disclosure occurred in that meeting, Loesch, Steve, and I somehow missed it. So we kept asking for the details. Finally, Stanek or Carlson told us they would send us the entire official MPD report. Looking straight at me, Carlson quipped, "It's yours. Go ahead, make a hundred copies, give it to anyone you want."

At one point in the meeting, Stanek and Carlson also gave us permission to have the BCA review Chris's case with the full blessing and cooperation of the MPD. With stunned faces, we said, "That's what we wanted, we're done." Within the next five minutes, the meeting ended. Cautiously optimistic, once again we skipped all the way to our car.

The following day, I sent an e-mail summarizing the agreement for a BCA review to Stanek and Carlson, copying Chief McManus. In the e-mail, I wrote: "Our questioning never had anything to do with usurping your authority or expertise. Based on what we have observed, and learned, we have no reason to believe a fair or thorough investigation took place for our son . . . What you do is critically important; you have an enormous responsibility as a role model. So do we; hundreds of people are intently watching our actions. We'd like nothing better than to see you succeed in the work you do and in the influence you generate . . . Kiss and hug your children extra hard tonight because you never know when it will be the last time. If you ever personally face this tragedy, we sincerely hope you are not left without a good-bye or one single answer about what happened to your child or sibling. No one deserves that."

McManus replied to the e-mail within fifteen minutes: "Please know that should the BCA decide to look at Christopher's file, the MPD will assist in any way possible." Stanek also responded via e-mail within the hour, pledging his support and stating that Lieutenant Carlson had already spoken with Tim O'Malley at the BCA. In a conversation with me two days later, O'Malley noted, "The BCA is ready to do whatever is necessary."

Permission Denied:
No Formal Request for BCA Review of Chris's Case

Yet again, our relief and gratitude were short-lived. On July 27, just eight days after our previous meeting, O'Malley told me, "The MPD are not making a formal request." I remember the stunning blow; I actually asked him to repeat that statement twice. O'Malley offered his deepest sympathy. Only at this point did I learn that the mission of the BCA is to support other agencies. The BCA engages only in response to a request from another law enforcement agency. Clearly, as private citizens, we did not fit that category. Feeling betrayed and duped, my shock turned to anger: "Wasn't losing Chris enough? This latest turn of events is a heinous crime in and of itself." In that conversation, I realized Tim O'Malley's desire to help and his genuine compassion regarding the situation our family faced. I told O'Malley he was the first true leader in law enforcement we had found in Minnesota.

When I described to Steve the latest move on the game board by the MPD, he responded with fury: "Jan, no way; this sucks. As former commissioner of public safety, surely Stanek knew the procedure required to work with the BCA!"

We were being played as pawns in the game called "Botched Investigation." People murdered our son; we would not leave the game without a fair and thorough investigation. That last move from the MPD demanded a response. Grandma Rose did just that. Her second e-mail to McManus carried a distinctly different tone from her first:

I'm convinced no one in authority gives a darn about Chris' death . . . What in heaven's name is going on down there? It's more of the same—unbelievable pathetic rhetoric . . .

A two-month-long battle ensued with many e-mails between Steve and Stanek. When Steve spoke with McManus on August 4, McManus sounded upset, saying he knew nothing about the reversal of the decision involving a BCA review of Chris's case. McManus promised to personally speak with Steve to give him an explanation. Though Steve phoned him several times and sent numerous e-mails, he received no response. Finally, on September 23, Steve sent McManus a comprehensive e-mail outlining key concerns and requesting a face-to-face meeting or phone conference. At the end of the e-mail, Steve made his position clear: "Let's trade shoes for a moment. This is your cherished son. Would you accept a partial investigation, a change in commitment to take this to the BCA, and a lack of promised follow up from you? Would you accept this? I guarantee you, I'm not." Steve never heard from McManus again.

Stanek did exchange many e-mails with Steve, offering to mail the MPD report, or make it available for Steve to pick up. Steve kept insisting he wanted to speak with Stanek or Carlson or even McManus in person; he wanted answers to key questions. No one would meet with Steve, so he finally agreed to have the report mailed to our home.

The MPD report arrived early on October 2, the morning of Sara's wedding. Though we chose not to open it until a few days after the wedding, the cover letter from Chief McManus, dated September 1, 2004, read: "The Minneapolis Police Department's investigation into the death of your son, Christopher, was concluded on July 30, 2004 . . . the case has been closed . . . Both reports document a thorough investigation by some of our most experienced investigators . . . unless there is new information, I agree with Lieutenant Carlson's decision to close this case . . . I have determined the investigation conducted by Central Investigation Division was thorough and complete . . . I find no reason that would warrant further review of this matter by the BCA or any other outside agency."

How does a case go from top priority on June 18, 2004, to closed on July 30? Considering that the MPD did not ask for the sealed evidence bags that remained in our possession, the question is even more perplexing.

CHAPTER 16

Sara and Jamie

October 2004

We are all angels with but one wing;
to fly we need to embrace each other.

AUTHOR UNKNOWN

Many little girls dream about their wedding day, when wishes come true. I don't remember Sara talking about a gorgeous white dress, a diamond ring, or even Prince Charming. She talked about the excitement of watching her brother walk down the aisle on the arm of one of her friends. Chris brought laughter and love to Sara's life, especially in tense moments. Now her deepest desire—sharing the joy of her wedding day with her brother—could not be fulfilled.

Steve and I wanted to shower Sara with abundant love and create a beautiful wedding day for her. We ached knowing the veil of innocence had been ripped from her at such a young age. Moreover, we had focused so much on Chris the past two years, Sara must have felt forgotten and alone many times. While we did our best to support her, our decision to seek justice for Chris left us drained and hurting much of the time. Though we could not spare our daughter from the harsh reality of our lives since Chris disappeared, we could share our enthusiasm about her upcoming wedding.

Sara lived in Cincinnati, I was still in Wisconsin preparing for the final move to Minnesota, and we were planning a wedding to be held on October 2, 2004, in Minnesota. During our two-year journey of loss and investigative work, we had improved our adaptability and focus—essential skills for organizing a celebration with two hundred guests. So now, when inevitable demands arose in preparing for the wedding, we rolled easily with them. We saw the world through new lenses; very few things mattered enough to waste precious time and energy dealing with them. How important are tablecloths, chairs, seating arrangements, even flowers? Laughing, Sara and I agreed not to let any last-minute challenges disappoint us. I remember telling her that if a heel fell off one of my shoes as I walked down the aisle, I would simply leave it there and keep walking. Sara didn't even consider wearing high heels. She wisely chose comfort instead, and ordered a pair of white Nikes with lace, and "Lightner" written across the back of the shoes. Since our investigation had caused enough trauma and disappointment, in other areas of our lives, we chose simplicity and ease whenever possible.

Imagine being a cop and marrying our only living child! Jamie must have felt like Nemo—the clown fish, stuck in an aquarium. Even my older sister Deborah jokingly said Sara's boyfriend would have to win Aunt Deborah's approval before becoming Sara's fiancé. When Steve first learned Sara was dating a cop, he freaked out and started asking Sara many questions. "So, what right does a cop have dating my daughter?" Swinging his arms as he paced back and forth, Steve's insistence on answers became more comical by the moment, sending Sara and me into fits of laughter. Of course our laughter fired him up even more.

The drama played out for about five minutes before I walked up to Steve and put my hand on his shoulder. Looking directly into his eyes, I gently reminded him, "Steve, your time for telling Sara what to do ended long ago." He blurted out, "Well, I only have one child left. I won't let anyone hurt her! *That's my job as her father.* I'm not going to mess up again." His response confirmed what I suspected—fear and guilt. Intellectually, Steve and I both understood that there was nothing we could have done to prevent what happened to Chris. Galaxies away, our hearts found that fact difficult to grasp. Protecting a child is primal for a parent. In the realm of the unknown—a missing child, a mysterious death—logic alone did not rule the day.

Steve calmed down and we all hugged. The following morning at work, Steve saw a three-page e-mail from Jamie written at 2:30 a.m. Jamie described his background, his values, and why he loved Sara. Oops. Steve phoned me immediately and asked sheepishly, "Jan, did I get a little carried away? Jamie sounds like a really neat guy." Trying not to laugh, I replied, "Steveo, you pretty much lost it. Sara must have told Jamie about your reaction. You might want to call him."

Steve did call Jamie to apologize for his outburst and to thank him for giving us a chance to know more about him and his love for Sara. Steve assured Jamie that we considered his chosen profession to be honorable and critically important. In fact, several of our close friends and family members served in various law enforcement agencies. More important, Steve wanted Jamie to know Chris and Sara had been raised to respect police officers. From an early age, they understood that if they ever found themselves in trouble, they should contact the police for help and protection.

After spending time with Jamie and Sara on vacation and during a few weekends, Steve and I realized how comfortable and happy they seemed together. We liked Jamie and recognized many wonderful traits in him. Sara and Jamie's engagement brought the possibility of a new measure of happiness and hope for the future. Delighted for Sara, Steve and I wondered if the addition of a new family member could help us begin to heal the crater in our hearts.

Of course we all struggled knowing Chris would not be physically present at Sara and Jamie's wedding. But he *was* present for almost twenty-two years as a vital person in our family, and a wedding *is* about family. A few concerned individuals told us not to mention Chris in the ceremony or at the reception, because doing so would spoil Sara's happiness. Steve, Sara, and I discussed the issue a couple of times and agreed we would *not* pretend Chris did not exist on one of the most important days in our lives. Chris felt as much a part of us as the air we breathed; we longed to acknowledge his place in our family and in our hearts.

It took me awhile to figure out why Sara showed no excitement about the wedding; she subtly resisted planning her special day. It was clear that she loved Jamie, and she seemed happy to start a new chapter in her life. I did not realize the *depth* of her sorrow regarding her wedding until she wrote several years later: "The excitement of getting engaged was bittersweet in my world. This event marked the first of many life-changing events Chris would not be a part of; now, or ever. Just the thought of planning a wedding my brother could not attend actually made me physically ill. I vividly recall driving in between dealer visits, crying to the point of throwing up, whenever simple wedding details crept into my mind. Though Jamie and I loved the thought of having a secluded beach getaway, we chose instead to get married in Minnesota. Since I was now an only child, my parents would never experience another child's wedding. Most of our friends and family lived in the Twin Cities area, and I knew my parents wanted to share happiness after so much sorrow. I didn't realize just being in Minneapolis would bring back the horror.

"Since Chris' funeral on March 4, 2003, I had not returned to the Twin Cities until the summer of 2004, to make important wedding decisions. As Jamie and I looked for a wedding cake, photographer, and flowers, we drove on streets I had traveled for years. Memories, once so alive and happy, now burst forth with grief and rage. Usually, I could bury those painful memories, not in the Twin Cities. I don't have a clue how my parents live there.

"One afternoon Jamie and I had to walk across the Hennepin Avenue Bridge to get back to our parked car. I knew Chris well; he did *not* jump or fall off that bridge. 'It's just another stupid college kid that jumped off a bridge' ranks as one of the most hurtful comments I read or heard. Seeing Minneapolis police cars driving by, now surfaced feelings of betrayal and confusion. I still cannot wrap my mind around why law enforcement did not do the right thing from day one. Many other missing person cases taught us a consistent reality: If Chris' name was Christina, abundant help would have magically appeared."

October 2, 2004

Sunshine woke us up on the big day. Jamie's mother, Sissy, is a professional hair stylist. She created beautiful up-dos for four bridesmaids and Sara in our master bath. The volume of hair spray in the air caused Steve to run throughout the house, opening up windows. I thought he was just getting rid of nervous energy, as well as fumes from the hair spray. When I learned the official MPD report on Chris's case had just arrived by way of FedEx, his behavior made more sense. Steve told me he put the envelope in the closet, behind the coats—out of sight, out of mind—for now.

Sara and Jamie's wedding was held at the Church of St. Therese in Deephaven, Minnesota, the same church in which Steve and I were married. About twenty minutes before Steve and I walked down the aisle on either side of Sara, I noted Sara's anxiety. Fearing she might drop Chris's turquoise ring (tightly clutched in her hand), she asked her father to stitch it to her bouquet, which he quickly did after someone retrieved the kit of "emergency supplies" from the bride's room at the church.

As the three of us stood looking at each other, we felt the enormity of all we had endured, and survived, as a family of three. Without a word, we held each other, forming our football huddle. We did not realize that Jamie witnessed our embrace. "Watching the connection between the three of you—your 'huddle'—touched me deeply," he later said. "You showed me love, commitment, and determination. I realized the character of the family I was joining. But I never got to meet Chris, never even heard the sound of his voice. I wanted Chris at our wedding, and there's no doubt in my mind, Chris and I would have developed a great friendship. Without him, we stand where we stand, feeling robbed."

The Wedding Ceremony and Reception

Archbishop Harry Flynn presided over the ceremony, thanks to Grandma Rose. When he delivered his sermon, he walked right up to Jamie and Sara, speaking directly to them. His key message—say yes to your spouse more often than to yourself—resonated with many people in the church, who later expressed the impact of Archbishop Flynn's words.

During the Mass, I saw Sara's tears and instinctively understood the origin. In her words: "I remember just before we walked down the aisle, Dad sewed Chris' ring to my bouquet. Any time my finger touched his ring, I felt stinging tears. Throughout the ceremony I stared at a huge cross bearing Jesus which hung on the wall behind the altar. 'Dear Jesus, please help me.' What I wanted most on my wedding day was to hold it together.

"Though I was marrying an amazing man and starting a new life, on this wondrous day, my constant companion—sorrow—did not go away. The impact of fully realizing I could never again share significant future events with my brother, hit hard. Some things, time cannot fix."

Following the ceremony, we ushered our guests into the adjoining community room, which had been adorned with balloons and artificial trees with small white lights. The small bride and groom figurines that had been used on Grandma Rose and Grandpa Gene's wedding cake in

Archbishop Flynn blesses Sara and Jamie's marriage.

1950 stood proudly on top of the magnificent wedding cake. The cake, surrounded by spectacular waterfalls, bridges, and flowers, created a sense of magic and wonder. Toasts, dancing, smiles, and laughter filled the room.

In Loving Memory of Chris

Sara and Jamie had chosen photos starting when they were born to tell the story of their lives through a slide show. The music accompanying each set of slides portrayed different periods in the lives of the Lightner and the Jenkins families. Shortly after our family pictures finished rolling, Steve and I stared at each other: there had been no pictures of Chris. Our confusion stemmed from the fact that we had helped pick some of the pictures, and Sara was adamant about including many photos of her brother. Then, just when we thought the slide show was finished, we saw "In Loving Memory of Chris." As we watched, Chris came to life in numerous pictures with his family and friends. Tears flowed as our guests acknowledged what we and they had lost.

"Mom, don't look, I'm hiding."

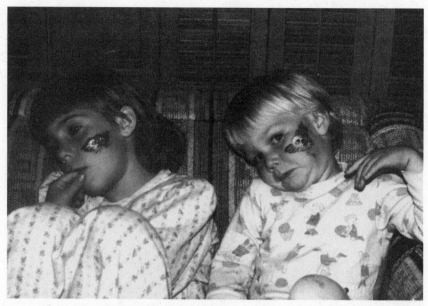

Sara and Chris proudly displaying their new face art.

Jan and Steve's three children.

Though we did our best to celebrate, sadness hung in the air. How could it not? We could not change what had happened to Chris, nor the two-year struggle for an investigation. Most of the people at the wedding knew and loved Chris; they too wanted answers to his death. Yet since Steve and I had lived in Wisconsin until 2004, the last time many of them had seen us was at Chris's memorial service. For that reason, several people struggled with not knowing how to relate to us. So we chose not to have a receiving line; it would have been too awkward. Instead, we circled amongst the tables, inviting people to dance.

The following day, we helped Sara and Jamie load their U-Haul and they headed home to Cincinnati. We loved them so much, we found it difficult to say good-bye.

Gut-Wrenching Disbelief

No longer able to avoid the inevitable, we opened the MPD report two days later. The cover letter from Chief McManus stated that the case had been closed on July 30, 2004. In utter disbelief, we reread that sentence numerous times. Looking at Steve, I whispered, "Oh my God. No one had the courage to face you when you learned for the first time, that our son's case is closed. So this is what it looks like to protect with courage and serve with compassion?"

An accounting of officers deployed for the water recovery effort comprised most of the report. Four or five pages covered investigative work. In our opinion, the statements written by the two MPD officers who were at the Lone Tree Bar on October 31, 2002—Officers Casey and Grant—represent the most disturbing part of the entire report.

First, both officers wrote several statements pertaining to where Chris was in the bar, what he was doing, and who he was with. How could they have made those comments unless they had spent a fair amount of time observing Chris in the bar? The question is even more troubling considering that both officers worked off-duty Halloween night as security guards at the Hennepin Center for the Arts, adjacent to the Lone Tree Bar.

Second, written statements from Officer Casey directly conflict with statements made by the bar manager. Bar manager Jill Krause has repeated the same story three times (one time in front of FBI and former

BCA agents) regarding the conversation she witnessed between Chris and Officer Casey on Halloween night.

Steve sent an e-mail to Chief of Police Bill McManus with two key questions: (1) What caused the reversal in the decision for the BCA to review the case? And (2) how could we accept closure of our son's case when critical data collected in the first six days and information from the recovery site had not been considered by the MPD?

Grandma Rose also sent an e-mail to Chief McManus asserting her grave disappointment. Included in that message she wrote: "No one did an investigation. Look up the definition of 'investigation.' Why, I could have done a better job all by myself."

Two Years without Chris

October 31, 2004, marked two years without our beloved Chris. More signs assured us he watched over us from heaven. Grandma Rose had lost a medal at search headquarters—an angel with "Hope" inscribed on the back. She looked in every place imaginable for months without success. Out of the clear blue, she opened her button box on October 31, 2004, to look for a particular button. She could not remember the last time she had opened the box. There, sitting on top, was the medal. Holding it in her cupped hands, she knew Chris sent his love.

Sara experienced a similar inexplicable occurrence. She and Jamie had just moved into a new home. Though Sara vowed to relax on October 31, 2004, she decided to unpack just one more box. Opening it, she gasped. A cross inscribed with the words "I am always with you" lay on top. She kept that cross in a plant in her bedroom, never anywhere else. Sara held the cross close to her heart and wept.

Sara's precious treasure.

CHAPTER 17

Two Years, No Investigation

November 2004–April 2005

*The strongest oak tree of the forest is not the one that is
protected from the storm and hidden from the sun. It's the one
that stands in the open where it is compelled to struggle for its
existence against the winds and rains and the scorching sun.*

NAPOLEON HILL

Chris could no longer speak for himself. Yet in 1998, he had spoken up by writing a letter to Arne Carlson, the governor of Minnesota, in which he stated: "My name is Chris Jenkins; I'm a junior at Eden Prairie High School. Recently I read an article in the paper that the 8th graders showed gains in reading, and slightly in math, according to the 1998 state's basic skills test . . . Though I'm proud to attend one of the best high schools in the nation, I'm saddened that many other students do not receive a great education. I believe schools could reach their goals with more government funding . . . then, children everywhere in this state can be well-educated and happy, leading to more knowledgeable and responsible citizens. Hopefully, with a stronger focus on education, some of our problems like crime, drugs, even racism, will be decreased. Thank you for reading this letter." Chris, the unstoppable optimist, hoped for a brighter future, one it turned out he would never see.

Now, two years after his death, we carefully unpacked a box marked "Chris' Memories." Prior to our move to Wisconsin in 2001, Chris and Sara each filled a cardboard box with items they chose to keep. In "Chris' Memories" we discovered his letter to Governor Carlson and a letter to Chris in 1997 from Congressman Jim Ramstad, who represented Minnesota's Third District. Ramstad wrote: "My heartfelt congratulations on your [Eden Prairie] football team's championship season! Chris, E.P.'s second straight state football title . . . places E.P.

as only the second team ever to win back-to-back championships in the largest class . . . Everyone in the E.P. School District is very proud of you, as you represent the best in young people . . . Chris, please let me know if I can ever be helpful to you or your family."

Key leaders in Minnesota state government recognized Chris's contribution as a young and engaged Minnesotan. What leaders in Minnesota are now stepping forth to bring a measure of justice to this young man's life?

Congressman Ramstad did respond. On Thanksgiving Day 2004, Steve and I met Ramstad and his wife at Sharing and Caring Hands, a Minneapolis-based organization that provides all sorts of services—meals, shelter, clothing, and so on—to the poor. Along with dozens of volunteers, the four of us served a warm meal to guests. Ramstad introduced himself to Steve and offered his condolences. When he asked Steve about the status of Chris's case, Steve highlighted our key concerns, adding that on the previous day, we had personally delivered a petition for assistance to the governor's office. Our petition requested a fair and thorough investigation by the BCA. Supporting documentation explained the request and included a list of critical data not reviewed by the MPD.

One week later, Ramstad sent us a letter letting us know that he had made an inquiry on our behalf to the appropriate officials at the BCA, the Department of Public Safety, and the governor's office.

Our appeal to Governor Tim Pawlenty did not yield results. Annie Paruccini, director of Board and Commission Appointments at the governor's office, did contact us after receiving our petition. She told us the governor's office would look into the matter. After a few months our request passed to Paul Anderson, special advisor to the governor. By April 2005, our key concerns regarding Chris's case still had not been answered, so we wrote Anderson a letter on May 5, 2005, asking for a face-to-face meeting. Remaining hopeful, we wrote: "We graciously thank you in advance for meeting with us . . . Chris deserves fairness . . . As his parents, we are speaking for him."

Upon returning to his office a week later, Anderson kindly e-mailed back: "Until the end of the legislative session adjournment, my schedule is extensive, and it will be difficult to meet with you prior to then . . . I will be out of the office the remainder of this week, but when I return from this weekend's Fishing Opener I will try and contact you to see what can be done." The first day of fishing is a big deal to Minnesotans, and the governor's attendance is a long-standing tradition.

By mid-June, we still had received no follow-up communication from Anderson, so Steve contacted him. Anderson's response remained essentially the same: "Until the legislature adjourns, I am unable to schedule a meeting . . . We are also in communication with the BCA and the City of Minneapolis to obtain further information from our law enforcement partners."

Wanting to build relationships, not destroy them, we patiently waited two more months. In August, Steve e-mailed Anderson again, but he received no response. Then, on September 2, 2005, Steve received an e-mail from Anderson: "Annie Paruccini is now the person in the office that will be in contact with you to discuss a potential meeting. I have assumed different duties within the office." We had waited all summer, only to receive this e-mail. In fact, we were back to where we started nine months earlier with the governor's office.

Searching for Dru Sjodin vs. Searching for Chris

Governors can, and do, step in, however. On November 26, 2003, the *Grand Forks Herald* reported: "When University of North Dakota senior, Dru Sjodin [from Pequot Lakes, Minnesota], did not show up at her part-time job on Saturday evening, November 22, 2003, her roommate said, 'Something is wrong, that's not like Dru.' . . . North Dakota Gov. John Hoeven promised 'all the resources available,' to aid the search, said Capt. Kirby of the Grand Forks Police Department. Calls from law enforcement agencies in other states, including Nebraska and Illinois, have come in, offering help, police said. Scores of airmen from Grand Forks Air Force Base helped with the search."

That same day, an article in the *St. Paul Pioneer Press* stated that "helicopters, horses, and ATV's were used . . . 'We also had law enforcement officers out there doing "knock and talks,"' said Lt. Byron Sieber of the Grand Forks Police Department. 'They stopped at farmsteads and homes in this area and interviewed people.'"

Massive search efforts led by hundreds of law enforcement personnel took place *within hours* of Dru Sjodin's disappearance. Yet *six days* after Chris disappeared, no one from any law enforcement agency had even checked out his residence! As of this writing, the MPD have not interviewed friends who accompanied Chris to the bar on Halloween night, nor have they questioned the bar employees who saw him at his last known location, the Lone Tree Bar.

Sjodin and Jenkins—college seniors, intelligent, enthusiastic, responsible citizens ready to graduate and step into very bright futures. They were strikingly similar young adults, yet radically different resources were made available after their disappearances.

Disappearances: Dalquist on October 30, 2002, and Jenkins on October 31, 2002

In Brainerd, Minnesota, about 150 miles north of the Twin Cities, another remarkable twenty-one-year-old, Erika Dalquist, vanished the day before Chris disappeared. Eighteen months later, in April 2004, Steve and I felt the double-edged sword likely experienced by the Dalquist family when a bloodhound named Calamity Jane broke away from her handler, Denny Adams, and located Dalquist's remains. Contrary to Sergeant Jackson's belief, bloodhounds apparently can, and do, track scents after one week. The Associated Press reported that Adams told Governor Tim Pawlenty the governor should be honored that the bloodhound chose to sit next to him in the front row at Dalquist's funeral. The governor responded by congratulating Adams.

Chris Jenkins disappeared in Minneapolis; in other words, in Governor Pawlenty's backyard. As of this writing, we have received no communication from Governor Pawlenty: not a phone call, e-mail, or letter.

Not for one moment do Steve, Sara, or I begrudge a single resource used for Dru or Erika. Thanks to the wonderful Dalquist family, one of our volunteers was allowed to watch the water search efforts for Erika, which eventually led to our discovery of global experts in water rescue and recovery. We have reached out to Linda Walker, Dru's loving mom, with heartfelt support. Linda has offered, on multiple occasions, to assist us in any way possible.

"Wait and See"

Ten days after the MPD looked into Chris's disappearance, Sergeant Jackson told us we were in a "wait and see" mode. Although he strongly believed Chris's body was in the Mississippi, he told us no divers were necessary because Chris's body would show up in the spring.

During the four months Chris was missing, *almost no ice* formed between the Hennepin Avenue Bridge and the Third Avenue Bridge in Minneapolis. In early December 2002, when the second bloodhound walked into the river in that area, our family's private investigator, Chuck Loesch, phoned the Hennepin County Sheriff's Office Water Patrol to request boat assistance. An official from that agency met us at the river. After hearing the facts, he told us that no boat would be put on the water due to ice on the ramp leading into the river and that no dragging of the river was necessary.

Yet three weeks after Dru Sjodin disappeared, the commitment to find her remained strong. The *Minneapolis Star Tribune* reported on December 13, 2003: "This weekend's search was announced by the governors of Minnesota and North Dakota after local officials asked for help as temperatures fell . . . National Guard troops drilled closely spaced holes in the ice . . . every 18 inches . . . across the 100-foot-wide Red River . . . to lower video cameras into the murky water in their search." That same day, the *Grand Forks Herald* reported that "close to 90 National Guard soldiers teamed up with 60 Highway Patrol troopers," and the Associated Press stated that "about 150 Guard members from Minnesota participated in the search." Then, on December 15, the AP reported that "despite the end of large-scale searches for now, authorities aren't giving up on finding Sjodin. 'This is ongoing,' said Polk County, Minnesota, Sheriff Mark LeTexier. 'Whether it's at this level or the patrol level, this is ongoing.'"

Searchers found Sjodin's body five months after she disappeared. That day is so clear in my mind; I was facilitating the Walton Institute, Walmart's flagship culture and leadership experience. In the cafeteria during lunch, CNN kept repeating the story: "Dru is home." In my aching for the Sjodin family, my own horror returned. The buzz continued in the lunch area as people debated, "Is she alive or not?" I couldn't breathe. As a mother who had lived that experience, I knew. Excusing myself, I found a ladies' room at the opposite end of the building, where I composed myself before guiding forty leaders through afternoon discussions.

Missing Young Women and Men
Deserve Equal Resources

As a nation, we must rethink the commonly held notion that young men are responsible for their own deaths, while young women are considered victims of crime. When a young adult is missing, the discrepancy in resources made available for women and for men is appalling.

Sadly, this fact plays into the hands of those who murder young men. The situation is bleak for these victims: young men are presumed reckless, so few resources are made available to find them; evidence is overlooked and destroyed; and the case is closed. To complicate the issue, bodies found in water are presumed to be drownings caused by suicide or accident; homicide is rarely, if ever, considered. When homicide is not regarded as a possible cause of death, a recovery scene is not viewed as a potential crime scene, and valuable evidence is irretrievably lost.

In the past decade dozens of young adult males have been found in bodies of water from October through April, primarily in northern states. Yet Red Cross statistics show that two-thirds of all drownings occur between May and August. Furthermore, when the Minnesota Department of Health analyzed the drowning rates in Minnesota between 1980 and 1985, their research concluded that most drownings occurred from May to August. Of those, 42 percent involved boating, and 35 percent resulted from swimming. The study also found that only 11 percent of drowning incidents happened in the winter (December–February), and 71 percent of those primarily involved snowmobiles and other vehicles breaking through ice on lakes and waterways.

Grandma Rose: A Volunteer on Speed Skates

Chris Jenkins's grandmother is fighting crime through awareness and prevention. My selfless mom, affectionately known by hundreds as Grandma Rose, channeled her grief and severe disappointment over the lack of effort in Chris's case into positive action. She volunteered one day a week at the Jacob Wetterling Foundation in St. Paul (now known as the Jacob Wetterling Resource Center), assisting with a variety of tasks to protect children from victimization and to educate families about personal safety. The organization recognized her as a "Volunteer on Speed

Skates" in its fall 2004 newsletter. Though my mom traveled fifty miles from her home to the foundation's offices every week, she declared: "I don't count the hours, measure the size, or judge the tedious nature of a task. If what I do at JWF helps find one child who goes missing, or provides assistance to one victim family like we received from JWF, then every minute is worth it." We are so proud of my mother; she is one awesome lady!

As Grandma Rose focused on crime prevention, Steve and I pursued our belief that Chris deserved an investigation by calling upon the MPD, BCA, Congressman Jim Ramstad, and Governor Tim Pawlenty. On December 17, 2004, Tim O'Malley, assistant superintendent of the BCA, wrote us a letter, copying the MPD, the Department of Public Safety, Congressman Ramstad, and Governor Pawlenty. Among other things, O'Malley stated, "The BCA's role is to assist, upon request, other law enforcement agencies in the investigation of crimes and the apprehension of criminals . . . In Chris' case, we have communicated regularly with the MPD. We have discussed the availability of our services including crime scene analysis, laboratory testing, polygraph examinations and investigative consultations . . . speaking with Lt. Carlson in July 2004 . . . the MPD opted not to have us review their file. The MPD is a fine law enforcement agency. We have worked closely with their homicide unit on many occasions and have respect for their investigative abilities . . . If the MPD requests assistance, we will respond promptly and cooperate fully."

Since the BCA only works with *formal* requests from law enforcement agencies, the commitment made to us in July by Carlson and Stanek did not make sense. Surely, as former commissioner of public safety, Stanek understood the process involved when working with the BCA, which reports to the Department of Public Safety. Stanek sent Steve the following explanation on December 1, 2004: "We support your right to have someone outside of MPD review the case (including the BCA if someone there will do so at your request), but MPD is confident in its investigation into Chris' death and is not requesting a formal review by an outside agency."

Unstoppable in our quest for fairness, we called upon Don Enger, who had worked with Loesch in the early days after Chris disappeared. A thirty-seven-year law enforcement veteran, Enger spent most of those years in homicide, including his tenure at the BCA. For various reasons, Enger believed Chris's death could have been a homicide. Ultimately members of the BCA met with Captain Stanek. That meeting resulted in an agreement for another law enforcement agency to review Chris's case.

When Stanek phoned in February 2005 to tell us about the intended "peer review," we strongly urged him to include key data gathered by our team for a fair assessment. Stanek told us he needed the information on his desk in three days so that the agency he chose could fit the review into its schedule. We replied, "Done. You'll have it on your desk by noon on Monday [February 7]." Two years of work resulted in compiling more than 150 pages of data, so we did not sleep that weekend. Grateful for the review, we organized our work into a user-friendly format that included a table of contents, an index, and references complete with updated contact information. In the cover letter placed inside the notebook, we expressed our heartfelt gratitude for the time and effort the peer review team would spend examining Chris's case.

After seeing the full three-ring binder, Stanek spoke with Steve to tell him that he hadn't realized we had amassed so much data and that it might take awhile for the team to complete its assessment. Assuring him that we wanted a thorough review, Steve conveyed our understanding with regards to timing and asked if we could meet with the peer review team to answer any questions members might have. The team did not want to meet with us, so we waited until the end of March, when Stanek phoned us with feedback. He read suggestions offered by the team that dealt primarily with internal processes, dealing with victim families, and the notation that the case contained little information. We listened in stunned silence as Stanek spoke: "It only took two weeks for the team to review this case. I knew they'd come up with the same conclusion we did." Worse yet, we heard, "The outside law enforcement agency that reviewed the investigative case file and the additional information you provided is not interested in meeting with you at this time."

Trust is not built behind closed doors. Left in a vacuum, we began to wonder if the data we provided had been taken seriously, so we phoned the professionals we listed to see if anyone had contacted them. No one had reached out to Dr. Ek, head of the Department of Forest Resources at the University; Dr. Mohseni, research engineer and authority on river currents and patterns; or Lynn Diederich, the office worker who spotted Chris's body in the river while walking across the Third Avenue Bridge. A review had been conducted by an outside agency that would not identify itself, allow us to meet the players, or even speak with us. As Chris's parents, how could we feel peace of mind or confidence in the process? We later learned that the Hennepin County Sheriff's Office had done the review. We spent about sixty hours documenting the work our team had accomplished, yet we had no opportunity to clarify critical points or ask questions. The Sheriff's Office has never contacted us.

Referring to the experience as the "phantom peer review," Steve and I understood that the mad mouse ride continued. Ripped by disbelief, we dug deep for courage.

CHAPTER 18

Renewed Hope

May–December 2005

It is better to light one candle than to curse the darkness.

If joy is a ray of sunshine infusing our spirits with hope, faith, and love, then the remainder of 2005 held bright spots of sunlight: wins on the lacrosse field, the expertise and commitment of global experts in water rescue and recovery, and the emergence of a leader in the MPD. Our greatest gift—the birth of Sara and Jamie's daughter, Cayman Rose—brought hope for the future. After losing a precious life and future dreams, what could possibly create more joy than a new life carrying the promise of happier days ahead?

On May 1, 2005, the UMN Men's Lacrosse team reached the top. They defeated the long-standing number 1 team, the Duluth Bulldogs, to win the Upper Midwest Lacrosse League tournament and advance to the nationals. Chris had often told me that Duluth was the team to beat, and he remained confident his team could do just that.

As Steve and I drove to that championship game between the Minnesota Gophers and Duluth Bulldogs, we played the CDs Chris burned for Steve for Father's Day, 2002. Both of us strongly felt Chris's presence and believed he would be with his team on the field. On that cloudy day, the rain stopped just before the game began. Shortly before the Gophers' win, the clouds parted, allowing bright sunshine to warm the air and intensify the glory of the final minutes of the game.

Christian Bailey, close friend of Chris's and former co-captain of the UMN Men's Lacrosse team, captured the impact and significance of that win: "Chris was definitely here today. I think he will always be on the field when Lars [Coach Larson] is coaching. He knows what Lars has been through these past three years, and he knows Lars deserved the win. I think the most incredible moment came right before Steve and Lars hugged. I'll never forget this; when the buzzer went off, I watched Lars like a hawk. He didn't visibly rejoice; he just watched as his guys gathered at midfield and celebrated. Then he turned around and walked right towards Steve and said, 'This one is for you.' Here is a man who has given almost all of himself to this team for the past twelve years, many times taking time away from his family and friends. Yet, there he stood, telling Steve it was for him, you, and Chris. I don't possess the vocabulary to describe the character of this exceptional human being named Lars."

Two weeks later, the UMN Men's Lacrosse team held its 2005 Awards Banquet. This marked the first year Lars gave the Chris Jenkins Leadership Award to the player demonstrating dedication to the team, the University, and the sport of lacrosse, while providing leadership both on and off the field. In the same way as the annual Chris Jenkins Spirit Award of the Eden Prairie Boys' Lacrosse team, the new UMN Lacrosse Leadership Award would be presented every year in Chris's honor. We continue to be humbled by the widespread love and appreciation of hundreds of people touched by Chris's goodness.

Our Desire to Build Bridges of Understanding

Chris taught us how to laugh, love, and celebrate life. Yet Steve and I were finding it so difficult to savor life because we had dedicated our lives to investigating Chris's death. It's amazing how responsible we felt to make things right. We took the job of parenting seriously, and we would not let our son down by excusing those who betrayed him before and after his death. Holding each other up in the toughest times, Steve and I had persisted for more than three years in standing solidly behind our son's character and his right to a proper investigation. The valleys of grave disappointment and despair ultimately strengthened our resolve.

Based on our experiences, we believed local law enforcement continued to demonstrate willful ignorance and a dismissive refusal to investigate the highly suspicious disappearance and death of our exuberant and accomplished twenty-one-year-old son.

Yet to reach our goal in the face of adversity, we had to figure out ways to build bridges, not burn them. One evening, as I discussed the situation with our superstar volunteer W.T., he described his experience watching a search in Trommald, Minnesota (east of Brainerd, in northern Minnesota), one year earlier. The Trident Foundation was searching a deep mine-pit lake for the body of Erika Dalquist, believed by authorities to be in that location. W.T. praised Dalquist's parents, who gave him permission to observe and speak with local law enforcement. He remembered one person in particular, Sergeant Neil Gaalswyk of the Crow Wing County Sheriff's Department Water Patrol, who seemed quite knowledgeable and experienced in water rescue and recovery.

Based on my conversation with W.T., Steve and I agreed that speaking with Gaalswyk might give us ideas for next steps. Steve's conversation with Gaalswyk, now Lieutenant Gaalswyk, confirmed key facts we had heard from Dr. Baden and the men who recovered Chris's body. Specifically, drowning victims are typically found floating facedown—slightly above water—arms out, legs slightly apart. Decomposition causes gas to form in the lungs, which keeps the body facedown due to the position of the lungs in the body. Lieutenant Gaalswyk added that oversized slip-on shoes would not still be on because in the final stages of drowning, involuntary thrashing of the arms and legs occurs, often throwing off even tied shoes. He asked Steve: "Was the ice retrieved from Chris's body melted and chemically tested to compare it to the fluids in Chris's lungs? This test can reveal if he drowned in the same location, or even the same body of water where he was recovered." Steve explained Chris had minimal water in his lungs, and the only tests performed screened for alcohol and other drugs.

Lieutenant Gaalswyk suggested we contact New York–based Lifeguard Systems, Inc., a team of recognized leaders in water rescue and recovery. He had attended some of their training and spoke very highly of their results, experience, and credentials. A few weeks later I talked with Deputy Sheriff Walt "Butch" Hendrick, president and founder of LGS. He confirmed that he had never heard of a drowning victim found floating faceup with the arms crossed on the chest. After asking me five or six very pointed questions, he hesitated and asked if I wanted to hear his initial thoughts. When I responded yes, I remember sliding down the kitchen cupboards to the floor as I heard him say, "Based on my thirty-five years of experience recovering victims from homicidal and accidental drownings, and participating in homicidal drowning investigations, I don't believe Chris was alive when he entered the river."

Sitting on the floor as I held my forehead in one hand and the phone in the other, I took a couple of long, slow, deep breaths and replied, "Deputy Sheriff Hendrick—" He interrupted with "Please call me Butch." "OK, Butch . . . Steve, Sara, and I have believed for many reasons that Chris died at the hands of others. You have confirmed our belief, and worst nightmare."

Stunned and intrigued by the facts I shared regarding Chris's case, Butch promised to help us. He requested several pieces of documentation that I agreed to send ASAP. Both of us needed a chance to go over the facts. As the LGS team reviewed Chris's case, we checked into their credentials and quickly realized we had struck gold.

For more than thirty-five years, and in fifteen countries, Butch Hendrick has been training public safety dive teams and rescue personnel; developing world-class rescue techniques, procedures, and programs; and performing surface and subsurface water rescues. In the 1970s he and the LGS staff provided the New York City Fire Department Rescue Companies Dive Team with more than a hundred hours of training annually for several years. The U.S. National Park Service, the Federal Aviation Administration, the Washington, D.C., Fire Department, and South African dive teams, among others, have benefited from LGS training. By the 1980s, more professional divers and trainers joined TeamLGS, which now operates in Canada, the United States, Asia, and the Caribbean. The Public Safety Diver Instructor Training courses created by TeamLGS represent the highest standards in the industry. LGS instructors are certified dive instructors, members of dive teams, emergency medical technicians, law enforcement and fire instructors, authors, and public speakers.

Many water and ice accident victims around the world are alive today because of Butch Hendrick's innovations, training, programs, equipment designs, publications, audiovisuals, public speaking, and actual rescue efforts. Due to these outstanding accomplishments, Butch has earned a reputation as an honored guest and speaker at conferences around the globe. Along with Andrea Zaferes, vice president of LGS, Craig Nelson MD, and others, Butch and his team members have more than seventy-five years' experience, and in excess of four hundred recoveries of bodies found in water.

Our work with Butch brought a breath of fresh air and hope to our lives. What we will remember about this extraordinary human being is his humility, servant leadership, and respect for life. No less stellar is our confidence in the ability and integrity of Andrea Zaferes.

Andrea also serves as vice president of RIPTIDE, Inc., which was created in 1998 by LGS as a nonprofit organization. One of the three missions of RIPTIDE is to assist law enforcement agencies with homicidal drowning investigations, thereby helping to bring justice to victims and their families. To create and maintain productive relationships, RIPTIDE strives to work in concert with the local law enforcement agencies involved, unless, on rare occasions, these agencies are not interested in investigating a case.

Andrea has received recognition and several awards as a researcher, author, public speaker, and trainer for water death investigations and rescue/recovery operations. Her contributions to water safety and rescue include developing and training scores of public safety certification programs, publishing numerous articles annually, coauthoring several books with Hendrick, and speaking at many national and international conferences.

Meeting with TeamLGS

As luck would have it, in early June 2005, Steve attended a business conference in New York City. I joined him so that we could meet with the LGS team in Poughkeepsie, New York, after Steve's trade show. On the train ride from Manhattan to LGS headquarters, Steve and I discussed the burning questions surrounding Chris's recovery scene. Wanting answers and dreading what they might prove, we forged ahead with the mixed and colliding emotions that were now our everyday reality.

We met with RIPTIDE team members Butch Hendrick, Andrea Zaferes, Detective Sergeant Eric Benjamin of the Ulster County Sheriff's Office, Criminal Division, and Sergeant Cameron Jones of the Winnipeg, Canada, Police Service Division. Since the team members had already reviewed the Minneapolis Police Department's report, as well as autopsy and recovery photos, they came prepared to offer insights. They expressed utter disbelief in the brevity of the MPD report and in the lack of basic investigative protocol. Yet the quality of the autopsy report impressed them. At the meeting, the team created and agreed upon the following five opinion statements:

1. It is not logical for Chris to have floated on February 27 due to the still-cold water temperatures.
2. Chris's body position as found on the surface is out of character for someone found in water, and the ice found attached to his body is also unusual.
3. It is very unlikely for his clothes and shoes to have been so well in place if he had been in the fast-moving river for four months.
4. The chances of Chris coming off the bridge in question are not logical in regards to where he was found.
5. Based on the condition of Chris's body and clothes, his recovery location and posture, and the case history, we do not believe he came off the bridge and was stuck in the bottom substrate for a period of time as theorized by Sergeant Jackson.

Since Butch would be working near the Minneapolis area in early July, he agreed to check out the Mississippi River in the area between the Hennepin Avenue and Third Avenue bridges, paying particular attention to the flow patterns around Nicollet Island. After expressing our deep gratitude, Steve and I returned to New York City by train. Totally exhausted and lost in our own thoughts, we didn't say much to each other. I remember closing my eyes, hearing the *clickety-clack* of the train on the track, and silently saying to Chris, *Oh my God, you really did die at the hands of others. Chris, I'm so sorry. Dad and I won't let you down.*

Full Steam Ahead

"Full steam ahead" accurately described our efforts and those of Andrea and Butch. Andrea sent copies of the autopsy report and photos to three medical examiners to seek additional input. The feedback from these MEs conveyed many similar opinions: the autopsy photos and report were well done and thorough, the condition of the body did not look like Chris had been submerged for four months, and the desiccation of his right hand was abnormal for a submerged body. One ME in particular, who had vast experience with bodies found in water, noted that bodies submerged for more than a month exhibited much more travel damage and degloving (i.e., the separation of the skin from underlying tissue) when touched.

One of the other MEs noted that Chris's body looked more as if he had been frozen rather than submerged for a long period of time in a river. Was Chris's body on land for a period of time? If he had been lying on a riverbank, was pulled into the river when the water rose, and then the water iced over, that could account for the ice on his body at the recovery scene, because the bottom layer of ice looked like ice created on water: it was clear and smooth. If Chris's body was frozen along the shoreline, this explanation also worked.

Something Is Terribly Wrong

When we met with Butch in early July, he was visibly shaken. He explained the purpose and outcomes of a meeting he had just left, a meeting he arranged before coming to Minnesota. He decided to seek advice from members of dive teams within a hundred-mile radius of Minneapolis, since they would be knowledgeable about local waterways. A trainer for the Hennepin County Sheriff's dive team, who had trained many of the teams in the area for over twenty years, was at that meeting. He knew Butch because of LGS training he had attended.

Employing the same process he uses when gathering opinions from several people at the same time, Butch opened the meeting by asking for help in determining what might have happened to a body found in water. Three possibilities existed: accident, suicide, or homicide. Creating a hypothetical scenario, Butch explained the particulars (time of year, water temperature, body size, no wounds found on body, lying on back, arms and hands crossed on chest, desiccated hand, clothing and oversized slip-on shoes in place, encased in inches of ice, etc.) without stating where this had occurred or naming the victim.

After much discussion, members of the group concluded that the manner of death could not be accident or suicide. They proceeded to clarify why those options did not work. When they had wrapped up their discussion, Butch laid down pictures of Chris Jenkins in the middle of the table. Astounded, Butch listened to comments such as: "We know that kid. He committed suicide by jumping off a bridge." Then one by one, every diver present attempted to justify his reversed opinion. Colored by a prior position adopted by local law enforcement, this reversal did not stem from an objective assessment of the facts.

Butch assured us he had never experienced anything like it. "Law enforcement in this state knows this case. I don't see how Chris will get a fair shake." Disgusted and angry, Steve and I told Butch we had been experiencing this type of illogical and disingenuous behavior from law enforcement for almost four years, so we were not surprised.

Worse yet, several months following Butch's meeting with local divers in Minnesota, a couple of them continued to call him, justifying why they had changed their minds. In fact, a trainer for the Hennepin County Sheriff's dive team called Butch numerous times trying to convince him to see the situation differently.

Over the years, Andrea and Butch have continued this same process and discussion with regard to Chris's case. Outside of Minnesota, the universal opinion of public safety divers, law enforcement, and death investigators is that Chris's case raises numerous red flags warranting a thorough investigation that did not appear to have been done.

Testing River Flow

While in Minnesota, Butch walked the area between the Hennepin Avenue and Third Avenue bridges, as well as along the shoreline of Nicollet Island between those two bridges. He threw a total of fifty tennis balls into the river from various points on the Iron and Hennepin Avenue bridges, as well as from the southwest shoreline of Nicollet Island, to see where the current took the balls. The results proved identical to Chuck Loesch's experiments with the orange dummy, and were consistent with the information received from Dr. Mohseni and Marlowe Peterson regarding how the river flows around Nicollet Island. Every ball thrown into the water from the Iron Bridge (connecting the eastern side of Nicollet Island with the east bank of the Mississippi River), and from the eastern, southern, and western shoreline of Nicollet Island (south of the Hennepin Avenue Bridge) ended up at the Xcel Energy Hydropower Plant. In fact, even the balls thrown west of Nicollet Island from the east side of Hennepin Avenue Bridge, up to about midway on the bridge, heading west toward Minneapolis, still ended up by the Xcel Plant. The first tennis ball to reach the Horseshoe Dam, where Chris's body was recovered, was thrown just beyond the midpoint on the bridge. As anticipated, the balls thrown even farther west of that midpoint, nearing downtown Minneapolis, also arrived at the Horseshoe Dam.

Butch did meet with Dr. Mohseni to discuss his findings. Convinced that Chris's body had entered the river north of the Hennepin Avenue Bridge, Butch also met with FBI Special Agent in Charge (SAC) Don Thompson (Chris's uncle), who happened to be in town visiting his family. Thompson agreed that further work involving a mannequin weighted to the size of Chris's body would lend more credibility to the results of the initial experiments already conducted by Butch and Chuck.

Before embarking on a river reenactment requiring extensive preparation, time, and expense, Butch requested verification of a key fact. He wanted to see one of Chris's oversized slip-on shoes to be certain those shoes would not have stayed on Chris's feet if he had gone off a bridge or drowned. All the evidence bags we received remained unopened in a secure container in a controlled environment. Understanding the importance of Butch's request, Steve opened the evidence bag with Chris's shoes. Butch shook his head as he looked at one of the shoes. "No way would those shoes have stayed on his feet, especially since they were big on him."

Preparations Begin

Realizing we needed cooperation from numerous agencies and permission for RIPTIDE to conduct a river reenactment, we contacted Annie Paruccini of Governor Pawlenty's office. Paruccini agreed to facilitate communication by contacting the following departments:

1. The Minneapolis Police Department, which maintained jurisdiction over Chris's case;
2. The Hennepin County Sheriff's Office (HCSO), which had jurisdiction over the river; and
3. The Department of Transportation (Mn/DOT), which controlled the bridges and roads where Butch would be working with a life-size mannequin for river flow analysis.

We encouraged Paruccini to offer the opportunity of watching Butch work on the river to members of these departments. This rare opportunity to learn from a globally recognized leader in water rescue and recovery could benefit Hennepin County personnel, at no expense to the public. RIPTIDE team members donated their time, and the Jenkins family paid all related costs.

Ideally, the river reenactment would occur around the time of year Chris disappeared—late October, early November. Paruccini understood that Butch would only move forward with the permission and partnership of the MPD. Paruccini's e-mail to us read: "As I indicated during our last phone conversation, because the Minneapolis Police Department is the necessary component in any re-enactment or further investigation . . . they would coordinate the effort . . . working directly with Captain Stanek." Paruccini did receive an e-mail from Stanek: "Annie, I will give it due consideration and get back to you next week." Both Captain Stanek and Sheriff's Office Inspector Bill Chandler wished to speak directly with Butch Hendrick. Butch did try several times to contact them. Considering he spends more than 320 days a year on customer sites (often in water or on ice), Butch did everything possible to arrange the work on the Mississippi at the end of October, following a previously scheduled commitment in Stillwater, Minnesota. By the time Hendrick spoke with Chandler, we had missed the window of opportunity of open days on Butch's calendar in late October. Although we had given four weeks' notice requesting approval, it did not happen. We could not get on RIPTIDE'S calendar till the first quarter of 2006, which meant our family needed to cover many additional expenses, since RIPTIDE was not already scheduled to work in the general vicinity of Minneapolis in early 2006.

On November 3, 2005, we received an e-mail from Paruccini: "The decisions for further review are at the discretion of the MPD and HCSO. The Commissioner's offices at the Department of Public Safety and the Minnesota BCA have kept our offices informed of their correspondence with you since your original visit to our office on December 1, 2004. However, the Governor will not be ordering those agencies to usurp the jurisdiction of the MPD on this case." Usurp? We're looking for a fair and complete investigation, which necessitates collaboration and teamwork between the agencies involved.

The Twin Cities 5K: Chris Deserves Justice

During the fall of 2005, we worked diligently to facilitate the river re-enactment efforts. We also participated in the annual Twin Cities 5K. Two years earlier my sister Linda had run in the Twin City Marathon for Chris. I came up with the bright idea that the UMN Men's Lacrosse team, along with as many others as we could persuade to join us, could run or walk the 5K race to honor Chris and remind others that he deserved justice. Any donations we received would be split between the lacrosse team and the Chris Jenkins Memorial Fund. We designed T-shirts and purchased blue bandanas—Chris's signature accessory. Anyone joining us received one of each. Gathering on the steps of the Capitol near the start of the race course, we thanked everyone, listened to a few of Chris's friends and Coach Lars describe what Chris meant to them, shared a few details regarding the investigation, and encouraged everyone to live his or her best life.

It didn't matter if we ran, walked, or crawled; anyone who crossed the finish line wearing a CJ#3 T-shirt received loud cheers from our

Faithful family and friends listening intently.

team. That first year, about sixty people participated. We've run every year since, with numbers of participants almost doubling each year. In addition to honoring Chris, and helping the men's lacrosse team get in shape, we've raised several thousand dollars every year for the Twin Cities, since our participants register for the 5K and pay the twenty-two-dollar fee.

New York FBI Dive Team

Thinking a new perspective might prove valuable, Don Thompson sent photos of Chris's recovery to the FBI's New York office, where the FBI Dive/Recovery team is based. In early October he spoke with members of the team, who told him the photos raised more questions than they provided answers. Thompson suggested that the dive team contact Butch. They knew Butch and agreed to do so. I sent a complete package of information regarding Chris's case to the dive team.

It is not clear whether any new ideas evolved from the FBI Dive Team's analysis. It is interesting to note, though, that they shared many of the same concerns as Loesch, Dr. Baden, Butch, and those who recovered Chris's body. We fail to understand why no agency in Hennepin County involved in the recovery, examination, or investigation of Chris's case had any questions or concerns regarding how Chris's body presented itself. Nor do we comprehend why the Minneapolis Police Department, the Hennepin County Sheriff's Office Water Patrol, and the Medical Examiner's Office failed to compare notes to help determine what happened in the death of a healthy twenty-one-year-old University student athlete. Even more disturbing is that the two men who recovered Chris's body had not been contacted by any of these agencies for facts or perspective when we spoke with them after the case closed. We could only wonder why.

An Open-Minded Leader Emerges

In November 2005, one of our contacts spoke with a member of the Minneapolis City Council about the lack of an investigation for Chris. After reviewing case information we provided, the council member decided to speak directly with Interim Police Chief Tim Dolan to voice his concerns about Chris's case. Dolan listened to the facts and decided he wanted to meet with us to better understand the situation. Prior to our meeting with Dolan, we sent him a key summary of our concerns, which included interviews and follow-up that had never been done, as well as opinions from numerous professionals gathered during our three-year investigation.

Interim Chief Dolan met with us early in December 2005, already aware of many key facts in Chris's case. Shortly into our meeting, he looked us straight in the eye and said, "Your son has never had a complete investigation." Almost too stunned to respond, I replied, "We know. That's why we're speaking with you, the third administration since Chris's shocking death."

Dolan had attended De La Salle High School, located on Nicollet Island, and often jogged along the riverbanks, so he quickly understood the concerns regarding how Chris's body showed up, as well as the results of experiments conducted by Loesch and Hendrick. Understanding the purpose and possible results from a river reenactment, he agreed to pursue the possibility of bringing RIPTIDE to Minneapolis.

Expressing our gratitude to Dolan for listening with an open mind, Steve and I left that meeting happy yet numb. It took awhile for it to sink in that Dolan, who would become chief of the MPD early in 2006, had begun to understand what had and had not happened to investigate Chris's death, and seemed willing to move the case forward. Interim Chief Dolan had broken the chain of ignorance.

Christmas 2005 arrived early for the Jenkins family. In November, precious Cayman Rose joined our family; then in December, our three

Cayman Rose's
first Christmas.

years of grueling work received consideration from an official in the MPD. Sara, Jamie, and Cayman spent Christmas with us in Minnesota. This would be the first time we found ourselves able to decorate for the holidays since 2001. This year as we looked at the stocking labeled "Christopher," we experienced a small measure of peace, believing that his death would finally be dignified by a proper investigation.

CHAPTER 19

Obstruction of Justice

January–March 2006

Obstacles cannot crush me, every obstacle yields to stern resolve.
He who is fixed to a star does not change his mind.

LEONARDO DA VINCI

In January 2006, Tim Dolan was named chief of the Minneapolis Police Department. With a leader in law enforcement, a reopened case, and the assistance of some of the most accomplished divers, instructors, and experts in the water rescue and recovery industry, we awakened each day with hope and cautious optimism. After so many setbacks, we saw the possibility of unraveling the mystery of Chris's death that had plagued our daily thoughts and ghoulish nightmares.

What happened to Chris? Who was involved? Chief Dolan assured us that both he and the previous chief, Bill McManus, believed RIPTIDE's work on the Mississippi River might produce information to point Chris's case in the right direction. If RIPTIDE could ascertain where Chris's body most likely entered the river in relation to the Hennepin Avenue Bridge, the answer would shed light on the question of foul play.

We spoke with Dolan a couple of times early in 2006 to update him on the river reenactment and to encourage him to invite anyone in law enforcement in Minneapolis who felt they could benefit by watching the river work. This rare opportunity to learn from experts would not cost Hennepin County a penny. RIPTIDE donated the time, and we paid the expenses.

Early in February 2006, Dolan let us know he had received verbal permission from Hennepin County for the work to proceed. Settling on the end of March for the river reenactment, we immediately began the necessary preparations.

Our resolve to find answers strengthened when we learned that another bright, fun-loving college man, Scot Radel, had disappeared from a bar in St. Cloud, Minnesota. Nine days after Chris's disappearance, Josh Guimond had vanished from Collegeville, a mere ten miles from St. Cloud. Watching all the news reports, we ached for Scot and his family. Frustration rose as Steve and I asked ourselves, "How many more?" Scot's eyes captured my heart; they reminded me so much of Chris's—bright, laughing, shining with goodness.

Semi-Incomprehensible Constraints

"We are overwhelmed here." I received an e-mail from Andrea Zaferes, vice president of RIPTIDE, requesting our help with requirements noted on the form the Hennepin County Sheriff's Office (HCSO) had sent to RIPTIDE. The form requested proof of permission from the Coast Guard to work on the river, and no less than a million-dollar liability insurance rider designating Hennepin County as the sole beneficiary. All documentation had to accompany the form before notarization. Since our family was paying all expenses, we would incur these additional fees.

In shock and disbelief, I reread the e-mail several times. In addition to being a New York State EMT and Ulster County Deputy Sheriff, Butch Hendrick is a fifty-ton U.S. Coast Guard–approved captain. Why was this accomplished man, who has dedicated his life to rescue/ recovery water operations and diving safety, being asked for a Coast Guard permit? These requests seemed not only outrageous but also bogus, so we began digging for facts.

Our trusted volunteer, W.T., spent countless hours tracking down the necessity of a Coast Guard permit. Eventually, he ended up speaking with personnel at the Coast Guard office in St. Louis, Missouri, whose area of responsibility covers the Mississippi River in Minnesota. Office personnel chuckled at the request for a Coast Guard permit, stating they had never heard of it. Interestingly enough, the St. Louis office is a "Marine Safety Office" that has a branch office at Fort Snelling near the Minneapolis–St. Paul International Airport.

Upon further exploration, W.T. saw the Coast Guard boat on its trailer in the parking lot at the Fort Snelling location, waiting to be towed to a body of water and deployed. This taxpayer-financed boat with two engines is perfect for use on the river. Since our understanding was that Hennepin County would provide a boat, we had not requested one from the Coast Guard.

Meanwhile, we contacted FBI Special Agent in Charge (SAC) Don Thompson (who has more than thirty-five years' experience in the FBI) to see if he could shed light on the issue of permission from the Coast Guard or the necessity of our providing a million-dollar insurance rider for Hennepin County. Don responded, "A Coast Guard permit and one-million-dollar insurance rider for Hennepin County? That's semi-incomprehensible." Ultimately, we told Andrea to complete the form, get it notarized, and disregard the permit and insurance. Stripped of our naïveté, and now of our compliance, we forged ahead.

Ready to Roll—Not So Fast

Preparations continued throughout February and March, and it appeared the river reenactment would go forward without a hitch. Then, the night before Butch Hendrick and Andrea Zaferes were scheduled to arrive, our phone rang. Butch asked Steve if he and Andrea should board the plane the following morning. He explained to Steve that from previous conversations with Hennepin County Sheriff's Office Inspector Bill Chandler, Butch had understood a boat would be provided by the county. Now, at the eleventh hour, Butch learned that the county would *not* be furnishing a boat. Since we were paying expenses, Butch did not want to waste our resources. Steve probed for exactly what Butch needed. He told Butch to come and said we'd find a boat.

For several hours we phoned friends and colleagues who might be able to help by providing a boat. In late March in Minnesota, boats are tucked away in storage, often behind several others. Unfortunately we did not locate an available boat that night. Feeling anxious, we somehow managed to maintain our unstoppable mind-set. Since July 2005, we had prepared for this day. Surely if we stayed focused on the goal, we would find a boat. The setbacks over the past four years forced us to learn resilience if we wanted to succeed. I often hugged pictures of Chris, breathing in my deep love for the son we raised. Every time I connected with "why" we pushed forward, I knew giving up was *not* acceptable.

Steve spoke with W.T., who spent the next twenty-four hours checking possible options, including the Army Corps of Engineers and the Fire Department.

Tireless Trio

During that long night, Steve, Sara, and I resumed our role of "tireless trio." Having Sara with us bolstered our resolve. Our granddaughter, Cayman Rose, accompanied Sara from Cincinnati and proved to be the greatest lift of all. Innocent little Cayman brought joy during a very tense week. Cayman's Great-Grandpa Gene and Great-Grandma Rose planned to arrive early on the morning of the reenactment. Gene wanted to accompany us to understand the process, and Rose delighted in staying at our home to watch over Cayman.

Steve's phone call to a colleague, Ron Lenling, director of purchasing at Genmar Holdings, Inc., produced results. Irwin Jacobs/Genmar is one of the world's largest manufacturers of recreational boats. Through networking at Genmar the following morning, Lenling learned of a distributor, Crystal-Pierz Marine in Rogers, Minnesota (about twenty-five miles northwest of Minneapolis). Lenling phoned Crystal-Pierz, explained the situation, and received a firm commitment from the company to provide a boat and experienced captain, who was also their top salesman. Steve received a phone call from this seasoned professional at Genmar, who communicated the plan. Crystal-Pierz had a brand-new

boat in stock, which the company planned to rig with the necessary equipment to safely navigate the frigid March waters of the Mississippi River

"Where's the beach, Mommy?"

in Minneapolis. Dedicating the day to helping our family learn more about what happened to Chris, the salesman would bring the boat to Nicollet Island the following morning.

As Crystal-Pierz prepared the boat, Butch and Andrea spent time with Dr. Mohseni and Chuck Loesch to review current river conditions before walking areas around Nicollet Island with Loesch, W.T., and Steve to finalize the overall plan. Next, Butch and Andrea met with Lieutenant Edwards, Inspector Chandler, FBI SAC Don Thompson, and Sergeant Jackson to discuss logistics and to communicate the plan. Basically, a mannequin weighted to the size of Chris's body would be used to ascertain where Chris's body likely originated based on his final resting place in the river. The boat would make it possible to drop the mannequin at various spots in the Mississippi River to prove or disprove earlier experiments on the river conducted by Butch and Loesch on separate occasions. The costly mannequin could also be retrieved by the boat if it went over the falls at the Horseshoe Dam.

The Reenactment

After months of preparation, the big day dawned. Shortly after arriving at the river, we met MPD Lieutenant Edwards, Homicide, and Hennepin County Sheriff's Office Lieutenant Storms, Water Patrol. Representing Hennepin County, they came to observe the process. Sadly, no other law enforcement personnel spent time at the river on that sunny day, to glean knowledge from Butch and Andrea, global leaders in water rescue and recovery operations.

We greeted Don Thompson, who had come from Virginia at our request to observe, assist if needed, and interpret results. Over the years we learned that in these emotionally charged situations, it helped to have another person present whom we trusted, to later provide us with objective feedback. Loesch arrived with a colleague, who also offered assistance. Hugging W.T., I remember how proud I was of our team and how grateful I was to these team members who offered encouragement and support during the toughest times.

Crystal-Pierz's representative arrived at the river with the boat about

10:00 a.m. As soon as Steve saw him, he ran up, introduced himself, and suggested they go upriver to determine where to launch the boat. Leaving in Steve's vehicle, they stopped at the first boat launch, located in a secluded area on Boom Island Park, just north of Nicollet Island on the eastern shore of the Mississippi. The iced-in boat launch prompted them to continue north to the next available launch site, River Ridge Park, about five miles north of Nicollet Island. There was no ice there, so the boat could easily be launched.

Reversed Decision

Shortly after Steve and Crystal-Pierz's experienced captain returned to the group gathered on Nicollet Island to begin the river reenactment, Lieutenant Storms delivered a gut punch. The boat would not be allowed in the river due to dangerous conditions. This decision made no sense to us. Though we are not experts on the dynamics of the river, how could the conditions be too dangerous for an experienced captain in a new boat and Butch, a veteran captain and diver? The river level was at 10,000 cubic feet per second, much less than the 14,000 cfs on the day Chris's body was recovered in the same area. Clearly, Lieutenant Storms had jurisdiction, so RIPTIDE obeyed.

Intrigued by all that transpired, Crystal-Pierz's representative stayed for a couple of hours just in case the decision was reversed and Butch could follow through with his original plan. No such luck. Forced to devise a new strategy, Butch then had to don a dry suit and put himself in the icy waters of the Mississippi.

Sara, Steve, and I watched the mannequin floating in the water, crushed by thoughts of what Chris must have endured. Holding on

with steely resolve, we also felt the sting of nine months of work blowing up in our face, as the intended strategy to produce results was not allowed. It's hard to say if our grief, anger, or sense of betrayal won out on that cold, harsh day at the river.

New Strategy

Butch's new plan required additional materials and safety precautions: a long floating rope so that the mannequin could move freely, and numerous tennis balls to confirm river flow characteristics previously tested around Nicollet Island. Steve, W.T., Sara, and I met for about sixty seconds, quickly figuring out a plan. Steve left with W.T. to buy the rope while Sara and I headed to the UMN tennis courts to request used tennis balls. The tennis coach happened to be at the courts. When he understood what we needed, he exclaimed, "I remember Chris's disappearance; he was one of our athletes. I'm so sorry. You can have all the used tennis balls you want." Sara and I rapidly gathered two huge garbage bags full of tennis balls; then we hopped in the car and headed back to the river, a scene that rocked us to the core. When Steve returned with the rope, the three of us just held each other for a moment, promising Chris our best efforts.

By this time, local media as well as FOXNews New York had gathered. Reminding the media to stay far out of the way so as not to disrupt the work, we also asked them to grant us some privacy. For four and a half years, we had kept our profile in the news to help Chris and other young men who met with a similar death. Though we've been called media hogs on a few occasions, we challenge any parent or sibling to stand in front of numerous microphones and cameras, communicating for the hundredth time what might have happened to their loved one. Media appearances did not benefit our health or well-being. We put ourselves through those gut-wrenching interviews because we sought truth and justice.

I'm glad Sara and I did not see what Steve witnessed just before Butch went into the water. If Sara and I had watched this exchange unfold, we might have gone postal. Holding the rescue throw rope bag he designed (one used all over the world), Butch stood in front of Lieutenant Storms and said, "Since you are the only one here who really knows how to use this, I'd like you to hold it and help me out if I run into trouble." Steve watched Storms back up, put his hands in the air, and reply, "I won't do that. I'm here as an observer only." Another deftly thrown gut punch from Hennepin County—but wait, the day wasn't over yet.

Who Is Being Protected? Who Is Being Served?

Over the next couple of hours, our tireless trio watched in grave silence. Sara had brought Chris's turquoise ring and we passed it among the three of us. Standing on Nicollet Island, and believing that Chris was likely murdered in the vicinity, a chill descended upon us, as much from our anguish as from the cold temperature and biting wind.

When Butch completed everything he could, based on the limitations thrown at him, he indicated that to prove or disprove his findings, he needed to cut the rope to allow the mannequin to reach its final destination. The eight-hundred-dollar mannequin might go over the falls, and without a boat, we could not retrieve it. After so many years of work, Steve and I wanted results. Taking responsibility for the cost, we uttered, "Cut the rope." Lieutenant Storms would not allow Butch to do that. He justified his decision by saying, "Too many people would phone in to the HCSO saying there is a body in the river."

Hendrick, Zaferes, Thompson, Edwards, and Storms met in the pavilion on the island and spoke for about forty-five minutes. While we waited, we offered drinks, chips, and a tray of ham and cheese croissant sandwiches purchased from our local Sam's Club to everyone present. Knowing forthcoming information might change the course of the investigation, the media waited to catch the highlights and our reaction.

Thompson walked outside and called our family into the pavilion. Grandpa Gene accompanied Steve, Sara, and me. Putting his arm around my shoulders, my dad's stoic expression throughout the day, now turned to great sadness. Walking into that pavilion, the tension in the air was palpable. Something serious clearly had gone down, though we did not know specifics until years later.

Loesch, Grandpa Gene, Butch, Andrea, and the three Jenkinses sat around a huge circular table with Storms and Edwards off to the side. Butch started by saying, "We cannot definitively say Chris's body entered the river north of the Hennepin Avenue Bridge." As we knew all along, that would have lent considerable weight to the likelihood of foul play. The anxiety of the past several days caught up with me, and I burst into tears.

Butch looked so sorry and tried to apologize. Putting my hands on the table, palms up, I looked him straight in the eyes and said, "Butch, you have no reason to be ashamed of anything. In the midst of a tight work schedule around the globe, you came here, generously offering your time, talent, and expertise. I applaud your efforts, and thank you from the entire Jenkins team."

At that point Lieutenant Edwards added, "If we [the MPD] conducted this type of work, we would never allow the family to watch." Sara's fiery eyes focused on Edwards, mirroring the rage I felt. If the Minneapolis police had investigated Chris's case or even considered the key data we provided multiple times, the Jenkins family would not have been put through the past four years of unnecessary hell. We wisely kept our mouths shut, knowing only ugly words could escape.

The meeting lasted about thirty minutes. Butch and Andrea promised to summarize their findings. After speaking with Storms several times during the day, Andrea wanted to reconnect with him in a few days to follow up on key points.

For the first time ever, we could not face the media. More than anything, we probably needed a punching bag. Leaving the pavilion, we hustled to our car and drove off.

Now for the rest of the story, which we learned several years later: standing on Nicollet Island, shivering from having been in the frigid river, Butch again explained to Storms the necessity of cutting the rope to get results. Storms snapped back, "Cut that rope, and we'll prosecute you to the fullest extent of the law."

Although Butch complied by not cutting the rope, we cannot find a law that he would have broken if he had cut that rope. If Lieutenant Storms's ominous warning wasn't intended to block our search for answers, why did he threaten Butch?

CHAPTER 20

Gutsy Decisions, Outrageous Results

April–May 2006

*Do what you feel in your heart to be right—
for you'll be criticized anyway.*

ELEANOR ROOSEVELT

"To this day, I still believe Chris was murdered. I just wasn't allowed to get the evidence." If he had been allowed to cut the rope, Butch Hendrick could have provided evidence that Chris's body most likely entered the river north of the Hennepin Avenue Bridge, which would have pointed to foul play. RIPTIDE's report addressed to Hennepin County Sheriff's Office Inspector Chandler clearly described the river project's goal and results. Because he was not allowed to track the mannequin from a boat as originally planned, Butch was forced to tether the mannequin and walk up to his chest in the river in numerous locations around Nicollet Island. Nonetheless, even those results indicated that because of water flow around the sandbar south of the island, Chris could not have come off the Iron Bridge and ended up in his recovery location.

Although testing showed Chris might have entered the river from a small area on the western shore of Nicollet Island, that possibility could not account for the large amounts of ice on his upper body. Particularly since his right hand must have been exposed to the elements for several days, the heavy foot and vehicular traffic in that area meant that someone would have spotted his body in that amount of time. Several of us reviewed video footage of the recovery scene, and FBI Special Agent in Charge (SAC) Don Thompson wrote: "There is no discernible ice formation along the west bank of Nicollet Island with the exception of some limited icing along the western tip of the island."

If Chris's body had come from under the midsection of the Hennepin

Avenue Bridge, he could have also ended up in his recovery location. Yet security camera footage; the positioning of his clothes, shoes, arms, and hands; and the fact that there were no broken bones (as there probably would have been from hitting the I-beam ledge or steel cable of the bridge)—all made coming off that bridge seem impossible.

Hendrick and Zaferes, Thompson, Edwards, and Storms agreed that the Iron Bridge and the east side of Nicollet Island could be eliminated as possible areas where Chris's body entered the water. The same individuals also agreed that river currents would likely have prevented Chris's body from being held under the ice at the southern tip of Nicollet Island. Since the only discernible buildup of ice visible around the island appeared at the southern tip, that conclusion held particular significance.

Based on the mannequin observations from Nicollet Island during the river work, tennis ball trials from the Hennepin Avenue Bridge and other areas around the island, and information provided by Dr. Ek and Dr. Mohseni, a third area existed where Chris may have entered the Mississippi River. This area, north of the Hennepin Avenue Bridge, included the east and west riverbanks, approximately a mile or more upriver. This possibility could account for the formation of thick ice on Chris's upper body.

Boyle's Law

Lieutenant Storms told Andrea that many bodies show up in the same position as Chris's, and in the same location. Although Andrea asked for a picture of another body that showed up in the same position as Chris, Storms has not sent one to her, or made one available. Andrea sent us an e-mail in mid-April 2006, explaining the following key points, which were relevant to discussions she had with Storms during the river work.

First, Chris's hand must have been exposed to the air or in ice above water for at least a few days prior to his recovery. Therefore, he was at the surface for at least a few days. Second, the two observers who reported seeing a body in the river placed calls just a few minutes apart; Chris's body was clearly visible with no ice from the waist down. So the lieutenant's statement that Chris could have been at that location for a few days and not been seen is not plausible. In fact, Storms told

Butch he could not cut the rope because too many people would report a body in the river to the Hennepin County Sheriff's Office. The lieutenant also said Chris may have been less recognizable because of the ice formed at the recovery location. If so, a period of time existed with no ice—therefore, his body would have been visible.

Lastly, Andrea addressed Storms's statement that Chris's body may have been floating just below the surface for a while. No, a large part of him had to be at the surface or he wouldn't have been at the surface at all. Pressure increases with depth, so even a few inches below the surface has increased pressure. Increased pressure decreases gas volume, which in turn decreases buoyancy. The bottom line is that an object with gas is at the surface or sinking. Andrea added: "The majority of certified divers cannot make themselves neutral enough to hover at one depth in shallow water (less than thirty feet), so the notion that a body or an object could be neutral enough to hover just below the surface is not an option. The moment it rises an inch, the gas expands and it becomes more buoyant, causing it to rise further. This is Boyle's Law, established in 1662."

The only feedback Butch ever received from his river work in Minneapolis, at the end of March 2006, came in the form of a report from HCSO Inspector Bill Chandler. In that report Chandler notes that a witness placed Chris walking on the Hennepin Avenue Bridge from downtown toward Nicollet Island. Nowhere does he state that two security cameras mounted on the Federal Reserve Bank did not show Chris walking on the Hennepin Avenue Bridge from 11:00 p.m. October 31 to 4:00 a.m. on November 1, 2002. Like Storms, Chandler states that Hennepin County has many documented cases of bodies being in a similar condition and position in the river. He also wrote, "Captain Ken Schilling and Lt. Jeff Storms of HCSO reviewed Hendrick's letter . . . they are in agreement with my findings . . . I find nothing unusual with the body condition based on time in the water or the ice conditions around the body and shoreline . . . It is my opinion with reasonable certainty that Jenkins more than likely entered the water from the Hennepin Avenue Bridge/Nicollet Island area."

Left in a vacuum, Butch made numerous phone calls that were not returned. In the ensuing months, Captain Stanek, Sergeant Jackson, and Lieutenant Edwards denigrated RIPTIDE's work and integrity, even in front of Steve and me. This pattern of discounting the work and credibility of seasoned professionals outside of Minnesota continued. The tactic did not sway our confidence in the experts we worked with, who donated their services for a noble cause—truth. Rather, it strengthened our resolve.

As an accomplished professional and lifelong learner, Butch continued to seek feedback, to no avail. Embarrassed by the lack of cooperation or respect shown Butch by the sheriff's office, Steve and I apologized profusely to him on several occasions. We assured him many of us clearly understood he could not get conclusive results without commitment and cooperation from the Hennepin County Sheriff's Office.

The Question That Rocked Our World

On a lovely spring evening late in April, Steve and I enjoyed a walk through our neighborhood. We stopped to chat with one of our neighbors, who asked about the status of Chris's case. He was quite interested and continued with questions. In that discussion we learned he had several years of experience in the field of forensic pathology. The case piqued his curiosity and he asked if he could take a look at it. He was particularly interested in the autopsy photos and report, so we shared photos and various documents with him.

Three days later our neighbor called to say he had been working on the case almost nonstop and had compiled several pages of questions. Open to a new perspective, Steve answered as many questions as he could. Then came the question that rocked our world: "Steve, did you know Chris clutched hair in his left hand?" Steve responded by saying we knew Chris's left hand was clenched. "Steve, I've scrutinized the autopsy photos. It looks like Chris held mud containing hair in his left hand."

Steve did not immediately alert me regarding the shocking discovery. Instead, he phoned his brother-in-law, FBI SAC Don Thompson, and Butch Hendrick, asking them to look at the photos and give their opinion. Thompson was traveling and Hendrick was working out of the country. Steve's anxiety mounted and he could hardly sleep. One night while I shopped for groceries, Steve made the gutsy decision to look at the autopsy photos of the son he adored. There it was—photo number 21. In Chris's left hand, pried open in the autopsy, lay what the report referred to as "foreign matter," laced with what looked like human hair.

When I got home and saw Steve's white face, I froze. He was so irate, he could hardly speak. Anguish and fury flooded his eyes. Then he showed me the envelope. He had already looked through the labeled evidence bags, secured in a controlled environment, comparing them to the entries on the MPD Property Inventory list. There it was, a sealed manila envelope labeled, "Foreign Matter in Left Hand." The word "right" was crossed out and replaced with "left."

We sat and cried. I felt the familiar migraine starting at the base of my skull, working its way up. These miserable headaches started early in November 2002. Before then, I had only experienced a few "normal" headaches in my entire life. Steve raged that the hair probably belonged to one of Chris's murderers. We felt all along that more than one person was responsible for ending our son's life.

We knew from the autopsy report that three Hennepin County medical examiners and four people from the Minneapolis Police Department—two sergeants from homicide and two forensic scientists from the Bureau of Identification—had been present at Chris's autopsy. Not one of seven qualified individuals made certain the hair was tested. Instead, the "foreign matter in left hand" was photographed, placed in an envelope, labeled, sealed, and shelved in a warehouse. For God's sake, a young man whose goodness captured the hearts of thousands of people, disappeared under highly suspicious circumstances and was found four months later frozen in the Mississippi River, and not one of seven professionals questioned the hair in his hand.

A Surprise Phone Call

The end of April 2006 brought another startling surprise, one that would eventually shock the nation. We received a phone call from two retired New York Police Department (NYPD) homicide detectives: Detective Sergeant Kevin Gannon and Detective Second Grade (in the top two hundred of more than three thousand police officers in New York City) Anthony Duarte. Having researched Chris's case and our investigative work, they wanted to meet with us that very evening on Nicollet Island.

Over the years, we have received many crazy calls, so we remained skeptical, asking several tough questions. As Steve spoke with Sergeant Gannon at least forty-five minutes, I spoke with W.T., a whiz on the Internet, requesting information on Sergeant Gannon and Detective Duarte. Within twenty minutes, W.T. called back, assuring us they were the real deal. At this point, we figured we had nothing to lose, so we drove to Minneapolis to meet them. Just before getting out of Steve's car, we looked at each other with a hint of apprehension. With a shrug of our shoulders, our eyes met, and seemed to say, *Oh well, we came this far, why lose courage now?*

During the next two hours, we learned that Gannon had worked a similar case many years earlier in New York. A young man named Patrick McNeill disappeared, only to be found weeks later in the river. While working that case, Gannon discovered that many facts did not add up. When Gannon learned he had cancer, he promised the McNeill family that if he lived, he would find out what happened to their son. Once again working Patrick's case, Gannon researched online and discovered that many young men in the Upper Midwest, in particular, had met similar fates under suspicious conditions. Because our family had done so much work, and continuously tried to get attention on these cases in the media, Gannon read everything he could find about Chris's case.

Not wanting to be biased by parents, Gannon and Duarte told us they had already met with Sergeant Jackson, still lead investigator on Chris's case. They soon learned how much we knew about Chris's case and several others, since we had worked with a team of professionals for many years. We agreed to send them the data we had gathered so far, which involved more than two dozen young men.

Fascinated by Steve's recounting of Dr. Lee Gilbertson's work, they requested his contact information. Dr. Lee Gilbertson, associate professor of criminal justice studies at St. Cloud State University, in St. Cloud, Minnesota, had studied this alarming pattern of college-aged men disappearing and showing up days, weeks, or months later in bodies of water. Along with his graduate students, Dr. Gilbertson created a PowerPoint presentation that he had shared many times with the public. Introducing Dr. Gilbertson to retired detectives Gannon and Duarte gave new wings to the growing suspicions of serial homicide.

Steve and I kept asking ourselves on the drive home, *How did honest, responsible, caring people like us end up in this web of horror?* We wondered if Gannon and Duarte could connect the dots in a way that would garner attention from the Feds. We sure hoped so.

Our Purpose:
Create a Productive Relationship with the MPD

On May 11, 2006, Steve and I met with Chief Dolan, Lieutenant Edwards, and Sergeant Jackson. We wanted to meet with them to voice our concerns, highlight conclusions reached from the work with RIPTIDE, and understand the status of Chris's case, as well as next steps. We continued to think we could create a positive working relationship with the MPD; well, maybe we still believed in the tooth fairy.

Surprised to hear about hair in Chris's left hand, Dolan asked why it was never tested. No one responded. Finally Steve spoke up: "That's what we want to know, Chief." Before agreeing to return Chris's evidence, we wanted to understand the level of commitment to investigate the case. Steve and I had already discussed the possibility of having testing done by an outside agency, and researched a few possibilities.

During the meeting, we learned people were beginning to talk, so Sergeant Jackson now regarded Chris's death as suspicious. In May 2006, we still did not hear the phrase "possible homicide" despite the fact that information uncovered since November 1, 2002, pointed to foul play as a distinct possibility. Unfortunately, so much evidence was lost in the early weeks after Chris's disappearance and at the recovery scene as a result of preconceived notions of suicide or accident without facts to support those conclusions. How frustrating for Steve and me!

Although we asked several questions regarding the recovery photos, no one seemed to have ever looked at them. Through future discussions, it appeared that only the Jenkins family had requested copies and studied them. Apparently, the recovery photos had not been reviewed and placed in Chris's file by the MPD as of May 2006. Some aspects of the case are too disturbing for words.

After Edwards and Jackson left the meeting, Steve and I decided to stay, continuing our discussion for an additional twenty minutes or so with Chief Dolan. We reiterated that several professionals had viewed the helicopter footage of Chris's recovery, and some had put their findings in writing. Twice, the camera angle clearly showed the west bank of Nicollet Island, and there was no discernible ice. Yet Chris's upper body was encased in ice. RIPTIDE cleared Chris from coming off the Iron Bridge, and the eastern and southern shorelines of Nicollet Island. Edwards and Storms agreed with those conclusions. With no ice on the western shoreline, logic puts Chris entering the Mississippi north of the Hennepin Avenue Bridge. Thus, foul play was the logical conclusion, since Chris's residence was located in the opposite direction, and on Halloween night, Chris had already voiced to his group's designated driver that it was getting late and they should be leaving the bar soon. Thanking Dolan many times over, we drove home.

Shortly after arriving home, we received an e-mail from RIPTIDE, documenting opinions of hundreds of professionals who had looked at Chris's case. As Hendrick and Zaferes often do, they sought input from other experts. "Walt Hendrick and I have shown Chris' case to dozens of experienced public safety divers, marine patrol officers, and hundreds of medicolegal death investigators, coroners, and medical examiners, beginning in June 2005 . . ." (the entire letter can be viewed at www.FootprintsOfCourage.com). Key points: "Arms over chest is most unusual and the vast majority of people who saw the photos said they had never seen a body surface and travel downriver in that position. The position of Chris' arms, especially without the presence of rigor, is extremely unusual for a body to have been on the bottom, then ascended to the surface, and traveled downstream to a resting location. His desiccated hand meant it was out of water for at least a couple or a few days—that was a consensus opinion. Hence, he did not surface and float downstream to his recovery location in a day's time."

We forwarded the e-mail to Dolan and then took a long walk. Who murdered Chris, placed his body upstream—probably under or wedged into tree branches—crossed his arms, and laughed because they were getting away with murder? We've been told that two people have bragged about what they did to Chris. Sadly, they are still laughing. We have reason to believe at least one is walking the streets.

Part III

Seeking Justice

"Cadet Prayer"

. . . Make us to choose the harder right instead of the easier wrong, and never to be content with a half truth when the whole truth can be won. Endow us with courage that is born of loyalty to all that is noble and worthy, that scorns to compromise with vice and injustice and knows no fear when truth and right are in jeopardy . . .

(REPEATED DURING CHAPEL SERVICES AT
THE U.S. MILITARY ACADEMY)

CHAPTER 21

Manning Up

June–November 2006

The time is always right to do what is right.
MARTIN LUTHER KING JR. (1929–68)

"Your son was a victim of homicide." No parent can fathom these words, not even when they are spoken. Sitting in the homicide conference room at the MPD, that statement cut through our hearts like a sharp knife. Although we had believed for years that Chris died at the hands of cold-blooded murderers, hearing that statement from Sergeant Jackson, who for years insisted that Chris committed suicide or had an accident, was surreal.

We met on November 17 with Sergeant Jackson, Lieutenant Edwards, and Dr. Baker, now head medical examiner for Hennepin County. Jackson told us he had followed leads in Minnesota and out of the state over the past year. Based on his conversations with at least one of the suspects/witnesses, Chris fought incredibly hard for his life, the victim of a possible robbery. A few additional details emerged. Answering one of Steve's questions, Jackson noted that he did not understand why Chris couldn't get to shore. Immediately red flags popped up for Steve and me. From all indications, Chris was not alive when he entered the river.

Murderers often create various versions of the truth, usually divulging at most 70–80 percent of the facts. The job of a homicide investigator is to connect the dots, paying particular attention to details that could only be known by those present at the crime scene. Although Jackson shared few facts with us; he had worked the case over the past year and believed Chris's death was indeed a homicide based on the information he gathered.

Chris Fought for His Life

What rang true for Steve and me more than anything was that Chris would have fought for his life to his last breath, of that we are certain. Steve asked, "How could Chris possibly have been alive when he entered the river?" Jackson responded, "Maybe he was unconscious." Steve pushed, "How might that have happened?" Jackson said, "Maybe he was hit on the head with a blunt object." I looked straight across the table at Dr. Baker and said, "Dr. Baker, you and I have had several productive conversations, is that correct?" He nodded. Continuing, I noted, "Since Chris played lacrosse as the only goalie with no pads on his arms or legs for an entire weekend five days before he disappeared, we questioned why the autopsy report stated 'no bruising' at which point you said we correctly interpreted the report." Again Dr. Baker nodded. "So are you telling us now that Chris may have been hit on the head hard enough to render him unconscious, yet no marks showed up, just like no bruising?" Dr. Baker looked down to the end of the table at Jackson; Jackson nodded. Baker looked back at me, and nodded. Struggling to keep the anger out of my voice I asked, "If four months of decomposition and water destroy marks and bruising on a body, why didn't anyone consider homicide as a possibility?" Silence.

When I asked Dr. Baker why no one immediately ran the hair in hand to the BCA for testing, Jackson replied, "Dr. Baker doesn't know about the hair." I sat there thinking, *Au contraire, mon frère. Dr. Baker participated in the autopsy, you did not.*

Human Hair in Chris's Left Hand

The only information we had regarding testing of foreign matter in left hand, fingernails, and brushing clothing for evidence, was that the foreign matter did include human hair. We did not receive further information in the meeting. Dolan, Edwards, and FBI SAC Thompson had urged us to get the evidence bags back in the system. Against our better judgment, we did, allowing Lieutenant Edwards to pick up the sealed evidence bags in June 2006. Steve insisted on Edwards signing the MPD Property Inventory form to document the chain of custody. Before leaving, Edwards promised Steve the evidence would be tested.

We don't remember if Jackson or Edwards mentioned their thoughts in the meeting on how the hair got in Chris's hand. But during the summer and fall of 2006, we did hear from both of them on more than one occasion, "He probably picked the hair up in the river, maybe from a comb." When we challenged that curious notion, Jackson told us, "Maybe he got it from the mud in the bottom of the river."

"Incomprehensible" accurately describes our rational reaction over the years to these types of comments we heard from law enforcement and medical examiners ("Maybe he jumped in the river to save a duck"). Some we ignored, while others we challenged. A reasonably intelligent person wonders, *Does anyone expect us to believe this foolishness? What is going on here?*

The meeting concluded on that Friday afternoon with Lieutenant Edwards telling us he would register Chris's death as a homicide in the courthouse records, and hopefully, we'd have a quiet weekend to collect our thoughts before the media hit on Monday. He also requested we attend the press conference planned for Monday to announce homicide because he felt our presence would be a strong message to the community of how police and parents working together can bring results. Too emotionally shot to respond, we promised to call him by Monday morning at the latest.

Grief-stricken from coming in touch with our son's murder, and upset about "no marks, no bruising, human hair, etc.," I forced myself to reframe my attitude and take the high road. No matter what had occurred over the past several years, Sergeant Jackson had recently worked the case and I felt grateful to him for that. As Steve and I walked out the door, I hugged a stunned Sergeant Jackson, then turned and hugged Dr. Baker. "Thank you gentlemen for what you've done for our son. Moving forward is what counts now." Lieutenant Edwards smiled.

Walking to our car, Steve and I decided to drive out to my parents' farm, forty miles west of Minneapolis. Determined to protect my parents, we wanted them to hear the recent developments from us, not from the news. Twenty minutes into the drive, both of our cell phones started ringing. Caller I.D. showed the news had already reached the media. We would not speak with anyone before Sara and my parents.

Of course Sara had known about our meeting with the MPD since Tuesday night when we received the call from Lieutenant Edwards requesting the Friday appointment. As I spoke with her now, Sara expressed anger after hearing the highlights of the meeting. "Mom, the facts have pointed to foul play for years. Why did the MPD put us through four years of living hell?"

Before arriving at my parents' farm, we phoned to let them know we were on our way. As we joined them in their family room, Grandma Rose and Grandpa Gene didn't say much; they listened with heavy hearts. The homicide of a loved one is simply unbearable. The four of us tried to see the positive: now Chris's case would receive the diligent investigation that should have been conducted in the first place. Watching my parents, I saw the horror of losing their grandson to murder return with full force. Oh, that gaping hole inside each of us is a lonely place indeed. While others may help us along the way, at the end of the day, each of us must find our own path through the labyrinth of profound grief and loss. My mom and dad's faith held them together.

"Chris, today it's your voice being heard"

During the fifty-five minutes it took to drive from the farm to our home, our cell phones rang incessantly. The anxiety continued to build. As we entered our home, Steve ran to the bathroom and was violently ill. Unable to make it to another bathroom, I threw up in the kitchen sink. Holding it together no longer worked.

Soon the media came, ringing the front door bell. Initially, we tried to ward them off, saying family members didn't even know yet. We were both from large families, and it would take awhile to contact everyone. Within an hour, giving statements to the media seemed inevitable. So we phoned Chris's close friends, asking them to come to our home if they chose. We also gave them a heads-up regarding media, offering them the chance to speak. Rather quickly, the cul-de-sac in front of our house looked like a parking lot.

We welcomed Chris's friends, feeling a strong sense of our extended family created many years previous. Emotions from the days at search headquarters came flooding back; we needed each other now as we did then. On days like this, we sorely missed Sara's presence. Her statement expressed the closeness she shared with her brother, even now: "Mom, Chris is proud of us today."

Supporting each other. Clockwise from top left: Adam Gamradt, Coach Lars, Bethany Keepman, Jared Keepman, Jan Jenkins, Christian Bailey.

Some of Chris's friends and Steve spoke with the media from our driveway. "I never doubted for a moment Chris was murdered, too many things didn't add up," voiced Luke Fisher. Other comments included: "Bittersweet. It doesn't bring Jenks back." A day of mixed emotions, a deep sense of loss, and hope for the truth to finally be told, typified

Luke and Chris loving life.

our discussions. Being surrounded by people Chris loved made the day bearable.

KSTP, the Twin Cities ABC affiliate, put untold hours into helping bring awareness to Chris's case. We had worked extensively with their investigative team, who demonstrated the utmost integrity and respect to the case and to us. So we allowed KSTP's reporter Kristi Piehl and cameraman, into our home. "We've been fighting four long years for the truth, now we want the rest of the story," declared Steve. Looking to the heavens, I spoke directly to our son in a shaky, yet fervent voice, "Chris, today it's your voice being heard. Finally, today, your voice is heard."

A Public Apology—Manning Up

Over the weekend we left a message for Lieutenant Edwards, letting him know we planned to attend the press conference with some of Chris's friends. Sure enough, on Monday, several of Chris's friends,

and my faithful friend Sally Leivermann, attended the press conference. They stood behind us as Steve and I sat at a long rectangular table
covered with microphones. In front of us, we saw a sea of reporters and
cameras. Understandably, the media eagerly awaited additional information promised by MPD spokesperson Lieutenant Greg Reinhardt.

"We made an assumption that caused pain for the Jenkins family.
I want to apologize for that." As Chief Dolan uttered those words, I
remember thinking, *You did nothing wrong, you personally tried to right the
wrong.* We accepted his apology. Displaying leadership, Chief Dolan had
just sent a clear message to his department and to the public, "Sometimes
we make mistakes, we apologize."

Dolan, Edwards, and Jackson spoke briefly. Jackson gave a few details including, "Chris was thrown over a bridge." Hearing that statement for the first time, especially in front of media, delivered a gut
punch to Steve and me. All indications showed that Chris did not come
off a bridge; yet, hearing these words caused us to ask ourselves, "Is it
remotely possible?" Right then, it didn't matter. We felt the horror any
parents would feel when picturing that image of their child in his last
minutes of life.

Just breathe, Jan, I told myself. We knew we had to hold it together.
Once the meeting opened up for questions, reporters addressed Sergeant
Jackson. He replied guardedly that Chris's case was an open investigation. Steve and I answered a few questions directed to us. One stands
out in my mind, "Did you ever want to give up?" "Sure," I responded,
"but one look at Chris's eyes in a photo or hearing the agony in Sara's
voice, I was back on track. A few times, I lined up several large photos
of Chris on the mantel. Seeing the laughter, energy, and love in his eyes
brought stinging tears, yet I reconnected with my love and commitment
to him. That's all it took."

Sergeant Jackson confirmed that one suspect/witness was incarcerated and another was at large. He made it very clear that he would not
acknowledge the whereabouts of the incarcerated individual to maintain
the integrity of the case. After the meeting wrapped up, a few reporters
and journalists stayed to ask questions, though the majority left rather
quickly, scrambling to get the release on the evening news. Judging by
the media reports over the next few days, most of us believed a push to
find the killer(s) would ensue.

Jackson waited patiently for Steve and me to finish answering questions, since the three of us had previously agreed to discuss key points. I saw a couple of Chris's friends walk up to Jackson and shake his hand. Knowing their anger, grief, and frustration over the years, I thought, *Wow, what classy young adults. They get it—it's moving forward that counts.*

In our conversation following the press conference, we asked Jackson about results of testing. He gave us no further information, so we specifically asked about fingernails. We explained our understanding that the FBI picked the BCA in St. Paul to house one of its four federally funded labs, giving local law enforcement improved access to mitochondrial DNA testing. In Chris's situation, testing for mitochondrial DNA might prove invaluable since it can be recovered from hair, teeth, or extensively decomposed human remains. Nuclear DNA is plentiful yet limited in the information it can provide. Much less mitochondrial DNA is available, but the results are conclusive, and it has even been recovered from remains hundreds of years old. "What if DNA other than Chris's could be identified under his fingernails?" we asked. "That's an intriguing idea," Jackson mused. "I'll have to think about that."

Since Sergeant Jackson planned to retire by the end of 2006, he suggested we meet his partner, who would take over the case. He also wanted to take us to the river to give us the whole story. As tough as that sounded, at least some of our nightmares of differing scenarios might end. We thanked him several times, asking him to keep in touch regarding the person(s) at large and scheduling a time to meet the new investigator.

Information Leaks Out

A few days after the press conference, we joined Sara, Jamie, and Cayman in Cincinnati for Thanksgiving. That year gratitude overflowed as we celebrated the holiday. After Steve returned to Minneapolis, I stayed a couple of days longer to enjoy our precious granddaughter.

Once again, our joy was short-lived. Steve called us in Cincinnati to warn us that a news station had just aired information on Chris's case, including mug shots of one of the suspects/witnesses and a conversation with the felon's sister. The station also gave the location of the suspect. Sergeant Jackson had made it plain to the press that he did not want that information released. I prayed my mom and dad would not see the news report.

After speaking with several individuals at the station, Steve learned they did not have 100 percent approval from the MPD to report the facts released. Irate, he spoke with the news director, who argued and said, "This is the hottest story in Minnesota and Wisconsin in the past fifty years; we'll air whatever we want." I wondered if the news director had ever thought about the trauma unnecessarily inflicted on victims' families by the media. Mostly, I wondered if he had ever lost a child to murder.

Late that night Sara and I picked up the report online. We watched with numbing horror, rage, and disbelief. I literally felt like I was coming out of my skin. I grabbed my coat and ran outside to get fresh air. Once outside, I needed to walk off the searing pain. For an hour, maybe two, I walked around Sara's unfamiliar neighborhood. Overcome with grief, I finally just sat on the curb, wanting to evaporate. No such luck; instead, I noticed a gutter beneath my feet. Leaning over, I threw up until my ribs hurt. Sobbing and shaking, I stumbled back to Sara's house. Seeing a man putting up Christmas lights, I cried louder, no longer caring who saw me or what I looked like. He didn't look up or ask if I was OK. The world seemed cold, callous, and eminently evil.

CHAPTER 22

Destined to Shine a Light

December 2006–March 2007

*When you love someone with all your heart, their death claims
the sacred part of you tightly connected to them.*

JAN JENKINS

The buzz around the water coolers in Minneapolis, especially in legal offices, became "someone will be charged within days." That was not really true, however. Officials at the MPD had promised a meeting to introduce us to Sergeant Nancy Dunlap, the new lead investigator on Chris's case, set expectations, and discuss evidentiary testing. Frustrated by the lack of follow-up, I wrote a letter to Chief Dolan early in December 2006 and sent it by courier. A few days later I received a phone call from Deputy Chief Wurster assuring me "everything will be done right" regarding evidentiary tests, and Steve and I would have the opportunity to meet with appropriate homicide officials after the holidays; Wurster agreed to send an e-mail to document our agreement. But, no e-mail, no meeting, and no communication followed.

Late that month, Steve spoke with Homicide Lieutenant Hayhoe, who asked for a couple of weeks to get up to speed on the case, and then he'd phone us to set up a meeting to discuss the status of the case. Still waiting, one month later, Steve spoke with Homicide Captain Andy Smith, who told Steve either he or Hayhoe would contact him the following morning. Hayhoe did phone Steve to tell him the case remained in the hands of the Hennepin County Attorney's Office. Steve went nuclear when Hayhoe told him we could not discuss the evidentiary testing because the chain of custody had been broken, and we still had possession of Chris's clothing, shoes, and other items. No, Steve said; he had given everything back to Lieutenant Edwards in June 2006, seven months earlier.

By February 2007, three months after a public apology to our family and a change to homicide in Chris's case, our trust in the Minneapolis Police Department was back to square one. Sergeant Nancy Dunlap never once contacted us, and no meeting occurred between the MPD and the Jenkinses during the first half of 2007. In our opinion, the lack of communication and broken commitments were unconscionable.

Late in February I spoke with Amy Sweasy, prosecuting attorney on Chris's case. Sweasy told me she had already thoroughly reviewed the case and wanted to go over it at least one more time before making any decisions. I assured her that although the wait was extremely difficult, more than anything we wanted fairness and results. She gave me no time frame for completion, and I thanked her for working on Chris's behalf.

The Chris Jenkins Invitational and Andy Boyles Memorial Lacrosse Clinic

Much preferring to honor Chris's remarkable life than dig into the facts surrounding his death, we wholeheartedly supported Coach Larson and the UMN Men's Lacrosse team in hosting the Chris Jenkins Invitational and Andy Boyles Memorial Lacrosse Clinic at the end of February 2007. Three nationally ranked men's lacrosse teams would join the UMN Gophers in a round-robin tournament: the California Polytechnic State University Mustangs, the Lindenwood University Lions, and the UMN Duluth Bulldogs. The clinic, sponsored by North Star Lacrosse, was held between Saturday's invitational games. Open to boys in grades 9–12, former notable college players, as well as coaches and players in the CJ Invitational, staffed the clinic.

Remembering that Chris had served years earlier as a lacrosse coach at the Andy Boyles Memorial Clinic, I acknowledged the mysterious twists and turns in life. Andy was the manager of the Roseville Area High School Lacrosse team who died of muscular dystrophy in August 2000. Andy's family initiated the idea for a clinic to honor his love for the game, and build visibility and skill level of high school lacrosse players in the Twin Cities metro area. Now, the lacrosse community honored Chris as well: an All-American goalie and three-time captain of the UMN Gopher Men's Lacrosse team.

Cayman Rose, our adorable granddaughter, came to Minnesota with her mom and dad, Sara and Jamie, to honor Chris. Sara surprised us by dressing Cayman in a Minnesota Gopher T-shirt with matching skirt. Purchasing online the only size 2 shirt she could find anywhere, Sara stared in disbelief after opening the package. The back of the shirt showed the number 3—her brother Chris's number, retired from the UMN Men's Lacrosse team. What are the chances of such extraordinary synchronicity?

Grandma Rose made the matching skirt for her great-granddaughter, Cayman. Adorned in a navy blue bandana, her Uncle Chris's signature headgear, and her Gopher shirt and skirt, Cayman enjoyed the entire weekend of lacrosse. She delighted in running around the sidelines, playing with a lacrosse stick, trying dozens of times to get on the field to join a game. Only walking for three months, her little white baby shoes gave away her young age. One of Chris's lacrosse teammates said to me, "If I didn't know differently, I'd think Jenks jumped into her body." Hmm, I was thinking the same thing. Chris's spirit clearly comes alive through Cayman.

"Boys, you're blocking my view."

Stick at the ready. "C'mon, Coach, let me play!"

After the last game of the invitational, Steve, Cayman, Chad Lunaas, and I went to the river to throw roses where Chris's body was found. After serving four years in the Marines, Chad was home, attending the University of Minnesota and playing lacrosse for the Gopher Men's team. I remember when he was a sniper on top of the American Embassy in Afghanistan and I felt a gnawing sense of danger. Yet Chad was alive and well; he stood next to us on the Third Avenue Bridge, above the spot where Chris's body lay frozen. In a cruel twist of fate, it was Chris who would never see his twenty-second birthday, meeting death at the hands of others, in the city he knew and loved. Life has a way of grabbing our attention. What matters is what we do about what we've learned, and who we become because of it.

Cayman threw the first rose, the white rose, for her uncle Chris. Chad, Steve, and I each threw a red rose; then we watched them float on the water before going over the dam. What struck me, perhaps the most, every year we've thrown roses, was the finality of our earthly life with Chris. It felt harsh; I began to understand it always would.

"Chris, we will never forget."

The Lighthouse

A few weeks later, we returned to Grand Cayman, where Chris said our family would spend vacations every year. On March 4, 2007, exactly four years after we held a memorial service for our son, Steve and I ate dinner at a great restaurant on Grand Cayman, the Lighthouse. One table sat on the deck over the water. The remainder of the deck was destroyed during Ivan, a Category 5 hurricane that unleashed its fury on the tiny island in September 2004. When the waiter led us to this secluded table with a full view of the ocean and the heavens, our mouths dropped open in disbelief. The waiter told us that most nights it was too windy to seat guests at this table, but we could try it.

Delighted with our good fortune, we sat down, thanking the waiter. High waves crashed ashore, yet no wind bothered our table, go figure. We decided to go to the restaurant in time to see the sunset, but clouds filled the sky, as they had all day. It did not matter—the setting was truly magical. Sitting over the ocean lifted our spirits on that difficult day.

Deciding to throw out a challenge, Steve remarked, "Chris, if you're here with us, let us see a sunset." Yeah, right. Well, a few minutes later as I'm studying the menu, I looked up and saw a huge orange ball—the sun setting in a sky of only clouds. I thought I must be hallucinating. I pointed to the sky, telling Steve to turn around. Speechless, we teared up, knowing beyond the shadow of a doubt that we were witnessing a miracle.

Scarcely recovering from our emotional encounter with the divine, Steve pointed to the sky behind me. Turning, I noticed an ascending full moon had peeked through the clouds. Now, tears were freely falling. "Chris, you are really here with us. Your spirit is bursting with energy, light, and love, just as you did for almost twenty-two years on earth." We sat over the water with a setting sun on one side of us and an ascending full moon on the other. Held in wonder between two marvels of the heavens, we knew our journey must continue. We understood a power far greater than us would not let us rest. As Chris told me three years earlier on our deck in Wisconsin, "Mom, God really exists. You have to tell them, God really exists." We never asked for this path—what parent would choose it? It is the path we've been given. Chris was destined to touch thousands of lives, as we are destined to shine a light on a web of evil extending far beyond Chris.

An old, somewhat rusted lighthouse, a candleholder, sat on our table. Of course, we asked the waiter if we could buy it. He asked the owner, who responded no. So we explained the reason, our son's story, and this time when he spoke with the owner the answer changed to yes. The lighthouse sits on a shelf in our family room with a few other precious treasures reminding us of Chris, and the special place he will always hold in our hearts. Death may end a life. Death cannot destroy a relationship built on goodness, truth, and love. Goodness trumps evil, for in the end, goodness will prevail.

"Chris, you are really here with us."

CHAPTER 23

More Than We Can Bear

April–June 2007

The greatest glory in living lies not in never falling,
but in rising every time we fall.

NELSON MANDELA

Chris's high school coaches remember his drive and intelligence on the football field. "He was one of our kids. He was a tough kid," remarked Hennen, assistant head coach at Eden Prairie High School, and Chris's offensive line coach. "He was such a smart kid, and that's our number one thing. That's what made his disappearance so strange." Eden Prairie head football coach, Mike Grant, told Steve and me, "Chris was very small for an offensive tackle, but he stuck his nose in there and got the job done. He was a strong football player and a good athlete, which transferred well into lacrosse."

Intelligence, physical and mental toughness: we watched Chris display those traits his entire life in numerous situations. In his biggest battle, fighting for his life, we are quite certain he never gave in.

Chris Fought for His Life

We heard it again, this time from retired Detective Gannon, "Chris fought desperately for his life." Gannon and Duarte continued their quest to discover why dozens of healthy college-aged men were found dead in the chilly waters of winter, mostly in northern states from Minnesota to New York. Believing Chris's death might hold a key to unlock part of the mystery, they dug into his case.

A phone call from Gannon one spring night sent waves of nausea through our weary bodies. He told us he and Duarte discussed how to handle the information they had, both believing no parent should have to wonder how their child died. Deciding we had suffered enough from ridiculous responses, lack of respect, and broken promises, they decided to tell us what they heard through interviews with local law enforcement (not the Minneapolis police), and a suspect/witness to Chris's murder. Without telling us every heinous detail, we heard enough to know Chris met an ugly, painful, drawn-out death. Some of the facts corroborated with known information that was never in the news, yet dovetailed with what Sergeant Jackson told us.

Steve lost it about five minutes into the conversation. He ran into the bathroom and didn't return till after I hung up. Holding the phone in my trembling hand, I asked a few questions, staying on the phone long enough to understand. Somehow my logical brain still functioned. Then instinct kicked in, warning me that much of what he said likely occurred, for various reasons. I thanked Gannon and hung up.

Sliding down from my chair, I pounded the floor while screaming at God, asking why he allowed this to happen to an innocent, compassionate, and kind human being, our son Chris. I raged at killers who find humor in taking the lives of others in a torturous way. As we would discover more and more, hell must be the goal of these cowards. Satan worshippers, they boldly display their satanic ideations online.

When I stopped pounding the floor, I stood up and pounded the kitchen cupboards. I remember crying so hard, it felt like I broke a rib. Both Steve and I wanted to come out of our skin. I sobbed till the rage subsided and agonizing grief took its place. Steve walked around the kitchen holding his head. We waited an hour or so before calling Sara. Although we spared her as much as possible, we knew not to keep critical information from her.

During that conversation Sara and I sobbed more than we spoke. I felt her heart breaking, and mine shattered even more. Throughout that sleepless night, Steve and I wondered what kind of people stoop to a level of brutality no other species in the animal kingdom would exhibit. Animals kill for food, and they behave largely on instinct. Humans have the opportunity to choose their behavior. If people who commit these atrocious acts have no respect for human life, would they sit laughing as they watched someone murder their son, brother, father, friend?

We phoned Sara the following morning to check on her well-being. Her story of how she handled the hellish news was phenomenal. After hearing what likely happened at the scene of her brother's death, she decided to take a bath, vowing not to get out of the tub until she could make sense of the horror. Eventually, Sara arrived at two poignant realizations: (1) If Chris knew he would save dozens, maybe hundreds of lives by losing his own, he would have submitted to God's will; and (2) as hard as he fought for his life, now we must fight for ours. Now, almost five years after Chris disappeared, we must figure out how to live without him, a foregone luxury for a family who chose to actively pursue truth and justice for a murdered family member. To honor ourselves, and the remarkable life Chris led, we needed to create a life worth living.

Needing Spiritual Guidance to Cope

Steve and I could no longer suck it up. We couldn't eat, sleep, or concentrate on anything. Father Tim Power, who presided over Chris's First Communion and his memorial service, agreed to meet us at Pax Christi Church. Although Father Tim exudes calm and peacefulness, the news we shared clearly made an impact. Scarcely able to speak between sobs, I emptied the box of tissues sitting next to me. Steve looked like he was in shock. Father Tim assured us God never left Chris's side. Unable to answer the tough questions we asked (which he had probably heard before), he smiled, saying he too planned to ask God many questions when they met. The three of us agreed the irony was that once we got to heaven, none of this would matter anyway.

The following day Steve met with another spiritual leader, Pastor Rod Anderson. Pastor Rod knew Chris from Youth Ministry, and he served as a leader at Chris's memorial service. Steve told me Pastor Rod was truly shaken. He had counseled some of Chris's friends, and he understood the depth of loss of so many people close to Chris. Pastor Rod was also a father and grandfather. For him, as for us, the satanic element put the whole situation far over the edge.

CHAPTER 24

Murderapolis: No Charges, a Bridge Collapses

July–August 2007

A people that values its privileges above its principles soon loses both.
DWIGHT EISENHOWER

This demanding marathon of peaks and valleys had no training schedule, no warm-ups, not even a game plan. Now in limbo, we waited with no understanding of why a case changed to homicide seemed to have ground to a halt. We thought a homicide announcement indicated the start of the serious pursuit of a killer or killers. During the eight-month wait for a meeting with the Hennepin County Attorney's Office to hear whether anyone would be held accountable for murdering our son, another young man's body showed up in the Mississippi River in the Minneapolis area.

In early spring 2007, twenty-two-year-old Joshua Kaneakua disappeared after leaving Gabby's Saloon in Minneapolis. Less than two weeks later, his body was discovered floating in the Mississippi River. Watching the evening news, Steve and I listened to Lieutenant Storms from the Hennepin County Sheriff's Office state that Kaneakua was found with no clothing, which is typical of bodies found in the river. His statement did not ring true for us. Storms had already told several of us that finding Chris fully clothed (shirt tucked in drawstring pants, shoes on) was not the least bit unusual; indeed, it was typical of bodies found in the river. So, which way was it? It couldn't be both.

Justice for Whom?

We finally received a call from the Hennepin County Attorney's Office, late in May, informing us that the review of Chris's case was completed.

Since many MPD officials planned to attend the meeting, including the captain of homicide and Chief Dolan, as well as Dr. Baker, now head of the Hennepin County Medical Examiner's Office, coordinating schedules proved challenging. We settled on July 31, 2007.

While prioritizing our key questions and concerns, Steve and I realized we needed an objective person in that meeting. We weren't attorneys or investigators; we played a far more important role in Chris's life. We loved him and raised him to be a contributing member of society. Murderers stole his life and robbed us of innocence. An objective person we trusted could help us interpret the unimaginable—parents listening to an attorney's explanation of what most likely happened in the last moments of their son's life. FBI Special Agent in Charge (SAC) Don Thompson agreed to come to Minneapolis. After attending two meetings at the Hennepin County Medical Examiner's Office, at which attorneys were present to represent the city and the county, Steve and I decided to hire an attorney to represent us in the meeting.

July 31 marked another day we will never forget. The meeting lasted no more than one hour. Assistant County Attorney Amy Sweasy described the process she used in making a decision, and gave us the most likely scenario of what happened to Chris. He was the victim of a botched robbery and was then thrown over a bridge—the Iron Bridge was mentioned. More than one person participated in the heinous crime. Steve raised questions, since the person(s) of interest did not match the same description we had previously heard from Sergeant Jackson.

As troublesome, if not more so, was the fact that MPD Lieutenant Edwards and Lieutenant Storms of the Sheriff's Office both agreed that coming off the Iron Bridge, or anywhere east or south of Nicollet Island, did not make sense in terms of where Chris's body ended up. Hardly able to contain my frustration, I stood up and asked, "Has anyone in this room looked at one recovery photo of Chris Jenkins?" Silence. I waited, looking into the eyes of everyone in that room. Silence. The recovery scene held answers—many clues were visible in the photos. At that moment, I knew I was finished. We had done everything humanly possible to right the wrong committed against our son on November 1, 2002. I had no control over illogical conclusions based on partial facts, no power to hunt down or arrest person(s) at large, and no desire to spend time and energy uselessly. It didn't matter what or who we brought to

"The last time I hugged my mom. Less than one week later, I was murdered."

the table, we could not make a difference for Chris. I was done. I knew no charges would be filed, and we would need to accept the situation, all of it.

More Gut Punches

Steve asked about the hair in Chris's hand. Sweasy said it was indeed Chris's hair. When FBI SAC Thompson viewed the photo many months earlier, he told us it looked like scalp hair. Angered, Steve took an enlarged picture of the hair in Chris's palm out of his briefcase and slammed it on the table. "Whose hair is this? Don't tell me it's Chris's, his hair was much shorter than that!" As it turned out, we were wrong on that point.

Late in 2007, Thompson had the opportunity to speak with the scientists at the BCA lab to understand specifically the type of testing done. Mitochondrial testing had been done, and it is conclusive. Chris was clutching his own hair. Actually, months earlier, Loesch and Gannon both believed that was a distinct possibility. In the fight to save his own life, Chris probably struggled to remove hands from around his neck, grabbing his own hair in the process. The hair remained in his left hand, tightly clenched from the cadaveric spasm that must have occurred when he took his last breath.

About thirty minutes into the meeting, Sweasy's boss, Principal Managing Attorney Paul Scoggin, remarked impatiently, "It has already been five years; it's time to get the show on the road." That remark hit me hard. It seemed so callous. Trying to focus rather than let my stinging tears emerge, I wrote his words in my notes. Steve and I had come to hear about the last hours of Chris's life, and to understand whether charges would be brought against those who murdered the son we adored. Yes, five years had passed. In those five years, how many hours did Hennepin County spend investigating Chris's murder or running down his killers? Reeling in pain from Scoggin's impatient and heartless comment, I couldn't respond. Somewhere deep inside I knew it wasn't worth the effort.

Our team of four asked to be excused for a five-minute break. No one responded, so we left the room. When we returned, everyone was looking at the huge posters of the Mississippi River we had brought to help explain the work performed by RIPTIDE. Looking uncomfortable, they quickly returned to their chairs and sat down. We did not comprehend why we were perceived as the enemy. We gladly shared all the data and resources we had gathered. In fact, for five years, we made that information available to anyone in law enforcement who cared to look at it.

The decision regarding Chris's case did not surprise us: no charges would be filed. Committing a crime is much easier than being charged for it; criminals are well aware of that fact.

Two outstanding questions remained. One pertained to forensic testing that Thompson agreed to review; the other involved a description of the person(s) of interest, which Steve and the MPD agreed to clarify at a later date since Sergeant Dunlap, the lead investigator, was not available for the review of Chris's case that day.

We thanked everyone in the room for their efforts. As we prepared to leave, Commander Mike Martin walked up to us to express his sympathy. Shaking our hands, he stated sincerely, "I can't imagine . . ." *You're right, you can't,* I thought. By his kind and well-meaning gesture, Martin clearly referred to losing a child to murder. Yes, that is the ultimate loss. Yet what we'd had to do over the past five years to right the wrongs, all the wrongs, I doubted anyone could ever fathom.

The Muzzle Comes Off

In the summer of 2006, shortly after Steve e-mailed the photo of the hair in Chris's hand to key officials, Lieutenant Edwards contacted us. When we met with him a few weeks later, he told us to keep our mouths shut regarding Chris's case because we were ruining it. We shut up. In November 2006 Edwards asked us to attend the press conference announcing the reclassification to homicide to show the public a unified front. We attended and thanked the MPD for their efforts. In December, Sergeant Jackson told us to keep our mouths shut regarding information we knew about the case. We did not discuss Chris's case with anyone.

Nonetheless, a few weeks after the press conference in November 2006, the trust we had worked so hard to establish with the MPD fizzled due to lack of promised follow-up from several department officials.

We understood that personnel changes take time and energy. Yet, how much time does it take to send a two-sentence e-mail or make a brief phone call of introduction? Yes, if we met to set expectations, that would have taken a bit longer; yet the benefits could have been significant.

After leaving the Hennepin County Attorney's Office, Steve and I spoke briefly with Thompson and our attorney; then we went straight to the KSTP studio. It was time to remove the muzzle; the handwriting had been on the wall for years and we knew it. Our efforts could not make a difference for Chris, so at KSTP we told our story. Following that news coverage, we learned (not through the MPD) that at least one person of interest left Minneapolis.

The 35W Bridge Collapses

Who could forget August 1, 2007? The 35W bridge spanning the Mississippi River in Minneapolis collapsed, causing injury and death. Retired detectives Gannon and Duarte happened to be in Minneapolis at the time, eating a meal, when suddenly the lights and glasses on tables in the restaurant began to shake; the bridge was falling. They ran all the way to the bridge, offering to help in any way they could. Gannon even volunteered to dive, since he had the necessary training.

A few hours earlier, Steve had driven across that very bridge on his way to a client appointment. Now, standing in our family room watching the news, our mouths dropped open in disbelief. How eerie; many of the officials we had met with the day before stood at the river talking to the media. That catastrophe was an accident. Chris's death was purposeful, cruel, and cowardly. Steve and I watched the news in silence for several minutes. We both knew another bridge had collapsed—the bridge of trust, understanding, and hope we had tried for five years to build with the agencies in Hennepin County.

Sara Responds with Action

Completely distraught at the exchange of information and outcome of our meeting at the Hennepin County Attorney's Office, Sara sent an e-mail to more than sixty Minnesota politicians, at both the state and federal level. Asking for assistance, she summarized five years of effort on our part, including the resistance we so often encountered from Hennepin County. Noting Chris's contribution to the university, the community, and to the hundreds of lives he touched, she wrote, "Chris represented what is good and right in the world."

Sara received two or three responses expressing sympathy. One representative wrote of her intention to follow up with Chief Dolan. With regard to Sara's plea for help, we are unaware of any actions taken or results achieved from her having contacted more than five dozen politicians from the state of Minnesota, the state Chris lived in and loved. (The e-mail Sara sent is posted on www.FootprintsOfCourage.com.)

Not for a minute do we regret the path we chose, the only honorable path we saw. To this day, we wonder why we had to fight so hard for someone to do the right thing—the right thing, eminently clear from the beginning.

Part IV

Living with Hope

A Cowboy's Tribute to Chris Jenkins
03/03/03

Dear Parents, Family and Friends,

You knew him a lifetime.
Us Arizona folks? . . . a few days.
You treasured his everything.
Us Arizona Cowboys? . . . all of his ways.

Out here there's no stew'n.
No frett'n. No fuss'n.
The first time we met him,
A real mighty fine young cowboy.

His smile, his eyes,
His laughter, his cheer.
He noticed life's flowers.
And yes, we tipped a beer.

Those that he touched,
And it may'a been just once.
Knew he'd be there,
If ya got in a crunch.

So simple. So easy.
Really not all that complex.
A masterful mind.
A book with real text.

An outsider? No way!
But, a man with true grit.
Wherever he traveled,
He was "the" perfect fit.

Yes, he is missed.
And we all hurt a lot.
But, take this to the bank.
It's better than stock.

The Good Lord, He roped him.
We don't understand this.
But, his spirit . . . it rides.
We've all been touched by Chris!

JEK

Giddy Up, Cowboy Chris!
We miss you, Ride on!

Love,
Jimmy Coyote Kraus
"The Arizona Cowboy"

CHAPTER 25

Chris's Happy Place

September–October 2007

*Be glad of life because it gives you the chance to love and
to work and to play and to look up at the stars.*

HENRY VAN DYKE

We discovered the Van Dyke quotation amongst pages of Chris's hand-written notes in his desk. His character came alive through the engaging ideas he chose to write down—how he loved life and the chance to gaze at the stars! Now, when we look at the stars, we look for Chris's twinkling eyes and his easy laughter. In fact, the following star was named Chris Jenkins: Aquarius RA 22h 0m 51s D-5'48". It was registered in the International Star Registry on February 17, 2003, the day Chris would have turned twenty-two years old. A dear family friend, Deborah Wingert, purchased the star and framed the certificate, which is surrounded by signatures of Chris's friends. I gave Deb some maternity clothes I wore when I was pregnant with Chris. Some bonds are forever!

Based on his writings, this young man, our son, was clearly ready to contribute to the world in a significant way. A twenty-one-year-old engaged in clarifying his views on life, love, and business—what a cruel loss for us to bear. He did the work and so did we; yet we will never experience the fruits of our labor by sharing the joy of his adult life. We miss him so much; we still want him back. Longing for Chris and the joy he brought to our lives, Steve, Sara, and I undergo the heavy weight of learning to accept the utter finality of Chris's life on earth as a member of our family.

Chris Loving Life and Giving Back

At eight years old, Chris had mastered riding his new bike with no hands, including riding down the huge hill on Oxbow Drive, right in front of our home. One day I sat at the bottom of the driveway hugging my knees, watching him race down that hill with arms held up to the sky, dancing eyes, and a huge grin. "I'm so happy I'm Christopher Jenkins!" he yelled, to no one in particular. Those words brought immediate tears of gratitude to my eyes. One of my greatest hopes for our children stemmed from my belief that confidence and self-esteem provide a strong springboard for leading a fulfilling and meaningful life. Without his realizing it, Chris had just shown me he was well on his way.

That bike leans against the wall in our garage now. When Steve and I look at it, we see a young Chris sitting on the seat, ready to embark on his next adventure. We see an energetic, blond, blue-eyed boy with a bright future for himself and others. We taught Sara and Chris to look out for each other and to take care of others in need. Starting when they were quite young, we encouraged them to be generous with their time, talent, and belongings, often reminding them how fortunate they were. We explained that our family of four did not have to go hungry, walk without shoes, or endure a cold winter without warm hats and gloves. As young children, perhaps they did not completely understand. As they grew older, sometimes they laughed at us, as children love to do when testing their parents. Yet, based on the feedback we've received since Chris disappeared, the message got through: Sara and Chris offered compassion and help, especially to those who needed it most.

Steve and I believe that from those who have been given much, much is expected. Life was not handed to us on a silver platter; we've both worked hard since our early teens to purchase the "extras" our parents could not afford. How well I remember carefully saving babysitting money to buy my first pair of contact lenses. In 1968, it took months of babysitting to earn two hundred dollars. Steve and I also paid our way through college. Yet we enjoyed many blessings, and clearly understood that our gifts of health, intelligence, and loving families gave us a great start in life. We have done our best to give back. Small wonder the enormous responsibility we both felt in righting the wrong committed against Chris, our family, and dozens of other young men and their families.

Seeking Justice

Retired detectives Gannon and Duarte also felt responsibility to seek justice and stop the string of senseless murders over the past decade. In October 2007, Gannon and his team met with FBI agents in Minneapolis. They shared data and asked for federal involvement in the possible serial murders of more than forty young men between the ages of seventeen and twenty-seven, from across the United States, beginning in 1996 and continuing today. We were not privy to most of the information exchanged in that meeting, but we do know the FBI requested more data from Gannon's team. We hoped the unexplained deaths of dozens of high-achieving young men, future leaders of this country, would be seriously investigated. Although we understand the FBI works quietly, we remain unaware of any further interest or involvement in these cases on their part.

"CJ#3—We Will Never Forget"

Early October 2007 also marked our third annual participation in the Twin Cities 5K event. The UMN Men's Lacrosse team, friends, family, and strangers—totaling about 250 people—walked or ran in this inspiring tribute to Chris. Since Steve and I meet participants every year on the steps of the Capitol in St. Paul to hand out T-shirts ("CJ#3, We Will Never Forget") and bandanas, we arrived early. A huge rainbow greeted us that year. Along with several others, we believed that, somehow, Chris painted this splash of colors in the sky to remind us he will always be with us.

As we ran, or walked, whichever the case may be, any time we saw someone with one of Chris's T-shirts, we high-fived and yelled, "CJ3!" More than once, strangers walked up to us with encouragement. Several asked for an update on the case. The easy answer was, "There are no updates. You know as much as we do regarding the MPD's activity on Chris's case."

At eighty years old, Grandpa Gene made a statement by walking the entire 5K in his favorite moccasins. If Chris's Native American costume had anything to do with his demise, his grandfather would not react to the hate crime by compromising his own deep respect for

The number of participants multiplies.

American Indians. We are so proud of my dad's integrity and courage. After completing the 5K, Steve and I ran back to join Grandpa Gene on the remainder of his walk. He may have been the last person to finish, but he made it!

Unable to walk long distances due to pulmonary fibrosis, Grandma Rose wisely chose to stand near the end of the course, cheering all of us wearing CJ#3 T-shirts. We asked her to join Gene, Steve, and me in crossing the finish line so that Jeff Twidwell, my brother-in-law, could capture an awesome photo. Chris must be so proud of his grandparents for never once wavering in their belief in him, or the support they offered.

Coach Larson surprised us at the 5K by bringing Chris's goalie stick, which we had given the UMN Men's Lacrosse team at a team dinner held after Chris disappeared. Shortly after Steve and I left that team dinner, Lars had asked the players to each write a note to Chris. The shaft of the goalie stick, now a time capsule stuffed with those crumpled messages, awaits the right occasion to unveil the heartfelt words of teammates and celebrate Chris's life. Though the notes writ-

"The oldest runner just crossed the finish line," blared the announcer.

ten all those years ago were intended for Chris, they will be read by survivors, mostly teammates. As survivors, we continue to learn how to carry on Chris's well-lived life.

Chris's Happy Place—A Return Visit

If Chris took you to Grandpa Gene and Grandma Rose's farm, you were indeed a special friend. My parents' farm was Chris's "Happy Place" for twenty-one years.

The weekend following the Twin Cities 5K in October 2007, the UMN Men's Lacrosse team held its second team-building event at Chris's grandparents' place—the Sweet farm. The last time Chris visited the farm was in October 2002 with his teammates. I remember Chris calling me to ask for team-building games. After I shared a few ideas with him, he said they sounded dorky, yet I later learned he used some of the activities and they turned out to be smashing successes. The team played many hours of lacrosse, built a large bonfire around which they got to know each other better, then spent the night in tents.

Christian Bailey, co-captain with Chris in 2002, now held the position of head coach of the UMN Men's Gopher Lacrosse team. Since few players in the fall of 2007 had ever met Chris, Christian took time to explain the importance of the farm in Chris's life. "I knew how much this place meant to Chris," Christian stated in his interview with Todd Moen of the *Carver County News*. "I've been looking forward to this weekend. It feels really good to be out here and it's neat to see guys running around this field again after five years. It's the perfect spot for our weekend," said Christian.

Grandma Rose told Todd Moen, "We haven't had the courage to host it again until this year. Yet, it just warms the heart to see the team out here again. They're such a good group of guys."

Video footage of the team leaving the following morning has been played on local and national media numerous times. It's the last video of our son alive. Grandma Rose recalls her grandson's good-bye—the last time my parents would ever see Chris. He hugged her as he always did and said, "Well, I love you, Grandma!" Four days later, on Halloween night, Chris disappeared in front of the Lone Tree Bar in downtown Minneapolis, never to be seen again by those who loved him.

Second Gopher men's lacrosse retreat at Chris's Happy Place.

Your Son Brought Out the Best in Me

The following e-mail sent by Ben Uzlik sums up the strong connection and admiration of many of Chris's friends and lacrosse teammates:

I met Chris my junior year of high school on a lacrosse trip I made with the Eden Prairie team . . . I spoke with Chris during the Hotdish Classic (lacrosse tournament in Blaine) just a week before he disappeared. We brought each other up to date on our lives: school, lacrosse, etc. I had not seen him since the summer and wanted to thank him for helping my youth team. That was the last time I saw him . . . Chris forced me to do my best. He would always say something like, "C'mon Oz, you can beat that guy—just don't think about it!" He was always there with a smile when I messed up too. "Man, you got smoked, buddy!" Because of my connection with Chris through the sport of lacrosse, every time I play, I think of him. I look at the net and picture him in the crease, stick at the ready. His button and stickers are on my desk, reminding me how precious life is, and how much a smile can change a person's life. Thanks for raising such a great young man. I was never his best friend, and usually an opponent, but he had a very positive influence on the way I look at life. Chris was one of the funniest, nicest, and sincere individuals I have ever known. We all miss him.

CHAPTER 26

The River: Ending a Family's Dreams

November 2007

We can't change what happened.
All we can do is love each other more.

STEVE JENKINS

"Wearing that redskin costume, you don't deserve to be in white skin. We're gonna skin you alive, white man, you'll be in so much pain. You're gonna die tonight." These piercing words were confessed to detectives (not from the MPD), by one of the suspects/witnesses in Chris's murder. Imagine hearing those merciless, hateful words regarding the last hours of your beloved son's life.

We've received e-mails and read comments on blogs attacking our statements to the press pertaining to Chris's likely abduction and torturous ride in the back of a van, and his eventual murder. The common remark is, "How can you possibly believe Chris was tortured when no marks were found on his body?"

First, psychological torture is another brutal way to terrorize someone, especially if you threaten the person with pain and death. Second, even physical torture does not have to leave noticeable marks, particularly if a person is placed in water and not discovered for several months. You can drown someone, rather quickly, or you can make their death a living hell by dragging out their agony. What action would cold-blooded killers (still laughing about murdering Chris and getting away with it) most likely take? We know what has been stated. The only people who know for sure what happened are Chris, God, and those who committed or witnessed the crime.

When criminals think further outside the box than law enforcement and the rest of society, we can expect more crime. Are abducting and drowning someone, leaving no marks, doing it on the darkest nights each month, and drawing graffiti where the victim was murdered and/ or placed in the water so difficult to imagine? Not for ruthless killers who commit heinous crimes and brag about it.

The river—the murderous Mississippi River; it beckons me, and I avoid it at all costs. We believe our son's life ended in that muddy water at the hands of the darkest evil. A suspect/witness confessed to the location Chris was taken to be drowned. After the vicious crime forced Chris to gasp for his last breath, he was taken to another spot in the river to be thrown away like trash. Chris, adored by hundreds, was placed on his back with arms crossed—allegedly posed as a gift to Satan—and pushed into the Mississippi River. Demonic evil tortured and took the life of the son we brought into the world, loved more than life itself, and cared for, for almost twenty-two years. God help us. A significant part of Steve, Sara, and me died with Chris. When you love someone with all your heart, his death claims the sacred part of you that is tightly connected to him. The strongest love demands the greatest sacrifice.

A Soul's Journey

Before winter's harsh cold sets in, I strongly sensed I must go to certain locations along the dreaded river. For whatever reason, my soul wanted to connect with Chris and learn where he spent his last agonizing moments on earth. Steve tried several times to discourage me, finally realizing I needed to complete this walk.

Driving to the Nicollet Island area of the Mississippi River, Steve and I scarcely said a word. After parking the car on the east side of the river, we walked toward Nicollet Island. Before descending the riverbank, we stood and held each other. Then without a word, we looked up, and our eyes met. Drawing strength from a brief prayer, we held hands and walked to the area where a suspect stated Chris was murdered. Based on that information from detectives (not from the MPD), and our visceral reaction to walking in that area, we believe it is possible Chris was murdered there. The damp, thick air hung with wicked vibes and twisted, sick energy. After looking around for less than five minutes, I literally ran all the way back to the car. Shaking, I felt like I had just escaped morbid rot from the depths of hell.

Steve followed close behind, stopping once to look back and scream at the river of death. Shaken, we pounded on the car in utter frustration. Both of us sensed we would never know what really happened to our son or why. Inside, we raged at the gross unfairness and injustice of a world in which murder, the ultimate crime, continues its rampage against innocent people.

Knowing I needed to finish my soul journey, Steve agreed to drive along the road closest to the shoreline as I walked northward. He adamantly stated he had no intention of getting out of the car again. Clearly his soul did not require what mine demanded—I needed to walk along the shoreline to determine where my precious son's body was put in the dirty river.

After driving a short distance north, Steve stayed in the car while I walked back down to the river. I could feel myself maintaining a psychological distance from this dreaded area. Yet standing there, with no fear or tears, I experienced my surroundings as if from a distance. This must be one of the ways I've trained myself just to survive, to function, since evil ripped Chris from our lives.

Trees are great places to just hang out.

Continuing my walk for at least twenty minutes along the shore-line, north of the Hennepin Avenue Bridge, I stopped when the spirit moved me. Quieting myself to connect with Chris, I closed my eyes and listened. Hearing the wind whistling in the trees, I looked up, yet didn't see any leaves or branches moving. A tiny bird fluttered, hopping from one branch to another. I sensed Chris's presence; he seemed to be telling me it didn't matter anymore if his body was here or not, he had left us five years ago. Now he lived far, far away, happy, in a much better place.

For a few precious minutes, I just stood there. Looking up again, I remembered how many times over the years I had looked up, only to find Chris hanging out, just chilling, high up on a tree branch. *Chris, I love you with every cell in my body. Please watch over us, especially Sara,* my heart whispered.

Our Family's Incredible Legacy

Walking up the riverbank to the street, I thought of our family's in-credible legacy at the University of Minnesota. Steve, Sara, Chris, and I: all four of us graduated from this university—a whole family's aca-demic career, lived within a mile or two of this very spot. I could easily point to all the places we had lived as students.

Deep in thought, I stopped for a moment, gazing toward Pracna on Main, a restaurant near the Third Avenue Bridge. Under that bridge, walkers spotted our beloved son's frozen body. Chris was only twenty-one when murderers ended his chance for a promising future.

Steve and I had known Pracna in happier days; we were also twenty-one. More than thirty years ago, we accepted a personal invitation to attend the grand opening. Bill Naegele, restaurant owner and friend of Steve's, invited us to carve our initials into the bar to memorialize the special occasion. That night was a blast. Steve and I loved life, each other, and looked to the future with great enthusiasm. Carefree joy and fun—I don't recall what that feels like.

Looking upward with misty eyes, I saw the huge Pillsbury Mills sign. My father, Grandpa Gene, worked at Pillsbury for forty-seven years. Our family moved to Minneapolis from New York when I was in fourth grade.

*"Hi everyone!
I love my grandpa!"*

Grandpa Gene and Chris shared a very special bond. I pictured my dad, carrying little Chris through the cornfields of his farm, Chris's Happy Place. Especially during the summer Chris was about eighteen months old, we often saw Grandpa's gray hair alongside Chris's white-blond hair, periodically bobbing through or above the cornstalks as Grandpa carried Chris on one of their many walks. Grandma Rose asked Grandpa Gene, "What do the two of you talk about out there?" Grandpa smiled and replied, "Rose, we don't need to talk; we just understand each other."

No Accountability, No Justice

Oh my God, the story was surreal. It felt like a movie with a tragic ending. But it wasn't a movie; this actually happened, right here in the city whose high homicide rate in the mid-1990s had earned it the nickname "Murderapolis." This was our family's life; a hand we had been dealt that could not be reversed, a history that could not be rewritten.

A University of Minnesota student athlete brutally murdered and his family left to fight for justice for their remarkable son who deserved so much better. Betrayed and ostracized by some of the very people who drive in cars marked "To Protect With Courage, To Serve With Compassion"; for years the MPD saw Chris's disappearance as 'nothing unusual' or serious enough to investigate. Our family gave so much to this city. Standing here, stripped of our dreams, innocence, and faith in the systems we supported and believed in, I knew my time in Minneapolis was finished. Too many so-called authorities had lost our respect; I was done with this city.

Unlike a video game, death offers no do-over. Murderers don't care; they deal cards of death; often premeditated, planned, and hideously carried out. Animals kill for food to survive, but many murderers kill for sport. Trapped in egomania, these destroyers of life stoop to the bowels of hell.

Sara had hoped those who took Chris's life might feel some remorse; and if so, maybe one day they would confess, or at least feel some of the pain of losing a loved one to murder. Now she knows that chance is slimmer than winning the lottery.

No accountability, no justice, yet *dozens* of people had a hand in putting Chris on the street, discounting his disappearance, covering up the truth, and ending Chris's life. We must learn to live with this harsh reality for the rest of our lives.

My mom, Grandma Rose, recently shared something with me she had never told anyone. The night she learned from Sara that Chris was missing, she immediately phoned numerous people for several hours, desperately hoping to find her grandson. When she could think of no one else to call, she cried out to God in anxiety and frustration: "Where were you, why didn't you help Chris?" God answered, "I was with him. I wept. These evil deeds are recorded."

CHAPTER 27

Finishing Strong

December 2007–January 2009

When you start a game, you better be willing to finish it.
CHRIS JENKINS

How hard a hit can you take, then stand up again and move forward? We didn't grapple intellectually with the question because our belief and purpose remained crystal clear. At times though, we did struggle, emotionally and physically, to stand up again. No parent or sibling can endure the length and agonizing horror of the road we traveled without faltering from sheer exhaustion and temporary hopelessness. From the beginning I trusted we would recognize our last tour of battle. When we could not make a difference for Chris, it would be time to shift gears.

Periodically we talked about wanting a "fast-forward" button to end the relentless pain of unspeakable loss. Yet in any endeavor, knowing when and how to power up, let go, and ultimately complete the undertaking requires awareness and keen discernment. During a struggle such as ours, which has continued for so many years, timing fluctuated along the way for Sara, Steve, and me. Recognizing completion also differed amongst the three of us. Yet by honoring each other's individual journey, we remained committed to holding each other up.

Are parents and siblings of a missing and murdered loved one ever really "done"? What does recovery mean in this surreal life tragedy? People get over or recover from a cold or the flu. To date, I am not aware of a single parent who has said he or she got over losing a child, especially in cases of murder. The murder of a child—the brutal ripping apart of the very fabric of life and love in the profoundly sacred bond between parent and child: no, parents don't get over that. The bond transcends earthly understanding. Chris is part of us and always will be.

Enduring Love for Chris

Our compelling drive, rooted in enduring love for Chris, stayed strong as a result of our:

- unwavering *belief* in Chris;
- rock-solid *purpose*: find Chris, seek justice;
- acting with *courage* regardless of circumstances;
- *commitment* to stay the course; and
- *resilience* to keep going, in spite of setbacks.

As a ten-year-old boy, Chris reminded Steve during a baseball game that commitment includes finishing what you start. On that sultry August day, Steve was coaching Chris's team, which lagged three runs behind their opponents. The team looked listless and disappointed; some teammates even disengaged. Steve recalls that a few players had

*"I love my dad.
He's kind of silly,
just like me."*

reached the point of gazing more at butterflies than pop flies. Chris ran up to his dad, advocating in an excited voice, "Dad, you need to pump them up! Tell them, when they start a game, they have to be willing to finish it." Steve did not let Chris down in that baseball game. Indeed, his commitment as a father continued—demonstrating deep and enduring love, long after his adored son disappeared. Early in 2008, Steve received the following e-mail:

> Mr. Jenkins,
>
> Let me tell you one more time how incredible you have been in the last 5½ years. Chris and I often joked about you and my dad coaching us when we were pip-squeaks.
>
> Your coaching never stopped. You have lived by faith and in doing so have brought more positive out of such a terrible time than anyone could have ever imagined.
>
> From a friend of your son's, I appreciate all that you have done, and as a man I stand in awe of you and your strengths.
>
> Thanks for being such a great example of what a father and a man should be.
>
> Todd Downing

Todd graduated from the University of Minnesota in 2003. He and Chris did stay connected through their college years. Continuing his passion for football, Todd joined the offensive coaching staff of the Minnesota Vikings in 2002, remaining in that position until 2006, when he accepted a spot on the defensive coaching staff of the St. Louis Rams. In 2009, Todd became the assistant wide receivers coach for the Detroit Lions. Remembering Todd's excellence as a quarterback for many years in grade school and high school, Steve sees Todd's new opportunity as the perfect fit.

Finishing What We Started

Nor did Steve falter in his commitment to finding answers regarding Chris's murder. Before the end of 2007, he met with representatives from

MPD homicide: the lead investigator on Chris's case, Sergeant Nancy Dunlap, Sergeant John Holthusen, Lieutenant Amelia Huffman, and Captain David Hayhoe. More than a year had passed since Chris's death was reclassified as a homicide. Steve wanted a clear understanding of the suspect(s) at large, and an update on progress made in the case. He left the meeting frustrated, realizing that little, if anything, had been done on Chris's case. It appeared no one was even interrogating suspects at large. To this day, we fail to understand why a death that was changed from undetermined to homicide did not result in renewed effort to solve the murder.

Believing they had sufficient evidence to prosecute those who murdered Chris, retired detectives Gannon and Duarte met with the MPD and later spoke with Hennepin County Assistant Attorney Amy Sweasy in March 2008. Along with our private investigator Chuck Loesch, they met with Dunlap, Huffman, and Chief Dolan at the MPD. Based on information received from suspects/witnesses in Chris's murder, and forensic evidence visible in recovery and autopsy photos, Gannon and Duarte felt confident Chris's case could move forward. That did not prove true.

We suspect Gannon and Duarte referred to information they gleaned from the *FBI Law Enforcement Bulletin* available to the public on the FBI Web site (see Notes). An investigative reporter from out of state alerted Steve and me about the bulletin because many facts pertain to distinctive signs in determining cases of drowning. After reading the article numerous times, Steve and I just shook our heads—so many of the facts presented were true in Chris's situation, it seemed like the article was written about Chris.

First and foremost, the article states, *"The investigator's role in a drowning investigation is crucial to a medical examiner in establishing an accurate cause of death."* As we have believed all along, communication between those who investigate a case, those who recover the body, and those who examine the body is critical. Other than a few rare cases in which diatom tests are conducted, there are no universally accepted diagnostic tests to prove that a death was caused by drowning. So by itself, an autopsy usually proves insufficient in determining drowning as a cause of death.

While numerous indicators of drowning are cited in the FBI bulletin, the following pertained to Chris's body at the recovery scene: line in eye, cadaveric spasm, head rotation, and hand and arm positions: "If death occurred on land, a noticeable horizontal line should exist on the eyeball . . . Conversely, if the victim drowned and is submerged in water at the time of death, then . . . no lines will be present." The autopsy photos clearly show a ruler measuring the line in Chris's eye.

"Any person who has died on land and remained in a terrestrial environment during the onset of rigor mortis . . . will likely display the head rotated to one side, a position almost never found in a drowning victim." Recovery photos show Chris's head is rotated to one side.

"When initially recovered from the water, portions of the body—mainly hands and arms—may appear to be in full rigor mortis, even though only a short time has passed since death occurred. This phenomenon, cadaveric spasm, results from the typically violent struggling of an individual at the time of the drowning. Cadaveric spasm forms only under conditions of extreme mental stress and indicates the victim's last thoughts and actions. It occurs virtually instantly."

The autopsy pictures show Chris's left hand was pried open to photograph the "foreign matter" (mud laced with hair) appearing in that hand. "Often, victims clench their hands in a fist. These . . . hand positions are much less pronounced or not present at all in victims who drowned while intoxicated because these individuals generally do not struggle, but simply disappear below the surface of the water." Chris's blood alcohol level (BAC) was .12 and some research studies show BAC can rise up to 0.15% through decomposition and other factors (see Notes). Chris was missing for four months before his body was discovered. As noted by Dr. Baden and others, Chris may have had little if any alcohol in his system when he died.

Since we do not know all that was discussed in the meeting with MPD homicide, Gannon, Duarte, and Loesch, we can only speculate that some of the facts just mentioned were presented as evidence that Chris likely died on land, was drowned by others, remained on a shoreline near or in the water, possibly wedged in a tree because thick ice encased his upper body and he did not float right away.

We understand that any single fact does not tell the whole story. The specific information presented in the FBI bulletin that pertained to

Chris's case, along with additional data we collected along the way, led us to believe Chris was indeed a victim of homicide. The FBI bulletin was available in February 2006, Chris's case was changed to homicide by the MPD in November 2006 for other reasons.

Many answers to Chris's demise were present at the recovery scene, during the recovery (body position, iced, not wedged into tree, etc.) and in the autopsy. Minnesota is the state with 10,000 lakes. We hope drowning incidents in the future will be properly investigated from the moment the body is found until a determination of cause and manner of death can be named. Agencies involved must collaborate, communicating often and clearly, to shine as much light as possible on what may have happened to a victim.

Although Steve and I were not present at either of those meetings, we learned the MPD told Gannon and Duarte that we needed to present a video or picture of the murder of Chris Jenkins before the case would return to the Hennepin County Attorney's Office. Chief Dolan confirmed that preposterous statement in a face-to-face meeting with us several months later. He also added that from the perspective of MPD homicide, Gannon and Duarte did not present new evidence.

After realizing they would have no influence in moving Chris's case forward, Gannon and Duarte decided to go public with information gathered over the past decade of more than forty "drownings" of young men in eleven states. They knew the FBI needed to engage in order to investigate those deaths.

The "drownings" occurred primarily in northern states stretching from Minnesota to New York during the school year. Although they looked at more than eighty cases, the detectives saw that at least forty fit a specific profile: young men ages eighteen to twenty-seven who became separated from friends after nights at parties or in bars. Contrary to public opinion, not all of the men were drunk; some consumed no alcohol the night they vanished. The disappearances typically occurred on nights with little moonlight—a quarter moon or less—and often fell on or near holidays. The majority of the men were college students, many with high GPAs and several of them active in intercollegiate sports. Data gathered in 2004–5 showed that more than 75 percent of the deaths occurred within a hundred miles of Interstate 94. One by one the bodies—with no obvious signs of trauma—surfaced in lakes, rivers, even shallow ponds. Approximately one-third were found in the Mississippi River. In most cases, friends, family members, even college professors, stated that the sudden, unexplained disappearance was completely out of character with the young man's previous behavior. Curiously enough, though young women drink alcohol and binge drink, they aren't disappearing and showing up days, weeks, or months later in water. (See Notes: victim profiles.)

We had spent more than six years trying to prevent another family from facing the heartbreaking experience of losing a son who goes missing, and then living the rest of their lives with his unresolved death. Steve and I told the Gannon team on numerous occasions that our intense involvement in seeking answers and justice was finished. We wished them well in their future investigative work.

Since the Gannon team was determined to resolve these deaths, we promised to support their efforts by attending the national press conference they sponsored in New York on April 28, 2008. Other families of victims also attended: Jon Snell (brother of Josh Snell), Mr. & Mrs. McNeill (parents of Patrick), Mr. & Mrs. Falcon (parents of Adam), and Mr. Kruziki (father of Matt). Because we had worked extensively with KSTP's investigative reporter Kristi Piehl, she also helped by arranging interviews with *Good Morning America* and *20/20*.

Along with Gannon and Duarte, Associate Professor Lee Gilbertson and his grad student Adam Carlson spoke to the media assembled in New York. They presented their findings, which included a specific east–west repeated pattern of disappearances, a profile of the victims, examples of illogical occurrences in the last known hours of the victims' lives (cell phone, shoes, hat, or other personal items found in different areas; victim last seen walking in the opposite direction of where his belongings were found; etc.), and various clusters of graffiti. Although the team of four stated they had discovered thirteen different types of graffiti groupings, they only presented one type—a smiley face, located where they believe the victim was murdered and/or put in the water. The growing saga of unexplained drowning deaths of vibrant young men in the prime of their lives gripped a nation, and several other countries around the globe as well. Like falling dominos, each new disappearance jolted thousands of people.

"My daddy is the best."

Sara, her husband, Jamie, and their two-year-old daughter, Cayman Rose, met us in Manhattan. Steve and I felt it was extremely important for them to be a part of our family's "passing the baton" to the next wave of individuals pursuing justice. Because of his presence at the national press conference and interviews, Jamie later told us he caught a glimpse of the life we had led the previous five and a half years: "I finally understand, to a very small degree, what you've done in seeking justice for Chris and dozens of other young men. Witnessing the excruciating pain on your faces, I still can't imagine what you feel. It sucks I never got to meet Chris."

Cayman's presence in New York warmed our hearts and brought joy. She also caused us to think about Chris's new home in heaven. We met Kristi Piehl and her cameraman, Jim O'Connell, late one evening by the available laptops in the business center at our hotel on Times Square. We wanted to check the KSTP 10:00 p.m. coverage of the press conference online. As we waited, a smiling Cayman ran up and down the hall looking under chairs, tables, and behind curtains: "I find Uncle Chris." Soon her voice sounded more frantic and her searching intensified. It seemed as if she had played hide-and-seek with Chris and then he disappeared before she was done "playing." Shortly before going to bed, Cayman was jabbering about her previous dog, Bijou, a border collie she had not seen

"I love my 'Biji.'"

or spoken of in more than a year. Bijou looked like our deceased border collie, Coco, which left us wondering if Cayman had actually seen Chris and Coco earlier in the evening. Who knows? We had learned to trust the little voice inside, especially since Chris disappeared. That voice had steered us in the right direction every time.

The following day Steve, Sara, and I interviewed separately with *20/20,* so we took turns watching Cayman. At one point, she ran up to Sara, tugged on her mother's arm, and asked for Band-Aids: "Please, Mommy, we need lotsa Band-Aids for Uncle Chris. Then we can make a big Band-Aid and fix him so he can come back." Giant tears tumbled out of Sara's eyes, and her throat tightened as she tried to respond to her daughter's innocent plea.

While in New York, Steve and I also interviewed with reporters from *People* magazine, which published a long story in its May 2008 issue titled "Are Serial Killers Stalking College Men?" The Smiley Face Killer story traveled to several other countries, including Australia, the UK, and Russia. Due to KSTP's coverage of Chris's murder and possible link to dozens of cases around the United States, their Web site experienced 1.3 million hits in a two-week period prior to and following the national press conference (April 20–May 3, 2008). As of June 2009, the Chris Jenkins file on the KSTP Web site continued to receive about 10,000 hits monthly.

Jon Snell flew back to Minneapolis on the same plane as Steve and me. He thanked us for inspiring him to stand up for his brother Josh, who was begging for help on his cell phone, saying people were chasing him, the night he disappeared. We hugged Jon and told him how proud we were of his courage and actions. We also promised to help him in the future in any way possible.

We remain eternally grateful to KSTP for its ongoing efforts to accurately report Chris's case and others. We know several of the station's employees went the extra mile many times over. Early in 2008, I sent a thank-you card to anchor John Mason and one to Kristi Piehl for their unending commitment to report the facts. Writing the cards as if they originated from Chris, I signed his name. Kristi lost hers and had no idea where it ended up. As she packed her belongings, getting ready to leave the hotel in New York, an envelope fell out of her box of supplies. Stooping down to pick it up, she realized it was the thank-you card from Chris. After working tirelessly for months, and now spending the weekend away from her husband and young sons, she must have been exhausted as she packed up to return home. Kristi told us she sat on the edge of the bed for a few minutes with tears in her eyes, internalizing the thanks from Chris. Some events surely evoke divine intervention.

To finish what we started, we did follow up on a few details that haunted us. In the process, we heard through our own connections of a taped conversation between a suspect/witness in Chris's murder and a female. The two discussed that no one knew the whereabouts of their mutual friend—once considered a person of interest in Chris's murder. Apparently, he left Minneapolis after we spoke at KSTP on July 31, 2007. Now we dug further and learned that he had fled again, this time leaving Minnesota after the national press conference on April 28, 2008. We know where he is and have offered that information to the Minneapolis police on more than one occasion. To our knowledge, the police have not pursued him since Sergeant Jackson retired, in spite of his highly suspicious behavior.

Based on what we've discovered over the years, it appears that dozens of people have answers about what happened to Chris Jenkins on Halloween night 2002. Extreme fear of retribution or being held accountable for their hideous behavior must silence their guilt.

Chris's Footprints Blazing across the Sky

Chris's lacrosse teammate and close friend Jared Keepman phoned us late Halloween night 2008. He wanted to know if we had witnessed the marvel in the sky. His story was so compelling, we asked him to put it in writing so that we could include it in the book:

> On Halloween night, 2008, I experienced a phenomenal event. The dogs were being a bit restless and had recently been out, but I finally broke down and let them out again. When I stepped outside with them around 9:30 p.m., I was facing north. There in the northern sky blazed a shooting star—larger, brighter and longer than I had *ever* seen. As the star shot from east to west across the heavens, its brilliance lit up half the sky. Staring in utter amazement, I chuckled, knowing Chris had a hand in it! Jenks, even

now, you continue to spread love and joy. We often said we never knew what you would do next. You haven't changed a bit! We will meet again, so you better be ready!

On October 26, 2009, Jared and Bethany welcomed their daughter, Kennedy Adele Keepman, into the world. A coincidence, or magic from heaven?

CHAPTER 28

What Matters Now

February 2009–Eternity

Peace I leave with you; My peace I give to you . . .
Do not let your hearts be troubled and do not be afraid.

JOHN 14:27

We believe our chosen path proved honorable by seeking truth with dignity and grace. Yet to live more fully now, we must shift the focus. In our quest to find out what happened to Chris, the answers could only be found by looking in the rearview mirror. To create a more promising future we must now face forward and focus on the road ahead. Our greatest gift to Chris, ourselves, and others, will originate in our belief that brighter days are possible. That belief will fuel the desire to create new dreams, giving us a chance to live and lead from a healthier place.

We must honor where we've been by blessing the life our family enjoyed and accepting that our future will be radically different from what we once anticipated. Dreaming of a better life requires leaving behind hopes of what can never be and behaviors that no longer work. Is it possible to hold Chris while leaving the pain behind? I don't have a clue.

So, what did our tragic journey look and feel like?

Tumultuous Ocean

In the tumultuous ocean of grief, we found ourselves caught in the undertow. The first gargantuan wave struck with full force on November 1, 2002, when we learned that Chris was missing. Have you ever found yourself caught in an undertow? The power of that pull to carry you out to sea cannot be overcome. If you follow your natural instinct to fight it, madly paddling toward shore, toward safety, exhaustion sets in as the undertow pulls you out even further. Eventually, you give up

275

completely. You become a victim of circumstances. In the ocean, you will likely become fish food. In life, you may never truly love or laugh again. It takes tremendous will to resist that urge to fight the undertow of injustice by becoming bitter and focusing on what can never be. Surrendering to what is can eventually lead you to a measure of happiness.

The only way to reach shore is to stay with the undertow, accepting its fury and force, knowing you will be slammed into the sand and tossed around like seaweed. Of course, it's counterintuitive to ride out that frightening experience of danger with no control. Yet only by enduring can you make progress toward your goal of landing safely on shore.

When the undertow is behind, you can paddle diagonally toward shore.

Undertow in Minneapolis

We did our best to build bridges with law enforcement, believing that together we could bring Chris home faster than either of us working alone. Surrounding ourselves with people willing and able to help, staying in the media to create awareness, and challenging the nonsense along the way helped us unearth truth. Recognizing that resistance and skepticism are inherent when pushing the envelope, we faced the inevitable adversity. Bruised and battered, we stayed the course.

With Chris's homicide announced in November 2006, the undertow was behind us—or so we thought. Early in 2009, Steve and I requested a meeting with the third homicide investigator on Chris's case, Sergeant Holthusen, and the new lieutenant of homicide, Lieutenant Zimmerman. This was our last-ditch effort to understand the MPD's position on persons at large, and intent to investigate the case. In March 2009, we met with MPD homicide Captain Huffman and Lieutenant Zimmerman. Much to our surprise, the lead detective on Chris's case, Sergeant John Holthusen, was out of town. Holthusen was the second lead detective on our son's case who had not even contacted us. I never spoke with, or met Sergeant Dunlap or Sergeant Holthusen. I wouldn't recognize either one if I stood next to them, or overheard them speaking in an elevator.

In that meeting, Steve and I did get clarification that in order to take the case back to prosecuting attorney Amy Sweasy, the MPD needed us to bring a video, picture, or other irrefutable physical evidence of our son's murder. I asked a pointed question. The answer baffled us, so Steve responded with almost the exact wording I had used: "So, you're telling us that evidence has to walk in the door?" The reply was clear: "Yes, if evidence walks in the door, we'll look at it." In our opinion, the words used in the conversation and the subsequent implication were unmistakable: it remained our job to solve Chris's murder—unless of course, irrefutable evidence fell from the stratosphere and dropped in on MPD homicide. Captain Huffman told us there were no person(s) at large and that the homicide department had followed up on all requests from the Hennepin County Attorney's Office. Those statements offered no information and did not reassure us.

Although Captain Huffman and Lieutenant Zimmerman heard our key questions, and Zimmerman told us he would have Holthusen contact us when he returned, we have not heard from MPD homicide since the meeting in March 2009. This pattern of communication has not varied much in almost seven years. In our opinion, we're told anything, no matter how reasonable (or, conversely, illogical), just to make us go away. We understand that Chris's case is long and complicated, largely because the idea of homicide was discounted for several years. We also realize that sometimes there is not enough evidence to prosecute.

Our greatest hope is that when the next body is found in water in Minneapolis, homicide will be considered before it is eliminated. If so, the recovery scene needs to be treated as a potential crime scene, and evidence should be collected before it is lost. Conscientious work at the recovery scene is critical since water and time can destroy potential evidence, already presenting many challenges in reaching conclusive findings. (See Notes: Critical considerations when investigating a drowning incident.) When cases are reclassified as homicide years later, it's too late to get evidence from the scene. Furthermore, trace evidence is best preserved when the body is bagged before being moved (another procedure strongly recommended by Butch Hendrick of Team Lifeguard Systems, Inc.).

What matters is that all of us learn from what doesn't work and commit to doing things differently to be more effective in the future.

What We Focus on Now

Paddling to shore took much longer than expected because we stood up for more than seventy young adult men who disappeared in the past twelve years under similar, sometimes almost identical circumstances. By sharing all our data, including contacts, with those who carried the torch forward, the cry for justice could be strengthened.

Now, almost seven years later, we have reached shore. For our family, what matters now? We are certain to learn more along the way and to move forward with greater ease by continuing to cut each other slack. The following ideas represent our present thoughts.

Believing Chris Is in a Better Place and Will Always Be with Us

"My uncle Chris is an angel," declares Cayman Rose with all the certitude an innocent three-year-old can muster. Cayman's matter-of-fact, sincere belief that Uncle Chris watches over her from heaven is both touching and compelling. Her three-year-old wisdom challenges the rest of us to trust the connections we often sense with Chris.

We experienced one of those connections in February 2009 when Steve and I made our annual trek to the Third Avenue Bridge to throw roses in the river where Chris's body was found. As usual, just driving into Minneapolis brought waves of profound sadness. Shivering as we walked across the bridge in the cold winter wind, we held on to each other and the beautiful roses. Stopping at the spot just above the recovery scene, we noticed that a large area of the river was completely frozen. This was the first year we had thrown roses on ice rather than open water.

For some reason, I apologize to Chris every year for what happened. He must know that Steve and I would have done anything to help him, including giving our own lives. I told Chris he would be an uncle again and I thought Sara and Jamie's baby was a boy. A few weeks later, we learned Cayman would have a baby brother at the end of July.

Enveloped in grief, we drove home in silence. Just as we entered our subdivision, we looked up and witnessed a full sundog. That rare and beautiful halo around the sun, formed in a winter sky, will always remind us of our son, our special angel in heaven.

Trusting Chris Loves Us Dearly and Wants Us to Be Happy

Chris spoke directly to Steve in a dream and his words became part of Steve's eulogy for his beloved son: "In a dream-filled sleep, I saw a brilliant light approaching me, the intensity of the sun, but I didn't need to squint. Suddenly, I clearly saw Chris. As he reached out and embraced me, I was overcome with his intense love and pure joy . . . 'Dad, let me start by telling you, Mom, Sara, and Coco that I love you with an intensity I have never felt before in my life.'"

Over the years, many people have commented on how much Chris loved his family. My older sister Deborah told me numerous times in the year following Chris's disappearance that she often sensed his intense love for Sara, Steve, and me. About a year after Chris's memorial service, we received two glass mugs and a note from Deborah. "These are from Christopher," she wrote. "He wants you to know how dearly he loves you and to do your best about the fun, laughter, wonder, magic, and celebration of life he stood for. P.S. Glad I finally made it to Disneyland to get these mugs. I feel certain he wants you to have them." Minnie Mouse was etched on one side of my mug, and "Chris Loves Mom" on the other. Steve's mug had Mickey Mouse cradling a football on one side and "Chris Loves Dad" on the opposite side. Through Deborah, Chris gave us the gift of his eternal love.

At least three years passed before Steve could even look at his mug. Football, which had united father and son for so many fun-filled years, activated the searing pain of profound loss. Now, both Steve and I use the mugs in remembrance of our son, whose love radiates from the heavens.

Chris's love for us and his desire for us to live with abundant joy have also been shared with us through Grandma Rose. My mom and dad visited Lourdes, France, with a church group a few years after Chris disappeared. While at the grotto in Lourdes, Mom sensed a very clear message from Chris. He knew how hard Steve and I were struggling, and hoped with all his heart that we'd laugh more, live more fully, and find a way to leave more of the pain behind. Now that we've passed the

"Grandma Rose loves my hugs."

baton to others who seek answers to the unexplained drownings, maybe that's possible. The drive and focus needed to uncover details of these deaths did not leave room for living fully. We doubt one can be immersed in that level of horror as a parent of one of the victims, and experience true happiness at the same time.

Acknowledging Our Contribution to Chris's Remarkable Life

Someone asked Christian Bailey, a close friend of Chris's, to describe Steve. After watching Steve play with a five-year-old for at least an hour, Christian noted, "Steve is like a middle-aged Chris." Slowly, I've observed Steve displaying more humor and silliness, reminding me of the man I knew before November 1, 2002, when the world we knew crashed forever. During his teen-

"Poppi Steve is so silly!"

age years, Chris routinely challenged Steve. When Chris reached early adulthood, it was easy to see how much he and his dad were alike, which probably contributed to earlier struggles between them.

The last year or two of Chris's life, he told Steve and me quite often that he loved us and appreciated all we had done for him. I turned fifty in August 2002, just a couple of months before we lost so much. On the birthday card Chris gave me that year, he wrote:

"Mother, Happy Birthday!!! I hope that you have a FAN-TABULOUS B-DAY. You have blessed me with your love, wisdom, and guidance for 21 years. I appreciate all that you have given me and I just wanted to thank you once again. I couldn't ask for a better mom. I had a great time spending time with you in Scony [Chris's name for Wisconsin], and I look forward to seeing you in Arizona if all works out as planned. Have a great B-Day. I won't harass (sp?) you about your age even though it is an old one! Just kidding. I Love You. Your Son, Christopher"

♥ MOTHER ♥
- HAPPY BIRTHDAY!!!
I hope that you have a
FANTABULOUS B-DAY
You have blessed me with your
love, wisdom, and guidance for 21 years.
I appreciate all that you have given
me and I just wanted to Thank
You once again. I couldn't ask for
a better Mom. I had a great
time spending time with you

in Scony, and I look forward to
Seeing you in Chicaca if all works
out as planned. Have a great B-DAy
I won't harass you about your
age even though it is an

The four directions have blessed you
with wisdom and kindness,
because you are a special person.

May every wish you wish come true
on this your special day!

(Happy Birthday)

old on 😊! Just Kidding.

I LOVE YOU

Your Son,
Christopher

Trusting We Have Left Meaningful Footprints

Our children, Sara and Chris, were our two greatest gifts to the world, our most important footprints for future generations. While Sara has lived a good life, consistently helping others, including her brother, clearly her toughest test came when Chris disappeared. Tireless in her efforts to find him, her character shone brightly as she pursued endless paths, setting the pace for the rest of us. Many of the twenty-somethings spoke with admiration about Sara's strength and determination, as well as her obvious love for her brother. These traits stood her well when she did the unspeakable—literally crawling through woods side by side with her parents, hearing their soulful cry as they looked for their son or parts of his body. Not once did she lose faith in her brother. Lacrosse is a tough sport, yet even some of Chris's lacrosse teammates commented on Sara's extraordinary mental toughness. Sara showed hundreds of people what it looks like to stand up for someone you love by taking action and pushing forward with laser focus.

Though Chris's life was taken much too soon, throughout his nearly twenty-two years on earth, he had an impact on thousands of lives. Dozens of comments from the message board on his Web site praised our efforts in teaching him right principles. Mel Preczewski sent us an e-mail shortly after Chris's graduation: "When I saw Sara hold up Chris's diploma, it brought tears to my eyes. It was an amazing experience as everyone paused to honor him; you could *really* feel Chris in that huge auditorium. I have been so drawn to Chris because he clearly chose the right way over the easy way, which is how I live my life. Steve and Jan, my hat goes off to you. You raised a child who knew the value of life and the power of people, love, and compassion. Chris is with you, and I am sure he will demand of you the same quality of life you demanded in him."

When a Young Person Is Missing,
Take Action Immediately

While we did not accomplish one of our key goals—obtaining justice for Chris and dozens of other young men—we believe we blazed a trail of courage with valuable footprints for others to follow. Several parents and family members who have lost young college-age men (later found in water) have told us our journey inspired them to look for answers and to trust their instinct that the facts in their beloved young man's death did not support the idea of accidental "drowning" or suicide.

A brochure describing the AMBER Alert program in Minnesota, which is distributed by the Jacob Wetterling Resource Center, emphasizes that the first few hours after a child is abducted are critical: "Of those abducted children who are murdered, seventy-four percent are killed within the first three hours, according to a U.S. Department of Justice study." Although the AMBER alert is activated for children seventeen years of age or younger, many of the young men who disappeared under suspicious circumstances and later were found in water were only a few years older than seventeen. Whether these statistics are applicable for college-aged children or not, the numbers do highlight the critical nature of rapid response to a suspicious disappearance, particularly when this behavior is not typical of the individual.

Minnesota has recently passed legislation requiring law enforcement to take a missing person's report immediately when someone eighteen years or older disappears, especially if the person is endangered. This law is named Brandon's Law for nineteen-year-old Brandon Swanson, who was last seen in rural western Minnesota in May 2008. As Brandon spoke with his father on his cell phone, Brandon's phone suddenly went dead. Many searches have failed to locate him.

Brandon's Law is a good start, but laws must be funded to be operational. In addition, this law does not yet define specific documented protocol, which means that actions taken will be dependent upon individual interpretation.

Dale and Sally Zamlen also supported Brandon's Law in May 2009, a month after their son Dan, a freshman at the University of St. Thomas in St. Paul, disappeared under suspicious conditions. Dan also was speaking on his cell phone with a friend when his voice suddenly grew faint and could no longer be heard.

Based on our experience, the following steps need to be implemented *immediately* if someone eighteen years or older is missing:

- Phone, text, and/or e-mail the missing person's family, friends, roommates, neighbors, and others to establish the facts.
- Call authorities, request, and complete a missing person's report.

- Contact as many people as possible to initiate searches; choose a leader to organize the searches and volunteers.
- Designate someone to set up a command center.
- If help from local law enforcement will not be available immediately, consider hiring a private investigator if feasible.
- Make the media your new best friend—all local television and radio stations, and newspapers—and speak out every day.
- Seek to establish a good relationship with authorities.

These steps are by no means exhaustive. The key is to take action *immediately*. In the first few hours, every second counts. In fact, after forty-eight hours, the odds of finding the missing person alive drop dramatically.

Did we leave the "campsite" for missing young adults better than we found it? We certainly hope so. My sister Carol has continued to speak out: "On any college visit over the past six years, I make it a point to talk to parents and students about the dangers of college-age males and females being alone, especially at night. The issue becomes personal when I share a few key details about my nephew Chris's story; finishing by saying the buddy system could save their life. Parents have thanked me, even applauded. It's important for all of us to share the message, so other families don't have to experience the nightmare we endured. Simple steps like being constantly aware of surroundings, watching out for each other, never leaving a friend behind in a bar or at a party—especially if you don't know their whereabouts—watching your drink so drugs cannot be added by random people, and choosing a designated driver when drinking alcohol."

While these suggestions do not represent a comprehensive list, awareness and basic safety precautions may save a life. We caution our daughters; we must remember our sons are even more likely to be victims of murder since they tend to see themselves as invincible, and society shows more sympathy for young women.

Another reality is that many young adults who grew up in rural and suburban areas attend universities located in large cities. These students start their collegiate years with a new sense of independence and spirit of adventure. They freely walk the streets with no real experience or understanding of the danger lurking around the corner.

Whether our efforts hastened law enforcement's response to the disappearance of Dan Zamlen early on April 5, 2009 or not, we were relieved and gratified to see the fast action of Minnesota State Patrol and the St. Paul police. Within twelve hours of Dan's disappearance, a State Patrol helicopter was in the air, and fire fighters were on the banks of the Mississippi River near Dan's last known location. At twenty-four hours, St. Paul police engaged and used police search dogs in the first couple of days. On May 1, almost one month later, Dan's body was recovered in the Mississippi River in St. Paul, Minnesota. On February 27, 2003, Chris's body was found in the Mississippi River in Minneapolis, only one and a half miles from that location.

Steve did contact Dan's father, Dale Zamlen, offering support and suggestions. Each day in the two weeks after Dan disappeared, Steve and I remembered and relived the horror, hour by hour, of our desperate efforts to find Chris. The gut-wrenching terror returned full force. The entire episode affirmed our decision to leave Minnesota and reach for a brighter future. Our efforts to save lives must take on a new, less hands-on approach for our own sanity and well-being. Nonetheless, we'll never forget the Zamlen family, or many of the other families. On a deep level, we know the survivor's cry of profound loss and gross injustice.

Continuing to Focus on Our New Family

As Sara and Jamie eagerly await the arrival of their second child at the end of July 2009, Sara reflects on her brother and parenthood. "Chris loved kids so much and I know he would have been the best uncle in the history of the world. Now he has to look over us from above. That's both a comfort and huge source of pain. As I sit here with this child growing inside of me, I think of all the hopes and dreams I have for our little boy. Then I think back to what it must have been like for my parents—all the hopes and dreams they had for their little boy, their son Christopher Mark Jenkins, brought into this world on February 17, 1981. People say that love for a child is so much different from any other kind of love. This baby is part of you; he will love you unconditionally. My parents loved Chris more than most parents could, and he turned into an amazing man because of it. They invested almost twenty-two years in Chris, teaching him to respect others, stick to high ethical and

Happy Chris—our pride and joy.

moral standards, and enjoy every day. He did all of that and then some. My parents were robbed of the joy of watching their amazing son live his dreams; we all were."

Sara, Jamie, Cayman Rose, and her little brother are precious to us. Their future will be influenced, but not defined, by the footprints Steve and I left behind from rearing Sara and Chris. Though we will always support them, their decisions will determine the footprints they leave and the lives they touch.

Since what happened to Chris will never make sense, perhaps following Cayman's three-year-old wisdom is the best solution. When I'm with Cayman, and she doesn't know the answer to a question, she looks at me while shrugging her shoulders, and then proclaims, "Gigi, it's a mystery."

Steve and I owe it to ourselves and to Sara and Jamie's family to look to the future with hope and positive expectations. Expectations compel us to find a way because they tap into the vast supply of resources in our lives. Now is our time to live more fully, savoring the meaningful moments along the way. It may be something as simple as enjoy-

Cayman and Gigi—
enjoying moments that
take our breath away.

ing the color of the sky, the warmth of the sun, a budding tree, and a tender hug from a grandchild. Or it might mean honoring the long-lasting riches of a grateful heart, an honest friend, and a compassionate stranger.

To share the best of ourselves with the people we care about most, we must remember to say, "I love you" on a regular basis. Steve, Sara, and I have done that since the day we became a family of three. That commitment has helped us appreciate and support each other. A personal favorite is, "I love you to the moon and back!"

Creating a Life Worth Living

In his short life, Chris embraced the people, excitement, fun, and wonder he discovered around him. We are quite certain he wants us to remember and celebrate his remarkable life rather than mourn his tragic death. By releasing ourselves from investigating his death, focusing on his life becomes possible.

We have stayed in touch with many of his friends and will continue to do so. They have been generous with their time, consideration, and concern. Their genuine love for our son, and kindness to our family, have helped us immeasurably in staying connected to Chris's love, energy, and generous spirit.

At the same time, we must reach for new dreams. One of those dreams is leaving Minnesota. Unlike Chris, who adored Minnesota and said he'd never leave, our memories here are not so grand. While we are eternally grateful to the hundreds of wonderful people in Minneapolis

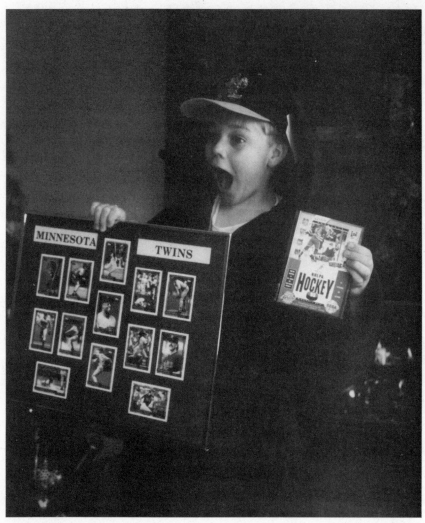

"Wow, this is so cool!"

and neighboring suburbs who reached out to help us, the reminders of the life we once had, are heartbreaking. In addition, though we can forgive the betrayal, harsh treatment, and lack of follow-up from those in key agencies in Hennepin County whom we entrusted to protect and serve us, that abuse left scars that cannot be erased. We hope things will be much better for the next family whose child is missing in Minneapolis, even if that child is eighteen years or older.

Steve and I love nature and enjoy several outdoor sports. We will look for a milder climate, healthy environment, beautiful scenery, and happy, energetic people for a new beginning. Whatever we choose to do and wherever we decide to live, we will carry on with grace and dignity. We expected nothing less of Sara and Chris; we can expect nothing less of ourselves.

Expressing Gratitude

Thank you, God, for the miracle—the wonder and blessing—of Sara and Chris in our lives. Steve and I are so proud of Sara's determination to live fully, honoring her brother in the process. No twenty-four-year-old should lose her only sibling and have to watch her parents struggle immeasurably with the injustice of missing, no investigation for years, and murder. Sara found a man she loved, built a marriage on hope for the future, and eagerly awaits their second child. She has realized much success in her professional life as well. We love Sara deeply, and respect her courage and tenacity in creating a new family and life for herself.

Though Chris left us way too soon, for twenty-one years we were fortunate enough to call him our son.

Accepting Jesus's Peace

A couple of years ago, I was rummaging through files of family keep-sakes, looking for information for this book. The handwritten program Steve and I created for our wedding day—August 9, 1975—fell out of one of the files. After picking it up and seeing the front cover, I burst into tears and sobbed for a long time. On that magical day, thank God we didn't know the horror that lay ahead. If we had known, would we have gotten married anyway? We've actually asked ourselves that question because the reality we have faced since November 1, 2002, could crush almost anyone's spirit forever.

There, on the front of our wedding program, I wrote, "To Jan and Steve, Christ Gives His Peace." My heart-wrenching sobs came from truly believing, maybe for the first time, that God does offer us peace. For so long, we felt abandoned, dumped on our heads, and forgotten by the God we had honored. I also felt, maybe for the first time since Chris vanished, that God did love us. It had been so hard to believe that God could love us and still allow such evil to end Chris's life.

Can Steve, Sara, or I realize complete peace ever again? I don't know. I do believe we can find a larger measure of peace than we've experienced up till now.

Believing Our Family Will Be Together Again

One of the incredible stories from the first message board on Chris's Web site gave me an image that I've held ever since. The young lady described a summer party at her home. Due to a recent breakup with a boyfriend, she was extremely upset. After arriving, Chris noted her great sadness and did everything he could think of to cheer her up. She wrote that nothing consoled her, and finally Chris said, "Well, if all else fails, jump in the kiddie pool!" Then, for everyone's amusement, he did a belly flop in the kiddie pool. The young lady said she laughed out loud and did feel a bit better for the rest of the evening.

Chris, your father, sister, and I love you beyond measure. We hold you in our hearts and we will be your voice until the day we join you in heaven. We can't say good-bye, so we'll just say, "See you on the other side. Save a spot for us in the kiddie pool."

Goodness Trumps Evil

This is a true story of love conquering fear. It's a story of those who loved Chris, including many who never met him. By facing adversity with courage, we forged precious bonds—a testament to the strength of the human spirit. Perhaps the greatest triumphs glow in the love shared and self-respect gained while seeking truth and justice.

Thank you for caring enough to read our family's journey through unthinkable tragedy. We hope you gained insight regarding the trauma endured by family and friends of a missing and murdered loved one. Most of us will suffer profound loss in our lives. At those times, the compassion, understanding, and love of others will help us through.

We must take care of each other. Please do not venture out alone at night. Walk in groups and make certain everyone in your group gets home safely. Saving a life is worth the extra effort.

If you found value in Chris's story, step forward with courage to improve your own life. Your footprints will touch the lives of many others. Creating a better world is within our reach.

Live fully while treasuring the gift of life. Our precious gift arrived on July 17, 2009, when we celebrated new life in our family—our grandson, Jace Christopher Lightner.

Love with all your heart, and may God bless you on your journey!

Sara and Chris's mom,
Jan Jenkins

Our Beautiful Rose

Rose Marie Sweet—1929–2010

A Legacy of Love, Laughter, and Unbridled Passion

Mom, when family and friends think about you, we remember your abiding faith, and love of the Lord. We cherish your devotion to family, and your huge, loving heart. We honor your generous spirit and concern and care for others. With delight, we recall your zany sense of humor and your laughter that filled a room. Your creativity and enthusiasm produced exquisite handmade gifts which you offered, expecting nothing in return. Showing spunk in standing up for fairness shines as a sparkling example of your well-lived life. You adored your grandson,

Chris, and gave us unflagging support in our efforts to find him and seek justice. You are a grand lady, one of God's great miracles, and we are blessed to call you mom, Rose, sis, Rosie, little Rose, Rose Marie, Grandma Rose, or great Grandma Rose.

Your great granddaughter, Cayman Rose, spoke on

Rose with her daughter, Jan, the author.

Cayman Radio in Grand Cayman early in March 2010, announcing to the entire island, "My great Grandma Rose is in heaven with Uncle Chris and they're having a party. *Actually,* Coco and Buster are at the party too!"

Watch over all of us, mom. It's comforting to know we have another angel in heaven. We will strive to live by the values you taught us through your actions every single day. You will live on in our hearts and through the extraordinary legacy you left behind.

Mom, every smile, every memory, every moment with you has been a treasured gift. You have touched us all with your essential goodness and unwavering love. May you always feel and know our abundant love for you.

Fly high beautiful mom; you are free!

Notes

Chapter 3. Loaded in Trunk

29 The AMBER (America's Missing: Broadcast Emergency Response) Alert programs have helped save the lives of 502 children nationwide. Retrieved on May 9, 2010, from http://www.crimealert.state.mn.us/AmberAlert/AA_Home.asp

Chapter 12. "Look, Mom, It's Not Hard to See"

138 The following chart lists the rate of flow over St. Anthony Falls in cubic feet per second (cfs) for the time during which Chris Jenkins was missing:

November 1, 2002	10,000 cfs
December 1, 2002	6,000 cfs
January 1, 2003	less than 6,000 cfs
February 1, 2003	less than 4,000 cfs
February 28, 2003	4,000 cfs

Climatological data from the National Weather Service recorded the following air temperatures (Fahrenheit) during the last week of February 2003: February 19—high of 38; February 20—high of 46, average of 39, low of 31; February 21—high of 40, average of 30, low of 20. Temperatures dropped below freezing for the next five days, until walkers saw Chris's body on February 27; on that day the temperature reached 37 degrees.

Chapter 14. A Lonely Path

155 M. G. F. Gilliland and R. O. Bost, "Alcohol in Decomposed Bodies: Postmortem Synthesis and Distribution." *Journal of Forensic Sciences* 38, no. 6 (1993): 1266–74.

Chapter 27. Finishing Strong

267 Gary Haupt, "Drowning Investigations," *FBI Law Enforcement Bulletin*. http://www.fbi.gov/publications/leb/2006/feb06leb.pdf.

268 M. G. F. Gilliland and R. O. Bost, "Alcohol in Decomposed Bodies: Postmortem Synthesis and Distribution." *Journal of Forensic Sciences* 38, no. 6 (1993): 1266–74.

270 Victim profiles of college-aged men who mysteriously disappeared and were later found in water:
Awareness = Answers—seeking answers in unexplained drowning deaths—http://www.sfkillers.com/
Footprints at the River's Edge—raising awareness about a series of mysterious disappearances in river towns across the United States and Canada—http://footprintsattheriversedge.blogspot.com/

Chapter 28. What Matters Now

277 **Critical considerations when investigating a drowning incident:** We offer this information to educate as many people as possible about what to do when investigating a drowning incident. The data comes from written documentation, conversations, and personal experience in working with Team Lifeguard Systems, Inc.

Law enforcement personnel and death investigators are typically well trained in many different causes and manners of death. The incident of bodies found in water is an exception. Unfortunately, such occurrences are assumed to be accidental drowning with the negative result that an effective investigation is not performed. In some cases a thorough investigation would reveal that cause of death was something other than drowning, and that manner of death was either suicide or homicide.

Death certificates list two determinations: cause of death and manner of death. The cause of death is the event or reason that led to the person's death, such as blunt trauma from a fall, a heart attack, a gunshot wound, or drowning. Manner of death is how the cause came to be.

Cause of Death

When a decedent is found in water with no obvious cause of death, the forensic pathologist or coroner responsible for diagnosing cause of death will almost always, if not always, rule it as drowning. *Drowning is a diagnosis of exclusion*—there is no other obvious cause of death; the victim was found in water, so the cause of death is deemed "drowning."

The only exception to this is a few rare cases in which diatom tests are conducted. Diatoms are unicellular algae with a silica shell that live in water exposed to sunlight. There are many thousands of species of diatoms worldwide, with each body of water having a fairly unique population pool of species. If a person drowns and inhales water with diatoms, and the person's heart beats long enough for the diatoms to be transported from the pulmonary capillaries, through the heart, to the femur bone marrow, then an examination of that marrow might result in finding a concentration of diatoms that match the supposed drowning medium. If yes, then a diagnosis of drowning can be made.

An important point is that it is possible for a person to drown without a noticeable concentration of diatoms reaching the femur marrow. This can occur if too little water is inhaled or if the heart stops quickly. Hence, a lack of diatoms found does not provide information on whether a person drowned. No diatoms found means you know nothing more than before the test was conducted.

Manner of Death

There are five standard manners of death: natural, accident, suicide, homicide, and undetermined. The following examples relate to cause of death diagnosed as drowning:

Natural: some offices would rule the following death as natural: a person with a history of epilepsy has a seizure and drowns in a bathtub that the person voluntarily got into.

Accident: a person falls off a boat without a life jacket and drowns.

Suicide: a person voluntarily jumps off a bridge with the intent to die and drowns.

Homicide: a person is involuntarily duct-taped alive to a chair and thrown off a boat and drowns.

Undetermined: a person's body is found floating in a lake. It is not known how the person came to be in the lake, there is no obvious cause of death, and there is no logical reason why the person would have been in that particular body of water or drowned in it.

The following points are articulated by Butch Hendrick, Andrea Zaferes, and Craig Nelson MD in *Homicidal Drowning Investigation:* "Compounding the perceived accident concept is the problem of little or no typical evidence of foul play on drowning sites or drowning victims. We have spoken with hundreds of patrol officers and detectives and almost all tell us they would recognize possible foul play in a drowning scene. When we ask them to give us the red flags they would be looking for, we are told: bruising or other signs of injury, signs of a struggle in the scene, and signs of past abuse. *The big problem is that rarely are any of these signs present in a homicidal drowning incident.*

"What reason do medical examiners have to rule a death 'accidental drowning' just because there is fluid in the lungs and no signs of injury? We have to say none! First, a cause of death due to drowning is usually determined by exclusion. Other than a few rare cases in which diatom tests are conducted, there are no universally accepted diagnostic tests to prove that a death was caused by drowning. Secondly, a lack of injury does not prove that the victim found in the water died by accident. To prove that the death was by accident, suicide, natural causes, or foul play requires a thorough investigation.

"Most cases of homicidal drownings are investigated by hindsight. *We cannot stress enough the importance of collecting and documenting as much evidence as possible at the scene of every drowning incident.*"

The following spiral-bound publication is available from Lifeguard Systems Inc.:

Homicidal Drowning Investigation, by Butch Hendrick, Andrea Zaferes, and Craig Nelson MD, Team Lifeguard Systems, Inc. Copyright 1998, 2001, 2002, 2003 (www.teamlgs.com; RIPTIDE: www.rip-tide.org; e-mail: LGS@Teamlgs.com).

Additional facts can be found in two articles published in the *Forensic Examiner* 15, no. 3 (Fall 2006):

Edward J. Rohn, MA, and Peter D. Frade, PhD, *The Role of Diatoms in Medicolegal Investigations I: The History, Contemporary Science, and Application of the Diatom Test for Drowning*

Leann Long, BS, *Multiple Mysterious Drownings: Accidents or Serial Murders?*

Index

Acknowledgments

Some people come into our lives and quietly go;
others stay for a while and leave footprints on our hearts
and we are never the same.

ANONYMOUS

Mom and Dad, you gave me life, and taught me about God, love, responsibility, compassion, and honesty through your personal examples. If I felt something was unfair, you encouraged me to speak up. You also helped me through the death of our son and your adored grandson, Chris. Our struggle for justice would not have been possible without your unflagging support. Dad and mom, I love you beyond measure and thank you for believing in us throughout the long journey. We counted on your acceptance of our tough decisions and you never once let us down.

Steve, you are the love of my life. You held me up when my heart broke, again and again. No father has ever loved a son more than you love Chris. You amazed me with your tenacity and unstoppable determination in searching for Chris and seeking truth. Late into the night you read this manuscript almost as many times as I did. Cheering me on for two years as I struggled to write our family's story, you were my biggest fan. We make a great team. Yes, I would have married you a million times over.

Sara and Jamie, thank you for understanding we couldn't stop until we saw the finish line—when we could no longer make a difference for Chris. Thank you also for recognizing that the mission to save lives chose us, we didn't choose the mission. We love you to the moon and back.

To the Sweet and Jenkins families and hundreds of faithful friends, your efforts lifted us so we could cope. Thanks for not judging us even when you may have thought our actions were crazy. We know you miss Chris too.

A private investigator with purpose and heart, that's you, Chuck

Loesch. You sacrificed so much in your unquenchable thirst for truth. Chris thanks you for leading the way with integrity, so do we.

W.T., simply put, you made our quest for justice possible. Through your intelligence and essential goodness, you found resources, helped us think logically, and offered a listening ear 24/7. We honor you with the MVP Volunteer Award for ongoing assistance in missing person cases. In every way possible, you "showed up" on innumerable tough days and nights.

To Rick Stein, Coach Lars, and John Wood, your leadership at search headquarters set the pace. You taught dozens of young adults what responsibility and purposeful action look like.

To our dear neighbors in Eden Prairie, Mary Davis and Phil Buchanan, you put your life on hold to help us find Chris. Your selfless dedication touched many lives.

Thousands of people provided the wind beneath our wings, holding us up throughout this surreal ordeal. Many of you we will never know. Our family is eternally grateful to you for your contribution—physical, emotional, spiritual or monetary.

My first three attempts to write Chris's story succeeded because of your dedication, Tim Katzman, our dear friend of forty years, and communication director for the San Diego Padres. Your invaluable feedback gave me the jump-start I needed to keep going. I hope you know how much I appreciate the time you somehow found to read the early drafts of a newbie author.

Next I found a group of brave and generous souls who agreed to read chapters as I completed them. Tricia Lorntson, W.T., Linda Walker, Gail Steining, Judy Zitzloff, April Shafer, Christian Bailey, Jamie and Sara Lightner, you rock!

Few friends would offer to read an entire manuscript over the course of a year. Deb Wingert, you did that and more. You believed in this story and my ability to write it from the beginning. I appreciate your talent and generosity; my readers thank you too!

We appreciate Rachel Holscher, Kyle Hunter, and others at Book-Mobile who made this book a reality. Your work pays tribute to Chris and will likely save others from a similar fate.

Then I found Mary Byers, the consummate professional editor. Mary, you have gently guided me through the painstaking task of writing our family's personal tragedy. I feel so fortunate you chose to walk this journey with me.

To Nikki Muehlhausen for pouring your heart into creating www .FootprintsOfCourage.com, your talent and dedication moved us.

To Mike Livingston and Chris Flynn, thanks for creating and maintaining our first two Web sites for Chris. Your efforts honored your friend and helped us tell the truth about what happened to our son.

Lifeguard Systems, Inc., brought help and hope when we needed it most. Butch Hendrick, and Andrea Zaferes, you personify servant leadership. We will continue to share what we've learned from your professional insight and experience so that countless lives can be saved.

Chief Dolan, you led the way with honesty and courage. To every individual in law enforcement who genuinely cared and helped us find Chris and truth, we hope you wear your badge proudly.

To Detective Mike Harvey and Lieutenant Gaalswyk, you serve with insight and compassion. Your contribution made a huge difference to the Jenkins family.

To Annie Sharma, Penny Bell, and Terry Kaminski, the invaluable work you did with Scrumpy and Hoover shed new light on Chris's case. We offer you our deepest gratitude.

Rick Harrison Site & Design Studio flew their Beech Bonanza A36 over the St. Croix River to take photos in hopes of spotting Chris. Although you did not know us, you stepped forward to offer your resources. Know that your unexpected and selfless action gave us a reason to smile.

To the YMCA on the University of Minnesota campus, thanks for providing us with our second home for search headquarters.

Compassion and assistance from the University of Minnesota made Sara, Steve, and me proud to be alumni. We graciously thank the Carlson School of Management, St. Anthony Falls Laboratory, the Department of Forest Resources, Counseling and Consulting Services, the Gopher Men's Lacrosse team, and the office of the president of the university, Dr. Robert Bruininks. To the dozens of students and staff who joined searches in hopes of finding Chris, you helped us remember that goodness trumps evil.

To the staff at the Jacob Wetterling Resource Center and to Patty Wetterling, you offered hope when we experienced only raw grief. Continue your work to prevent crimes against innocent children, the world needs you.

Expressing gratitude helps us move forward with more joy and less pain. So, to honor our desire to embrace life again, and to thank those who stood by us, we have created a full list of acknowledgments on our Web site, www.FootprintsOfCourage.com.

Allow me to apologize to those of you whom we have omitted, for surely there will be some.

Resources

Contact Organizations

Jacob Wetterling Resource Center (JWRC)
A Program of the National Child Protection Training Center (NCPTC)
2314 University Ave W., Suite 14, Saint Paul, MN 55114
Phone: 651-714-4673; fax: 651-714-9098; toll-free: 800-325-HOPE
www.jwrc.org
www.ncptc.org

The Jacob Wetterling Foundation (JWF) was founded in 1989 by Patty and Jerry Wetterling following their son's abduction near St. Joseph, Minnesota. To better reflect its work, JWF became the Jacob Wetterling Resource Center (JWRC) in September 2008, and launched a new Web site to arm the public with the tips, tools, and resources to build safer communities. The Web site includes a list of recommended books for children, teens, and adults. Effective February 1, 2010, JWRC merged with the National Child Protection Training Center (NCPTC). The NCPTC will maintain JWRC's core mission to educate children, families, and communities. JWRC will also continue to provide victim assistance to families who have a missing or exploited child and advocate for child protection legislation.

Parents of Murdered Children (POMC)
100 East Eighth Street, Suite 202, Cincinnati, OH 45202
Phone: 513-721-5683; fax: 513-345-4489; toll-free: 888-818-POMC
www.pomc.com; e-mail: natlpomc@aol.com

National organization with local chapters providing support for all survivors of murder, not just parents. Services and resources available include: monthly support groups and meetings, victims' advocacy, court accompaniment, second opinion services to provide answers to questions and concerns regarding a death and subsequent investigations, survivors' newsletter, education, training, consultation, murder response team, speaker's bureau, and more.

The National Center for Missing and Exploited Children (NCMEC)
Charles B. Wang International Children's Building
699 Prince Street, Alexandria, VA 22314-3175
Phone: 703-274-3900; fax: 703-274-2200;
toll-free: 800-THE-LOST® (800-843-5678)
www.missingkids.com

The National Center for Missing and Exploited Children spearheads national efforts to locate and recover missing children, and provides services nationwide for families and professionals in the prevention of abducted, endangered, and sexually exploited children. NCMEC deploys Team Adam, a rapid response and support system comprised of retired law enforcement officers, to provide on-site technical assistance to local law enforcement agencies investigating cases of child abduction and sexual exploitation.

FBI Headquarters
Special Investigations and Initiatives Unit,
Crimes Against Children Unit
935 Pennsylvania Avenue NW, Washington, DC 20535-0001
Phone: 202-324-3666; fax: 202-324-2731

Suggested Reading

Gavin De Becker. *Protecting the Gift: Keeping Children and Teenagers Safe (and Parents Sane).* New York: Dell Publishing, 1999.
Carrie M. Freitag and Margaret J. Kerouac. *Aftermath: In the Wake of Murder.* Ellicott City, MD: Chevron Publishing, 2003.
Michael W. Quinn. *Walking With the Devil: The Police Code of Silence.* Quinn and Associates, 2005.

A series of three booklets published through the Office of Juvenile Justice and Delinquency Prevention (OJJDP) through the Office of Justice Programs under the Department of Justice is available to help families and communities with missing children:

When Your Child is Missing: The Family Survival Guide;
What About Me? Coping with the Abduction of a Brother or Sister; and
You're Not Alone: The Journey from Abduction to Empowerment.

Each of these booklets can be found and downloaded free of charge at www.ojp.usdoj.gov.

WE INVITE YOU TO VISIT OUR WEB SITE AT:

www.FootprintsOfCourage.com

- Share how Chris's story has influenced your life.
- Leave a message detailing tips for staying safe, and making every day count.
- Learn more about Chris through reading some of his writings.
- View original documentation from law enforcement and outside agencies involved in the investigation into Chris's disappearance and death.
- Learn about upcoming newscasts and publications regarding Chris's unsolved case.
- Watch previous newscasts regarding Chris's investigation and the release of *Footprints of Courage: Our Family's Struggle for Justice*.
- Read a full list of acknowledgments.
- Order more copies of *Footprints of Courage;* quantity discounts available on our Web site.

**Contact Jan Jenkins for
speaking engagements and workshops:
Jan Jenkins: www.LegacyOfCourage.com
Jan@legacyofcourage.com • Office: 952-445-5261**

Onward and Upward!